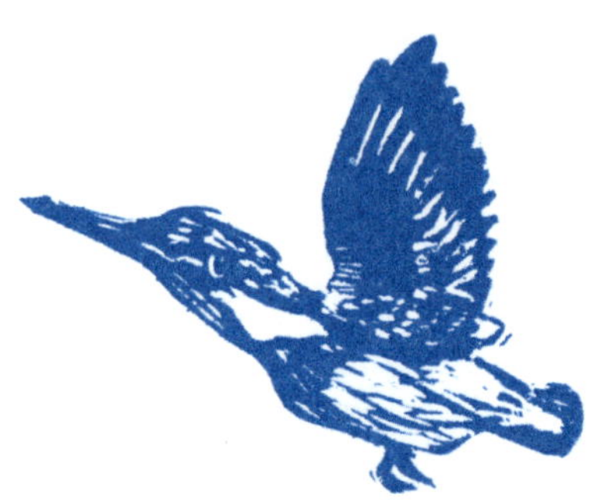

Ross Hair

Brilliant Absence

Pursuing the Kingfisher in
the work of Hans Waanders

Uniformbooks 2019

First published 2019
Copyright © Text: Ross Hair; Images: Estate of Hans Waanders
ISBN 978–1–910010–20–4

Uniformbooks
7 Hillhead Terrace, Axminster, Devon EX13 5JL
www.uniformbooks.co.uk

Trade distribution in the UK by Central Books
www.centralbooks.com

Printed and bound by T J International, Padstow, Cornwall

But as we readily follow an agreeable object that flies from us, so we love to contemplate blue, not because it advances to us, but because it draws us after it.

—Johann Wolfgang von Goethe, *Theory of Colours*

Illustrations

Contents

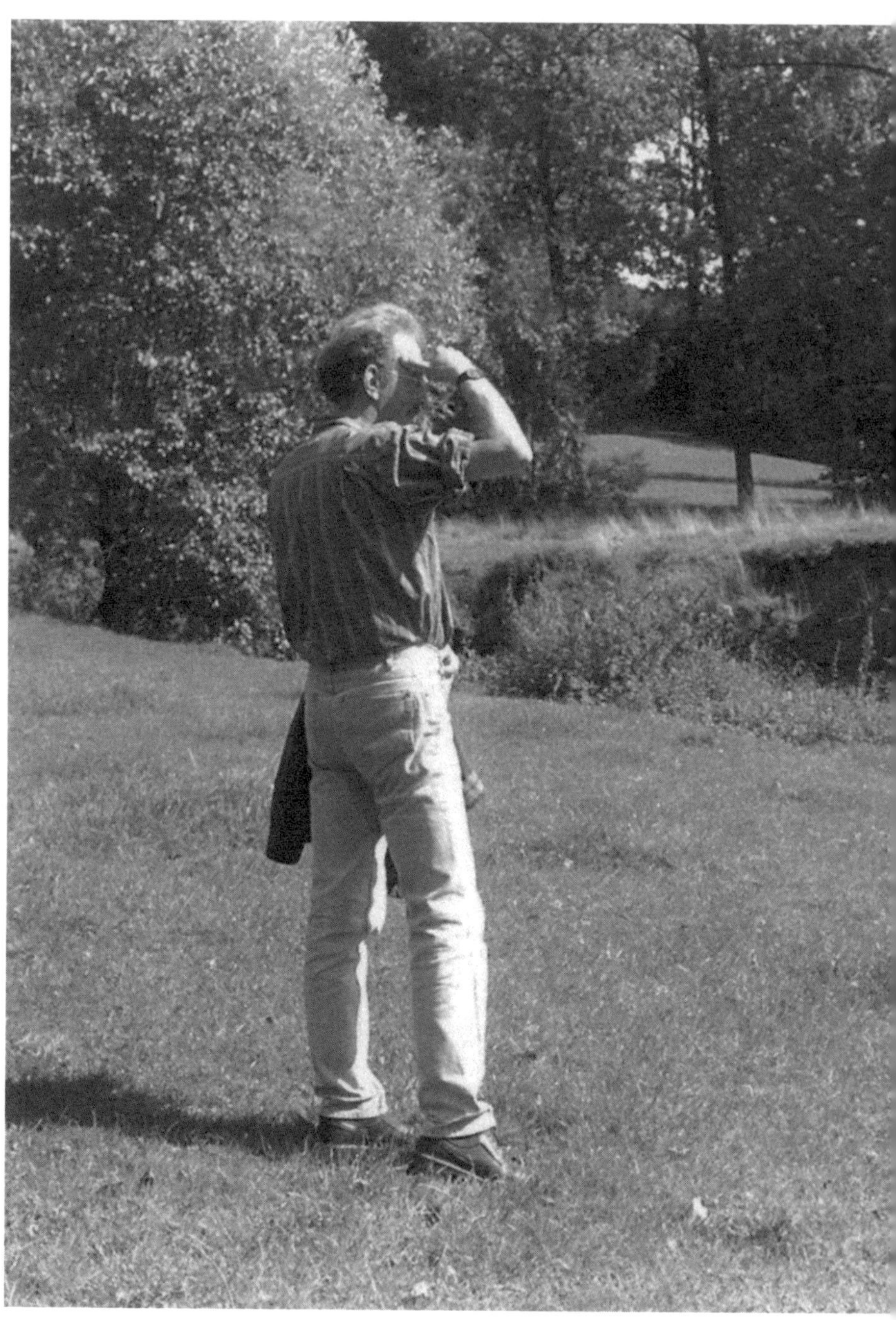

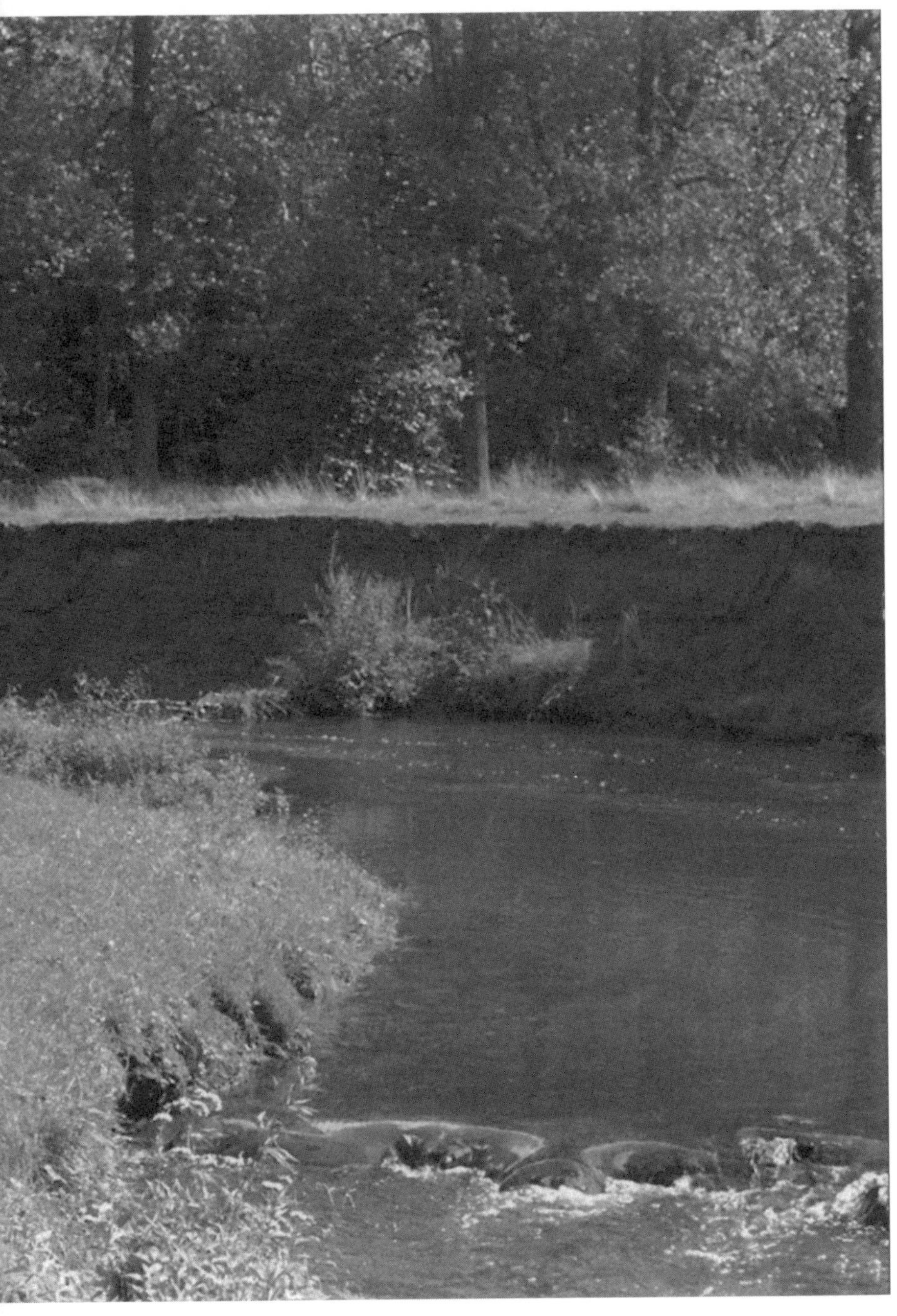

MARTINICO. m. fam. **Duende.**

MARTINIEGA. f. Tributo que se debía
pagar el día de San Martín.

MARTÍN PESCADOR. m. Ave trepa-
dora que vive a orillas de los ríos y lagunas, se alimenta de pececillos, que coge
con gran destreza, y de los países fríos
emigra por San Mar-
tín.

MÁRTIR. com.
Persona que padece
muerte por amor de
Jesucristo y en de-
fensa de la verdade-
ra religión. ‖ Por
ext., persona que
muere o padece mu-
ho en defensa de
ras creencias o
sas. ‖ fig. Perso-
que padece gran-
fanes y traba-
ntes mártir

sor. fr. fig. y fam. con que se
ificultad y resistencia que al-
ara declarar lo que se

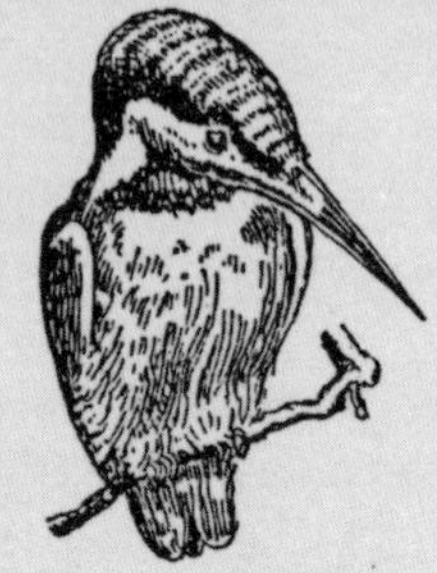

Martín pescador

tamb
Antoni.
Esto es ι.
las MÁS *d*ι
artículo e;
barbarismc
indetermin.
esta batalla
bres.‖ Denoι
rencia. MÁS *q*ι.
perder la honra.
El MÁS *y el menos.*
de la suma o adic
por una crucecita (
más, más. m. adv. A
grado posible. *En es*ι
MÁS *cien volúmer*ˆ
denota idea de
*pesetas de sue*ʲ
de renta. ‖
se denˀ
ᴦ

---

distinguished by their size, appearance,
etc.

KINGFISHER, [king'-fish-er]. *n.* the halcyon, a bird
of the genus *Alcedo*, distinguished
by its long beak and brightly
coloured plumage, dwelling near
streams and rivers, and feeding
on fish.

KINGHOOD, [king'-hŏŏd]. *n.*
condition of being a king.

KINGLESS, [king'-les], *adj.* without king.

KINGLET, [king'-let], *n.* a puppet
king; the golden-crested wren.

KINGLIKE, [king'-līk], *adj.* like a
king, kingly, regal, majestic.

KINGLINESS, [king'-li-nes], *n.* the
quality of being kingly.

NGLING, [king'-ling], *n.* an
nificant, pett'ˀ king.

Y, [kin⋯

⋯taining to a king; becoming,
⋯estic, noble; worthy
king.

⋯ a mach'

Origin

A chance sighting on October 4th, 1982 of *Alcedo atthis*—the bird more familarly known in English as the Common Kingfisher, and, in Dutch, *de IJsvogel*—prompted a notable sea change in the work of the Dutch artist Hans Waanders. A former student of the Minerva Art Academy in Groningen, Waanders specialised in painting "detailed watercolours, with vegetation, birds and water".[1] However, seeing the small brilliant blue bird flying low across a small pond near the river Maas was, as Waanders' friend and publisher Karen Davidson writes, "a magical encounter" that "transformed his life" as well as his art.[2]

Waanders had already witnessed the bird on two previous occasions. The first occurred on a cycling trip through the Dutch province of Overijssel in 1963. The second, fourteen years later, in 1977 (the same year that Waanders graduated from the Minerva Art Academy) was seen along the Amblève river in Belgium. Yet, according to Cathy Courtney, director of the *Artists' Lives* project at the British Library, it was the third sighting in 1982 that "initiated a poetic quest for further sightings abroad and at home" and precipitated "a quarrying for information about the species" that would occupy Waanders for the remaining nineteen years of his life.[3] Over this relatively brief period, Waanders produced over one hundred books in addition to numerous prints, stamps, and cards, site-specific installations, conceptual interventions, and a short radio programme, entitled *A Discussion Between a Kingfisher and Yuri Gagarin*, which was broadcast on Dutch radio in 1992.

The "spare and elegant visual language" of this work and its "evocative imagery" has led art historian Kristine Stiles to compare it to visual poetry: "As poetry condenses a world of meaning into a word, so Waanders' single images press ineffable private references into sharable cultural metaphors."[4] Echoing Stiles' sentiments, the poet and artist Alec Finlay, whose small press Morning Star published several titles by Waanders, finds in Waanders' ambitious project an underlying "romantic spirit" that "gives the work an essentially poetic character".[5] As "a collector of evidence, haunter of streams, survivor, witness of wonders", Waanders, the poet and publisher Thomas A. Clark writes,* is at once "poet, artist, [and] ornithologist".[6] Perhaps more so, the nature of Waanders' work casts him as a poet in the

---

* Waanders' work was exhibited on several occasions at the Cairn Gallery that Clark, with the artist and publisher Laurie Clark, ran in Nailsworth, Gloucestershire.

old sense of "maker" (*poiētēs*); a lyric "maker" of books, images, and impressions that combine the praxis of handwork with the Daedalian wings of "poesie".*

Like the pioneering figures of ornithology such as the eighteenth-century curate and amateur naturalist Gilbert White, Waanders was also a keen letter writer who sustained a large correspondence with numerous friends, publishers, and collaborators. Breaking down longstanding distinctions between art and life, this practice constitutes an additional component of Waanders' work that extends and enacts the themes and motifs of distance, travel, and communication that recur throughout it.

Waanders' interest in communication media and its infrastructures and systems, (and the emotive resonances of solitude and nostalgia they elicit), recalls what Craig Saper, in his 2001 book *Networked Art*, defines as "intimate bureaucracies":

> An intimate bureaucracy makes poetic use of the trappings of the large bureaucratic systems and procedures (e.g., logos, stamps) to create intimate aesthetic situations, including all the pleasures of sharing a special knowledge or new language among a small network of participants.[7]

Saper finds the rudiments of this intimate bureaucracy in the spheres of the Nouveau Realistes and Fluxus. The use of communication media in Yves Klein's blue postage stamp (c.1957), for example, or the *Flux Post Kit* (a collection of rubberstamps, postcards, and postage stamps contained in a small plastic box with the image of a mailbox on its lid that George Maciunas compiled in 1968) anticipate two closely related art forms invested in long-distance communication that burgeoned in the 1970s: correspondence art and mail art. These forms of networked art make extensive use of the bureaucratic processes, procedures, and systems of the postal service, albeit for slightly different ends.

Where correspondence art emphasises a "reciprocal or interactive communication correspondence", mail art functions on the basis of "unidirectional or one-way communication" which is "mailed out without any requirement for response".[8] Waanders' work invites comparison with both of these practices and has utilised many of

---

* "A Poet no industrie can make," Sidney writes in his "Defence of Poesie," "if his owne Genius be not carried into it. And therefore is an old Proverbe, *Orator fit, Poeta nascitur.* Yet confesse I alwaies, that as the fertilest ground must be manured, so must the highest flying wit have a Dedalus to guide him. That Dedalus they say both in this and in other, hath three wrings to beare itself up into the aire of due commendation: that is Art, Imitation, and Exercise." Sir Philip Sidney, *The Prose Works*, ed. Albert Feuillerat (Cambridge: Cambridge University Press, 1962), p.37.

the forms and mediums that, according to the former Fluxus artist Ken Friedman, "have become associated with correspondence art and mail art" such as "postcards, artists' books, printed ephemera, rubber stamps, artists' postage stamps, and posters of various kinds".[9]

Of all of these forms and mediums it is the book that is Waanders' "principle medium", Kristine Stiles writes.[10] Artists' books or "book-works"—to use an alternative term coined by the curator, librarian, and artists' book specialist Clive Phillpot—broadly denote "artworks in book form" that "sit provocatively at the juncture where art, documentation and literature all come together".[11] Such books, the book artist and visual theorist Johanna Drucker notes, also tend to be acutely "self-conscious about the structure, and meaning of the book as form".[12] According to the Mexican conceptual artist Ulises Carrión, a key pioneer of the form, the book constitutes a medium in its own right and is "an expressive unity" in which "the message is the sum of all material and formal elements".[13] The self-reflexive, hybrid forms of bookworks and artists' books, as Kristine Stiles suggests, have permitted Waanders "more whimsical constructions than the historically bound traditions of painting and sculpture" normally allow.[14] The "systemic" artists' books, as conceived by the art historian Robert Morgan, is especially relevant to Waanders' "whimsical constructions" which, similarly, often process "ideas and images in the form of 'information' which [are] transmitted bereft of traditional art objects".[15]

Waanders' systematic methods of documenting and processing information can be broadly aligned with what the writer Michael Hampton, in his revisionist history of the form, *Unshelfmarked: Reconceiving the Artists' Book*, describes describes as an "eco-idiom" and "cosmological thematic" in contemporary artists' books which tends to "collapse the categories 'art' and 'nature.'" "Be it collections of pressed flowers and ferns, the classic pocket field guide format, more conversational pond notes and hedgerow queries or *aurora borealis* holiday snaps", Hampton writes, "as the scientific probing of cosmic nature has grown more vertiginous and bewildering, the innate flexibility of the artists' book […] allows its technicians to hearken back to these publishing stalwarts or adopt and redo them with a modern twist".[16] In the case of Waanders, his appropriations of familiar, functional formats such as notebooks, field guides, bird books, and atlases (along with dictionaries, almanacs, and stamp stockbooks and albums) have proved apposite in articulating some of the principle themes of his work including travel, communication, philately, ornithology, taxonomy, and collecting.

Waanders' publications have also taken the form of accordions and leporellos, rolled sheets, and boxed editions of loose, unbound sheets that, like his more conventional codex formats, have often utilised a "splendid mixture of textures, images, photographs, words, and stamp prints", in addition to tipped- or pasted-in plates and material.[17] Like the personal form of the diary and the scrapbook, as well as the intimate bureaucracies of mail and correspondence art, Waanders' books are especially suited for incorporating "extra-artistic ephemera with an associative life and a history" that tacitly illuminate "the links between a personal life and the world".[18]

In their design and construction Waanders' books favour functionality over ostentation. Assembled "in the security of his own studio", as Waanders' friend and publisher Peter Foolen recalls, Waanders undertook most of "the copying, cutting, pasting, stamping, binding, and finishing" singlehandedly, making his books in small editions ranging from unique one-off copies to relatively larger runs rarely exceeding twenty-five copies.[19] The reproducible nature of Waanders' books is therefore subtly tempered by the manual methods of their construction and their extrinsic, by-hand, additions and finishes. In this respect, Waanders' books frequently possess what Johanna Drucker ascribes to certain artists' books as an "auratic quality, an often inexplicable air of power, attraction, or uniqueness" that may result from limited edition sizes, complicated production processes, "elaborate labor" or "an intense investment in obsessive work".[20] Obsessive work, elaborate labour, and complex methods of production, however, does not necessarily mean precious, rarefied, or "fine". As one of Waanders' longstanding supporters, the art historian and typographer Tjeu Teeuwen suggests, the auratic quality imparted in a typical book of Waanders' is one of "adequate simplicity".[21] This simplicity combines the spare, simple idiom of Waanders' images and books with a practicality of purpose more commonly found in the field guides, catalogues, and manuals that his books frequently evoke. "The only thing that counts, when choosing a medium, is its quality of expression—not its status", Waanders has claimed:

> The craftsmanship of a book is just as interesting (or: uninteresting) as the question what type of frame a painting should have, or on what kind of paper a watercolour should be made—it is hardly ever relevant for the contents of a work.[22]

In addition to his hand-assembled editions, a number of small presses including Pont La Vue Press (New York), Morning Star Publications (Edinburgh), Estampa Ediciones (Madrid), and the

Peninsula Foundation (Eindhoven) have published books by Waanders. Out of all these publications, it is *Kingfishers and Related Works*, published in 2000, that is perhaps the most salient. Published in an edition of a hundred copies with the support of Karen Davidson's Pont La Vue Press, Peter Foolen's October editions, and Alec Finlay's Morning Star press, this book, as Foolen writes "is a major publication, not only in size but also in richness of thought and vision".[23]

Perhaps in allusion to Joseph M. Forshaw's exhaustive six-volume work, *Kingfishers and Related Birds*, *Kingfishers and Related Works* is a definitive summary and statement of Waanders' work.* As well as reproducing selections from some of his key publications and prints, *Kingfishers* also includes a brief artist biography, lists of Waanders' books, cards, exhibitions, and collections of his work. A substantial bibliography of the books (a veritable reference library on *Alcedo atthis* and other Alcedinidae) that influenced and informed Waanders' works is also appended.** The result is 164 pages of black (and some colour) photocopied text and images, hand bound in dark blue boards baring a simple design of a single kingfisher image. Repeated as rigid formation ascending diagonally beyond the book's covers, Waanders' simple yet elegant design reflects the rote nature of his practices and the various systems of classification and cataloguing that he has adopted in his pursuit of the bird. [*See page 19*]

Although the quality of production makes *Kingfishers and Related Works* the closest that Waanders has come to fine printing, the book eschews unnecessary ornament and finish in favour of his earlier publications' simple, modest idioms. Furthermore, despite its relatively high quality production and large edition size, each copy of *Kingfishers and Related Works* retains the auratic quality of Waanders' earlier handmade books. Manually applied relief impressions, hand-coloured additions, pasted-in plates and ephemera, all serve to render each book discretely unique.

The auratic qualities of Waanders' books are, however, perhaps most pronounced in the interventions that he makes in the

* The first volume of Forshaw's *Kingfishers and Related Birds* is one of the many titles that Waanders' includes in the list of 'references' he provides in *Kingfishers and Related Works*.

** Didier Mathieu has aptly described Waanders' reference library as "the library of an amateur enlightened by the memory of the fleeting trail of blue left by a kingfisher" ("Bibliothèque de référence, bibliothèque d'un amateur éclairé par le souvenir de la fugace traînée de bleu laissée par un martin-pêcheur") and quotes Waanders' remark that *every book may be a reference for a new publication*. See Mathieu, Didier, 'On Hans Waanders', online PDF, 1. Originally published in *Herman de Vries, Lefevre Jean Claude, Oxo-Pascal Le Coq, Hans Waanders, Eric Watier* (Saint-Yrieix-la-Perche / Mariemont: Centre des livres d'artistes / Musée royal, 2007).

reclaimed field guides and bird books that, to use Drucker's term, he has methodologically "transformed".* In these unique found editions, Waanders systematically stamps, invariably in blue ink, his own hand-carved rubberstamp images of the kingfisher's profile over every bird illustration with the exception of *Alcedo atthis*. Hands-on craft meets the impersonality of mechanised reproduction, in these interventions, as Waanders' rote stamping essentially turns a pre-owned, mass produced book into an auratic art object. Contrasting markedly with the unique qualities of the specific copy in which they occur, the serial uniformity of Waanders' "marks", as the curator Jenny Brownrigg notes, "mingle with the traces of previous book owners": "A preserved newspaper cut out is trapped in the pages of one book. Small, precise handwriting appears in another."[24]

Yet, as much as these books assert their unique material presence, they also accentuate the very palpable absence of the bird they seek to invoke. Each blue stamp is essentially a tacit reminder that, as John Berger remarks in his seminal book *Ways of Seeing*: "Images were first made to conjure up the appearance of something that was absent."[25] "The repetition of [the kingfisher's] afterimage, its shadow" might, as Jenny Brownrigg writes of Waanders' interventions, be "the required incantation in the artist's quests to become closer", but each of these impressions also compounds its absence.[26] Throughout literature and art, the critic Richard Stamelman writes, "the image moves in a frenetic, always circular, self-repeating pattern around the event of the past it wishes to carry back into the present. Its relentless attempts at recuperation multiply the forms and meanings it expresses." In a similar manner, the systematic repetitions of Waanders' rubberstamped images of *Alcedo atthis* exceed their intended purpose and, as "sign, surrogate, and material for what lives no more", are also "endlessly proliferating, always different [and], forever ephemeral".[27]

It seems particularly apposite that Waanders should carve these rubberstamps out of old erasers. What was originally intended to efface and remove becomes, in Waanders' hands, the means for impressing, imprinting, and making indelible "what lives no more". It is also striking that these images are frequently impressed on *printed ephemera*—"the minor transient documents of everyday life" such as postcards, goods labels, trade cards, and catalogues—that, nominally, are as passing and fleet as Waanders' brilliant blue subject.[28]

* "Transformed books", Drucker writes, "use an existing work as their base, and then make a palimpsest which is a combination of textual, visual and material manipulation of the original". Drucker, *The Century of Artists' Books*, p.93.

Waanders' rubber stamp interventions are indicative blue micro-cosms of a series of larger dialectical tensions underpinning all of his work. Each book, print, or card invariably evokes notions of singularity and repetition, as well as retrieval and loss, which are borne out of the seminal encounter with *Alcedo atthis* in 1982 at what Waanders came to refer to as the *ijsvogelwiel* (kingfisherpond). Every work, every impression, is poignant testimony of how, as Thomas A. Clark, writes, "a brief glimpse" became for Waanders "a lasting memory".[29] By repeatedly evoking this seminal yet ephemeral experience, Waanders, with a mixture poignancy and vivacity, recalls how seeing the common kingfisher is, despite its moniker, a rare and exceptional experience. It would be another seven years before Waanders would see the bird again. "However brief", as the nature writers Mark Cocker and Richard Mabey suggest, seeing a kingfisher out in the field "often leaves a lasting impression and frequently a sense of privilege".[30] This sense of "lasting impression" finds an apposite equivalent in the countless impressions—the rubberstamps, prints, and books—that Waanders would make in response to his brief encounter with the bird.

The negotiations between ephemerality and durance that inform so much of Waanders' work are echoed in what Rosemary Eastman, the co-director of the acclaimed 1966 BBC documentary *The Private Life of the Kingfisher*, describes in her monograph, *The Kingfisher*, as the bird's "elusive and for the most part quiet" nature:

> Except in the spring when its noisy courtship proceedings are taking place and in the autumn when the parents are desperately trying to drive away their offspring with angry threats, one might question its very existence. One may explore their whole territory and flush neither of the pair, though they were seen only yesterday, leaving one puzzled by their apparent absence.[31]

Although the kingfisher will usually "disappear in a streak of blue, often before a good view of it can be had", in such privileged encounters, Eastman writes, "the ordinary commonplace of the bankside is transformed".[32] It is for similar reasons that Alfred Tennyson, in his poem 'The Progress of Spring', dubs the kingfisher "the secret splendour of the brooks".[33] Unobtrusive and eye-catching, discreet and conspicuous, imperceptible and dazzling, *Alcedo atthis* is, as these various accounts and observations imply, a paradox of apprehension.

Brilliant Absence is an attempt to track and comprehend this para-dox, the secret splendour of Waanders' work, as it haunts his books, prints, correspondence, and interventions. As bird and metaphor,

Waanders' elusive kingfisher limns a body of work that encompasses empirical study and lyric quest, and where the rigour of research meets the romance of the search. In scope and range, Waanders' singular endeavor is both epistemological and ontological—as much concerned with the acquisition and limits of knowledge as it is with questions of being and reality. This single-minded (one might say, eccentric) endeavour to understand, seek out, and represent *Alcedo atthis* in all its aspects is imbued with a wistful melancholy that marks and bides time in the blue space that hangs between past and future. Thus, Waanders' bird is, as Karen Davidson suggests, "both testimony and promise of significance". In this compelling dialectic of presence and absence, what started out as a "small project" is recast as "an archetypal engagement".[34]

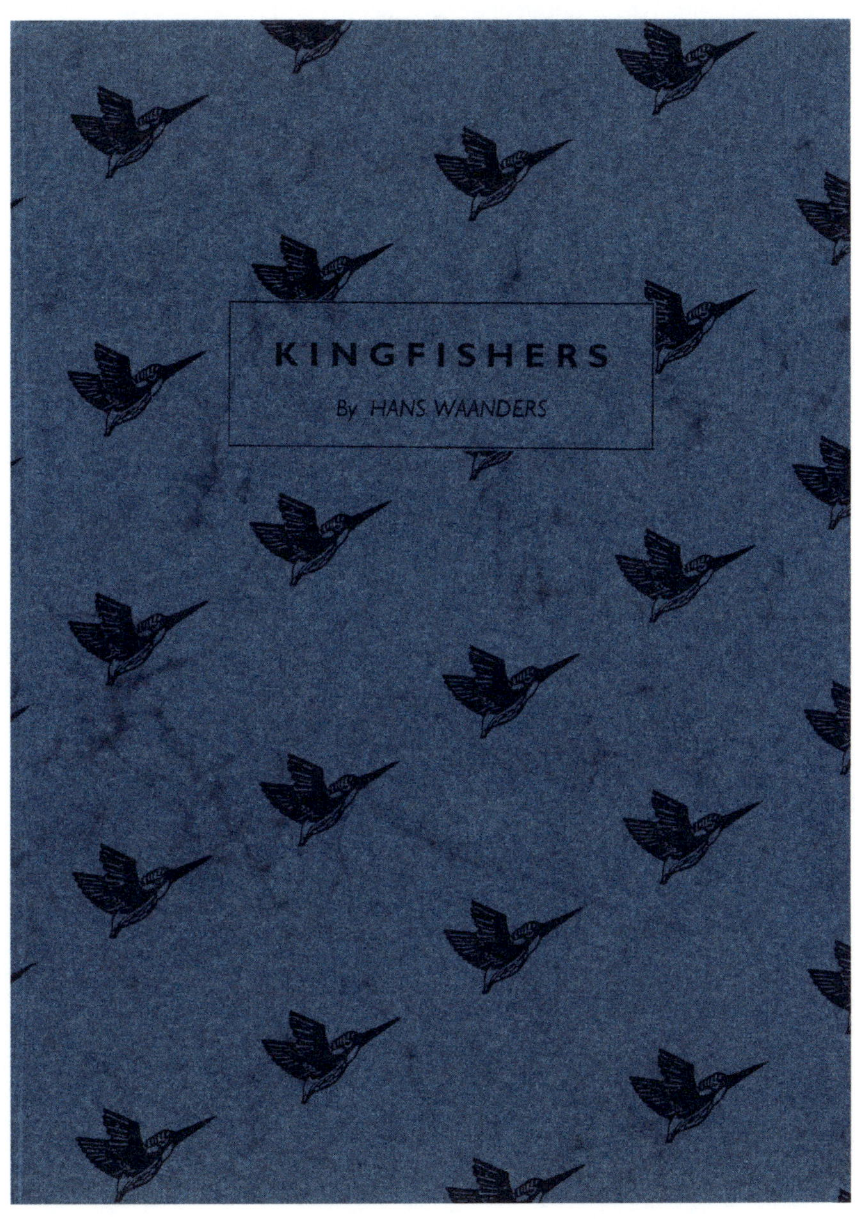

KINGFISHERS
By HANS WAANDERS

رتبة الشقراقيات
Order CORACIIFORMES

Family ALCEDINIDAE الفصيلة السماكية

Alcedo L. جنس السماك الاخضر

DE ZITVOETIGEN.

(INCESSORES)

Ordnung **Coraciiformes – Rackenvögel**

Familie **Alcedinidae – Eisvögel**

Vogels: Aves. Lichtsnaveligen, Levirostres.

IJsvogels, *Alcedines*

Ordning Coraciiformes

KUNGSFISKARE, familj *Alcedinidae*

familj *Alcedinidae*

Säihkylinnut (lahko **Coraciiformes**)

Kuningaskalastajat (heimo **Alcedinidae**)

Family ALCEDINIDAE (Halcyonidae)
Subfamily Alcedininae
Genus *Alcedo* Linnaeus

ORDER CORACIIFORMES
FAMILY ALCEDINIDAE
Kingfishers

파랑새 목 CORACIIFORMES

물촉새 과 Alcedinidae

Разред Синявицоподобни (Coraciiformes)

СЕМ. ЗЕМЕРОДНИ РИБАРЧЕТА (ALCEDINIDAE).

ORDEN CORACIIFORMES

FAMILIA ALCEDINIDAE (MARTIN-PESCADORES)

IJSVOGELS - *Alcedinidae*

CORACIIFORMES

Ordnung   Eisvögel — *Halcyones*

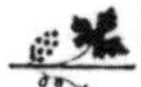

2º CORACIIFORMES

ALCEDINIDÉS.

Skrigefugle

ORDO CORACIIFORMES

Familia Alcedinidae

Gen Alcedo L., 1758

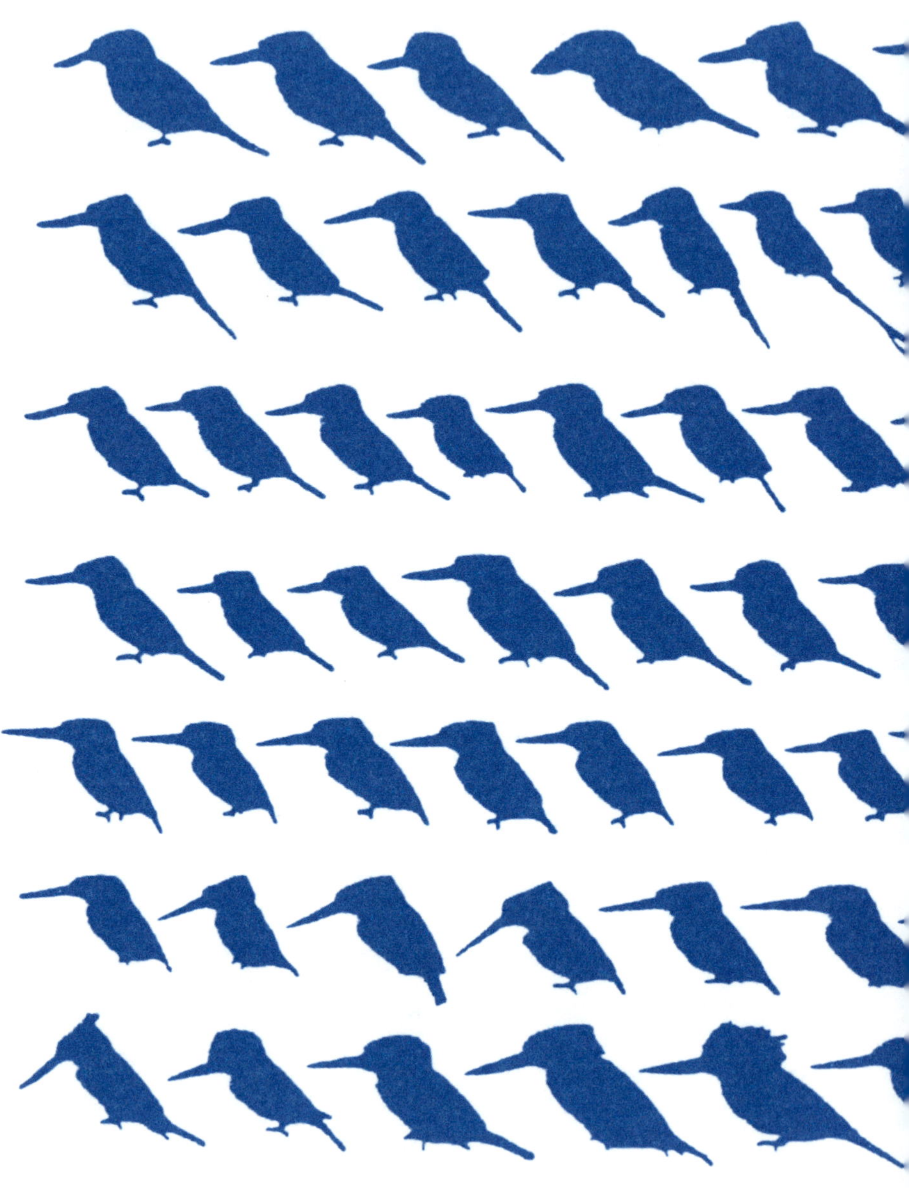

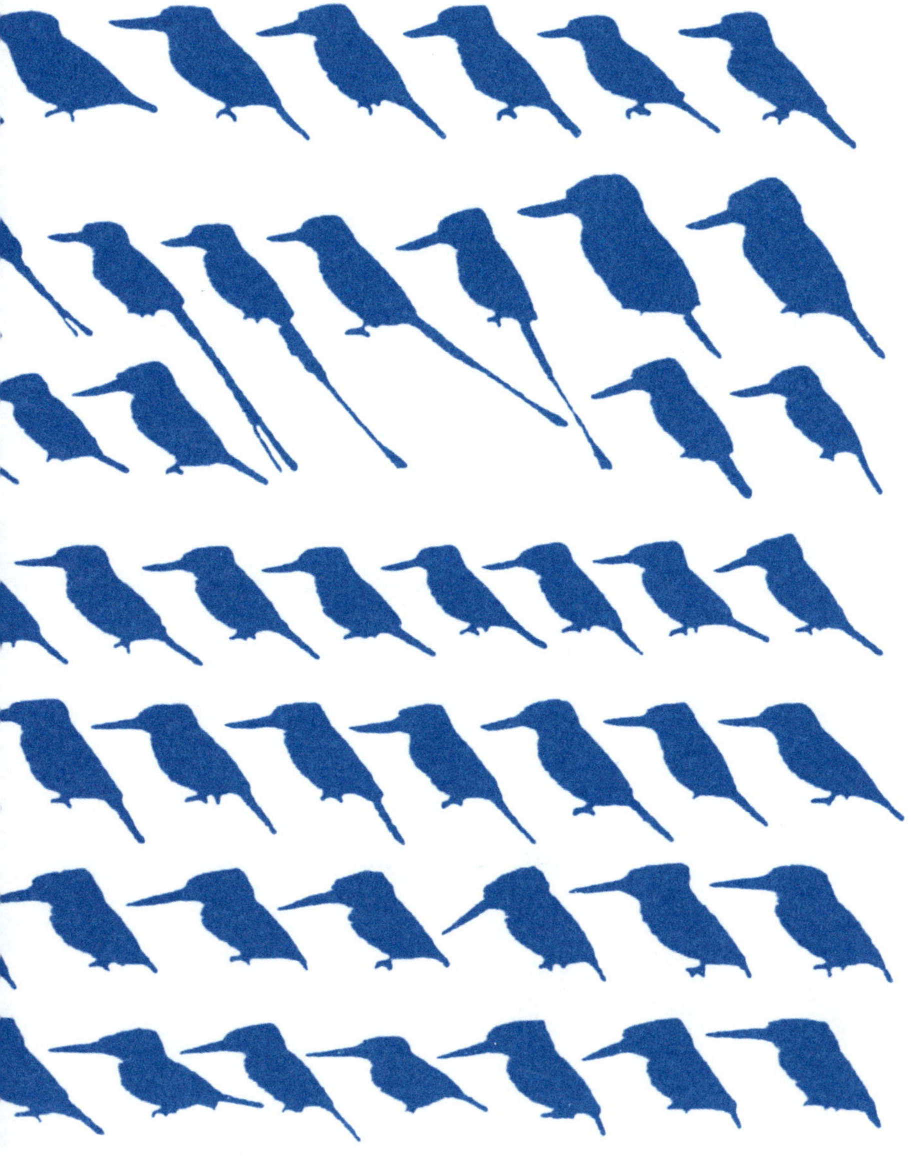

Solitair

Il vit seul

viver solitário

ein unverträglicher Einzelgänger

een schuwe vogel, ongezellig en onverdraagzaam

l'oiseau vit en solitaire

A solitary and unsocial bird

Meestal solitair

enkeltvis

Ungesellig

is usually seen solitary

Life

With the popularity of contemporary forms of nature writing, to focus one's attention on a single subject, as Waanders does with *Alcedo atthis*, is not especially unusual. "Bumblebees. Butterflies. Fields. Moorland. Otters. Osprey. Crows. Weeds. Footpaths", the natural history writer and critic Patrick Barkham wryly notes of this trend: "No creature or corner of the countryside appears too insignificant for a meandering exploration in 70,000 words."[1] However, in addition to the visual emphasis of his work, Waanders' obsessive study of *Alcedo atthis* is very different to the explorations of wildness and self that occur in popular contemporary nature, or, indeed the socio-economic bent that characterises much of the current trend in this particular genre.

Although his fascination with *Alcedo atthis* might, for example, invite comparison with the American writer and activist Susan Cerulean's relentless pursuit of the swallow-tailed kite (*Elanoides forficatus*) in *Tracking Desire*, Waanders' search bares very different fruits. Both quests begin with what Cerulean calls an "origin moment": "My memory is etched with a clear image of how that bird hung over me, suspended like an angel, so starkly black and white, with its wide scissored-slit of a tail."[2] Yet in comparison to Cerulean, Waanders' "origin moment" does not precipitate the kind of embrace or reverence of wildness that Cerulean is keen to share with her reader. "When that first fleet kite shadowed my face", Cerulean confides, "I knew that something essential connecting me viscerally to wildness had come into my life. I wanted that wildness."[3]

Far from valorizing "wildness"—or reassessing himself, or his life, in relation to it—Waanders' attention is frequently turned to human culture, technology, and commerce, including its most quotidian and prosaic ephemera. When it comes to seeking the elusive kingfisher, telephone directories, postage stamps, old encyclopedias, almanacs, prediction guides, and retail nomenclature are as illuminating or disclosing as riverbanks and waterways. Such nondescript intimations and traces of the kingfisher reflect a key aspect of the bird's elusive splendor—namely, its familiarity and its pervasive presence in popular imagination. "Its image", as Mark Cocker and Richard Mabey remark, "is now so ubiquitous—especially on crockery, calendars and anniversary cards—that even people who have never seen one are completely familiar with its appearance".[4]

As much as it differs from the popular contemporary forms of nature writing, Waanders' project also departs from birding memoirs and biographies such as Richard Millington's *A Twitcher's Diary*, published in 1981, or more recent titles such as Lynn E. Barber's *Extreme Birder: One Woman's Big Year*, and Noah Strycker's recent *Birding Without Borders: An Obsession, A Quest, and the Biggest Year in the World*. The narrow, specialised nature of this niche genre means that less dynamic accounts, as David Callahan suggests in *A History of Birdwatching in 100 Objects*, "have tended to anal retention, often being a listing memoir appealing to a limited but committed audience". For "only birders can travel the world and have little to say about the culture and avifauna of the countries visited, just the numbers and species names".[5]

While Waanders shows a similar predisposition for numbers and lists, even at his most myopic—most appositely perhaps in *Eyes* which records Waanders' daily ritual of stamping the same one single image of the kingfisher's eye to mark the time since sighting the bird in 1982—the circumambient world remains steadfastly in the wings of his work. As a peripheral presence, the world beyond *Alcedo atthis* not only provides context and enriches the meaning that accrues around Waanders' principal subject, but it also orients it. The world is put into limpid relief and illuminated in Waanders' pursuit of the kingfisher. As an opportunity for gaining further knowledge of Waanders' fugitive bird, the world is recast and renewed in its image.

If Waanders' work eschews the rhapsodic embrace of nature and landscape as it occurs in contemporary nature writing, or the niche myopia of the birding memoir, it does nevertheless invite certain comparisons with a close relative of these genres: J. A. Baker's *The Peregrine*. Published in 1967 and now univocally revered as a classic of nature writing, Baker's book recounts a ten-year obsession with *Falco peregrinus* that Baker distills into one hypothetical season lasting from October to April. Over this period of time, Baker's narrator assiduously tracks and observes his hawks on a daily basis:

> Be alone. Shun the furtive oddity of man, cringe from the hostile eyes of farms. Learn to fear. To share fear is the greatest bond of all. The hunter must become the thing he hunts. What is, is now, must have the quivering intensity of an arrow thudding into a tree. Yesterday is dim and monochrome. A week ago you were not born. Persist, endure, follow, watch.[6]

As with Waanders, a defining epiphanic encounter catalyses an all-consuming pursuit. "I saw my first peregrine on a December day at the estuary ten years ago", Baker's narrator recalls:

> That was my first peregrine. I have seen many since then, but
> none has excelled it for speed and fire of spirit. For ten years I
> spent all my winters searching for that restless brilliance, for the
> sudden passion and violence that peregrines flush from the sky.[7]

From that crucial moment on, Hetty Saunders suggests in *My House of Sky*, her biography of Baker, the hawks would "become Baker's own polestar: they were at the centre of everything that he wrote". "Perhaps he saw them as a lifeline", Saunders speculates: "anchors for his creativity and ambition, but also for knowing his place in the world".[8]

The pursuits of Waanders and Baker are both solitary ones. For Waanders this is very much in the spirit of his subject, as the concluding line of the cento "SOLITAIR", included in *Kingfishers and Related Works*, emphasises: "is usually seen solitary". [*See page 24*] This truncated fragment of a phrase lifted presumably from a bird guide might therefore reflect as much on how one observes *Alcedo atthis* as the bird's own well-documented solitary nature. Indeed, according to Davidson, Waanders' "gestures were quiet and solitary, akin to the bird he pursued".[9]

Where Baker shuns "the furtive oddity of man", Waanders situates himself on the edges of the social world and adopts a deliberately *eccentric* position in relation to it. Perhaps like the preeminent water-side solitaire Henry David Thoreau, operating at such a remove—from the margins rather than from the centre—put Waanders in a better position to gain a sharper perspective on things, and also, to best express his interest in communication, travel, and, above all, distance.

"Distance is always multiple and relative in its configurations", Norie Neumark writes in her introduction to a compelling collection of essays that address the theory and practice of networked art and activism as it occurs in mail art, sound art, telematic art, fax art, and Fluxus. As these forms and practices attest, Neumark writes, distance "is coloured by geography, technology, temporality, emotion; or it may reference the gap, space, or interval between two points, lines, or objects".[10] For Waanders, it is in the pregnant pauses of dispatch and reception—the liminal, transitory spaces between sender and receiver—where his own temporal, spatial, and psychological sense of distance is perhaps most acute. By taking distance from things, Waanders finds the means with, and vantage point for apprehending them more purposefully.

Differences between the solitary pursuits of Baker and Waanders
are also revealed in their mutual eschewal of the autobiograph-
ical. As Saunders stresses, "always the observer and never the
observed", Baker "gave little away about the personal details of his
life" and "remained as enigmatic as the birds" he obsessed over.[11]
This eschewal of the biographical is, as Robert Macfarlane suggests,
a means of "self-depletion" and "extreme interspecies identification", so that the narrator of *The Peregrine*, in a form of *participation
mystique*, gets closer to becoming his quarry.[12]

By contrast, Waanders' limited biographical details increase rather
than collapse the distance between subject and object. Instead of
suggesting interspecies identification, Waanders' neutral biographies
further impress the image of a detached, dispassionate observer out
on the periphery of things. Despite his practice of including biographies in books such as *Kingfishers and Related Works*, these documents
disclose a minimum of information regarding Waanders' personal
life and are more akin to a birder's "life list"—a cumulative record of
species identified over a lifetime—than a typical biography.

A typical birder's list, the sociologists John Law and Michael
Lynch write, provides the motives for "searching the environment;
regarding, disregarding and selecting among potential experiences;
remarking upon or saying nothing about an observed event; and
treating an announced sighting as a notable, doubtful or unre-
markable claim".[13] Thus, as a representation of observations and
taxonomical tool, the list orders and arranges perception by elimination and exclusion as well as by accounting and inclusion.

Like the birder's list, Waanders' biographies are the inventories
of very specific details. Waanders lists his sightings of *Alcedo atthis*
and his travels in search of it, along (in earlier versions) with some
rudimentary information regarding his education, career, publications, and exhibitions.* Information of a more personal nature, such
as family or social life, is omitted. One might read this is as Waanders'
attempt to distinguish his art from his everyday affairs. Yet, Waanders
also excludes any information that might reveal something about his
relationship to the larger art world. These biographical lists reveal
nothing about influences, contemporaries, collaborators, or endors-
ers of Waanders' work. Removed from any readily identifiable art

* The biography included in *Standard Catalogue*, for example, includes information about
Waanders' education and teaching career as well as travels abroad that are omitted from
later versions. One assumes this is because these do not relate directly to *Alcedo atthis* or the
'narrative' that Waanders constructs around the bird. The biography included in *Brilliant
Absence* assimilates some of the information that Waanders omits with the later biographies.
[*See pages 156–157*]

historical context and operating outside of its common landmarks and parameters, Waanders (like the avian subject of his work) evades reductive classification. On the single occasion when Waanders' biography does allude to another artist, it is one of the old masters, and fellow Dutchman, Hieronymus Bosch. Bosch merits inclusion not because of his reputation within the Western art tradition but because laying eyes on the kingfisher (as Waanders did in Madrid's Prado Museum in 1990) in the center panel of his *The Garden of Earthly Delights* constitutes a sighting of *Alcedo atthis* (See 'Biography' p.156). Presenting his biography as a pragmatic, self-effacing list devoid of discursive embellishment Waanders conveys a life that appears to have been lived, privately and publicly, for *Alcedo atthis*.

One notable biographical detail that Waanders and Baker do share is their respective longstanding health problems. Complications in Waanders' health involved multiple heart operations, including triple bypass surgery. Baker was a long-term sufferer of mental ill health. "This is never declared outright in the book", Robert Macfarlane remarks of the latter, "but it is nevertheless made clear that the narrator is suffering from some deep wound, mental or physical, which tinged his perception with 'dimness' and 'desolation,' as well as sharpening his awareness of beauty.Although only implicit, Baker's illness, Macfarlane continues, is pivotal to *The Peregrine*: "For to abolish yourself through intense focus on another creature is, in a way, to evade death."[14] For Waanders, however, his own concentrated focus on *Alcedo atthis*—what W. H. Hudson considered to be "perhaps the most medicinal of all birds to see"—is not so much a matter of evading mortality as it is a means for contending with it.[15]

"Very often the feeling overwhelms that there is no time to lose", Waanders writes in a letter to Kristine Stiles: "I've got to work! And that's good. There is the need to tell so much. My work is about survival too."[16] "During the last months of his life", Peter Foolen recalls, Waanders "kept spending as much time as he could in his studio":

> Being busy—surrounded by his books and encyclopedias, his globes and stamps, the archive with his correspondence and above all the kingfishers—seemed to relieve the pain and gave him the strength to carry on.[17] [*See page 157*]

Foolen's recollections adumbrate Thomas A. Clark's observation that underpinning Waanders' work there "is an urgent sense of mortality: that we might live, but without the spirit, without curiosity, piety, and revelation, we indeed die".[18] Clark's sentiments recall those of Julia Kristeva and her suggestion that, "if the meaning of life is lost, life can be easily lost: when meaning shatters, life no longer matters".[19] In the face of such very tangible loss, and living with a constant reminder of one's own mortality, *Alcedo atthis* becomes the sustainer of meaning, presenting Waanders, as Karen Davidson suggests, with "a quest, a romance, and sense of adventure—possibilities, survival, flight, and fall".[20] From the perspective of such mortality and mutability—of "Life and Death" as Waanders writes in a letter to Kristine Stiles—it is possible to see how the kingfisher, according to Tjeu Teeuwen, serves crucially as both "a metaphor of life (and the life of the artist) in the margin of existence".[21]

INTRODUCTION

Ter inleiding

この本の使い方

Einleitung

ПРЕДИСЛОВИЕ

Inledning

INTRODUZIONE

УВОД

INTRODUÇÃO

Introducción

enkonduko

ÚVOD

Indledning

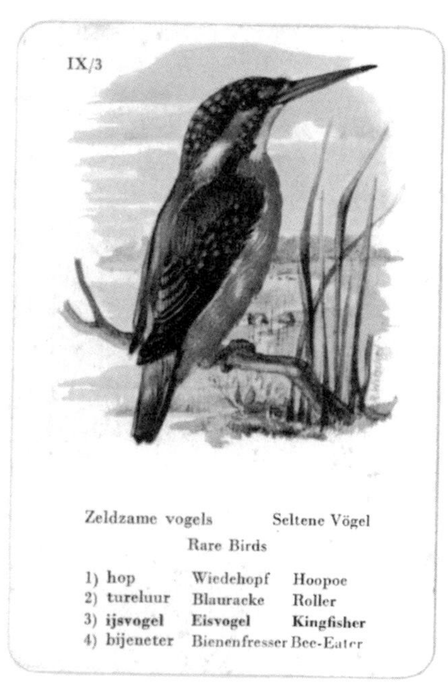

Zeldzame vogels   Seltene Vögel
Rare Birds

1) hop — Wiedehopf — Hoopoe
2) tureluur — Blauracke — Roller
3) ijsvogel — Eisvogel — Kingfisher
4) bijeneter — Bienenfresser — Bee-Eater

Kingfisher (*Alcedo ispida*).—The Kingfisher is, without exception, the brightest plumaged of all our common resident birds; for, despite of what many people say and write, the Kingfisher is still, happily, a very common bird, though its beautiful appearance causes it much persecution. Many are shot in order to be stuffed as specimens, and more still are netted, as the bird flashes like a jewelled arrow from its perch to follow the course of the small ditch or stream on which it has been fishing. Its tactics in pursuit of fish are exactly similar to those of the Spotted Flycatcher after insects. Motionless, it sits on some pendant spray or overhanging stump, until some small fish approaches its perch; then headlong the bird dives and rarely misses its prey. It then returns to its perch, and after banging the fish against it until it is quite limp, it tosses it up and swallows it head first. The curious nest is made at the end of a long burrow in the bank-side. In a sort of chamber at the end of the hole, the minute bones of its finny prey are disgorged, and in this small heap of broken up bones and scales the rounded white eggs are deposited. Both sexes of this bird are equally brilliant in appearance—and the young also, in their first plumage, are almost equally so.

Kuningaskalastaja *Alcedo atthis* P 18. Pesii harvinaisena hitaasti virtaavien purojen ja jokien jyrkissä hiekkatörmissä, joihin kaivaa pesänsä. Esiintyminen vaihtelee talvien ankaruudesta johtuen. Kalastelee usein lammilla. Lajille on tunnusomaista *hohtavan sininen ja vihreä yläpuoli* – selkä ja pyrstö loistavat ikäänkuin itsestäänvalaisevina. *Alapuoli oranssinpunainen*. Pää suuri, *nokka pitkä*, siivet leveät, jalat ja pyrstö lyhyet. Laskeutuu veden yläpuolella oleville paaluille ja oksille, istuu pitkiä aikoja aivan hiljaa, mutta nykii myös luonteenomaisesti päätään ja pyrstöään. Lentää nopeasti ja suoraviivaisesti matalalla vedenpinnan yläpuolella. Värit vaikeasti nähtävissä, ainoastaan selkä/pyrstö loistavat. Melko arka. Lekuttelee toisinaan. Saalistaessaan kaloja syöksyy suoraan istuinpaikaltaan pää edellä veteen. Ääni korkea ja läpitunkeva "tí-ii, tí-i-ii". Poikueääni pesästä yksitoikkoinen rahiseva "vuerrvuerrvuerrvuerr".

الفصيلة السماكية Family ALCEDINIDAE

تتصف طيور هذه الفصيلة برأس كبير قياسا الى حجم الجسم ، ومنقار ضخم مستقيم ، بادي الطول ومستدق في طرفه · القدم ضعيفة لا تمكن الطير من المشي على الارض ، والاصبعان الوحشية والوسطية ملتحمتان في الجزء الاكبر منهما ، ويقتصر الالتحام بين الانسية والوسطية على المفصل القاعدى منهما (شكل ـ ١٩٢ أ) · القوادم ١١ ولكن الاولى صغيرة · ريشات الذنب ١٢ (ونادرا ١٠) · اللسان قصير ، والانبوبان الاعوريان أثريان · لمعظم الانواع ريش زاهي الالوان · غذاؤها حيواني ، ويعتاش كثير منها على الاسماك ، بينما يكتفي بعضها بالحشرات والحيوانات الصغيرة الاخرى · تبيض هذه الطيور في أنفاق تحفرها في الجروف الرملية المطلة على الماء عادة ، وقد تستعمل ثقوب الاشجار لهذا الغرض · بيضها قريب من الاستدارة ، وهو أبيض لامع · وتنتمي الانواع العراقية الى (٣) أجناس ·

물촉새 *Alcedo atthis* (Linné)

영국에서 일본까지, 북쪽은 북위 60°까지의 구세계. 아프리카, 동남
아시아.

야외특징─길이 17 cm. 혼동되지 않는다. 배면은 진주빛 청색과 선록색(鮮綠色)이
다. 후(喉)는 백색이고 나머지 하면은 밤색이다. 목(頸) 측면에는 밤색과 백색 반
문이 있다. 부리는 흑색을 띠며 부리 기부는 적색이다. 다리는 진홍색이다.

서식지─물가. 여름에는 내륙, 겨울에는 해안에서도 본다.

현 황─호수 주변의 뚝이나 개울가에 번식하는 혼한 여름새이다. 또한 드문 겨울새
이다.

alced/o ৪ Birdo el la ordo de koracioformaj birdoj, kun verda k lazura koloroj k longa, rekta beko, vivanta ĉe riveroj k manĝanta fiŝojn (*Alcedo, Alcyone*). ~edoj. Fam. de koracioformaj birdoj, al kiu apartenas i.a. la ~oj (*Alcedinidæ*).

Min of meer verwante soorten zijn: de IJsvogel (Alcédo ispida), de mooiste van onze inlandsche vogels. Op den rug heeft een metaalglanzend blauw en aan den buik zijdeachtig menierood de overhand. De kin en de keel zijn wit, de pooten steenrood en de snavel is zwart. Hij leeft hoofdzakelijk van visch, kreeften en waterinsekten en woont dus ook bij het water. Met de kleine pooten kan hij niet goed loopen maar op de „zitvoeten" stevig zitten. Uren lang doodstil op een over het water hangenden tak gezeten, loert hij op buit als een kat op de muis. Heeft hij een vischje gezien dan stort hij zich, met den kop vooruit in het water, pakt het met den grooten, scherp geranden snavel beet, werkt zich door een paar riemslagen met de vleugels weer uit het water en neemt zijne vorige plaats weer in. Als zijne prooi dood is, werkt hij die, met den kop 't eerst, door het wijde keelgaat naar binnen. Omdat de vogel zijn voedsel uit het water haalt zijn de veeren stijf, nauw aansluitend en vetachtig. Hij is niet groot (17 cM.) en eet dus geen grootere visschen, maar hij is zeer vraatzuchtig en niet altijd onschadelijk voor de visscherij. Na sterke regenbuien, als het water troebel is en des winters als ijs de oppervlakte bedekt, moeten de ijsvogels vaak bitter honger lijden. In veel streken van ons land zijn zij zeldzaam, omdat zij alleen nestelen kunnen in steile, zandige oevers. Hierin graven zij met den groven snavel diepe, nauwe, horizontale gangen en aan het einde daarvan een ruimere broedplaats.

Daarin maken zij een nest van graten en vischafval en leggen zij witte eieren. Het vleesch is zoo tranig van smaak, dat zelfs roofdieren het niet lusten. Het is een standvogel.

Visvangers. Familie HALCYONIDAE. Slegs vier van die nege visvangers wat gereeld in die Wildtuin voorkom is ware visvreters. Die res vreet insekte wat op die grond weg van die water af gevang word, alhoewel sommiges van tyd tot tyd in die water duik om 'n waterdiertjie te vang. Alle visvangers het groot snawels, klein voetjies en bene wat nie vir loop geskik is nie. Baie is helderkleurig. Hulle jag meestal van 'n uitkykpos vanwaar hulle die grond of water kan bespied. Die prooi word met kragtige, sywaartse houe van die snawel teen 'n klip of tak geslaan totdat dit nie meer roer nie. Visvangers broei in gate wat hulle self in grondwalle uithol, of in reedsbestaande gate in bome.

ΑΛΚΥΩΝΑ: Πουλί κοινό στίς ἀκτές, τά ποτάμια καί τίς λίμνες ὅπου ζεῖ τρώγοντας ψάρια. Τά πιάνει μέ τή σουβλερή μύτη του πετώντας ξυστά πάνω στό νερό κι ὕστερα κάθεται σ᾽ ἕνα κλαδί γιά νά τά καταπιεῖ. Φτιάχνει τή φωλιά του σκάβοντας μιά τρύπα στό κάθετο μέρος μιᾶς ἀπόκρημνης ἀκτῆς. Ζεῖ στήν Ἑλλάδα ὅλο τόν χρόνο. Μῆκος 17 ἑκ.

EISVOGEL

Alcédo átthis íspida L.

Größe: Deutlich größer als ein Sperling.

Aussehen: ♂ ≈ ♀. Oberseite, Bartstreif, Flügel und Steuerfedern grün bis blaugrün mit hellen Tropfenflecken, Bürzel seegrün, Schwanz blau. Unterseite rostbraun, Kehle weißlich. Kleiner schwarzer Zügelstrich. Schnabel beim ♂ schwarz, beim ♀ ganz oder an der Wurzel rot. — Juv. fahler.

Flugbild: Der Vogel fliegt wie ein grüner Pfeil gerade, schnell und schnurrend meist niedrig über dem Wasser. Dabei fallen der gedrungene Körper, der vorgestreckte Schnabel und der kurze Schwanz auf. Rüttelt gelegentlich über seiner Beute.

Stimme: Scharfes, durchdringendes tieht, zuweilen mit angehängtem oder gereihtem tit tit, manchmal pfeifend tszie.

Eier: 6—8 rein weiße, glänzende, nahezu kugelige Eier.

Lebensweise: Der Eisvogel ist Stand-, zuweilen auch Strich- oder Zugvogel. Er liebt klare Bäche und stehende Gewässer, die er besonders zur Strichzeit oft besucht. Bei Verschmutzung bleibt er den Gewässern fern. Lauert gern auf Ästen über dem Wasser oder auf Steinen auf Beute, die er stoßtauchend im Wasser fängt. Nistort sind steile Erd- oder Lehmwände in Wassernähe, in Notfällen auch weiter davon entfernt. Das Nest ist ein 80 cm langer Gang mit einem rundlichen Brutraum am Ende. Die Eier werden ohne Unterlage, zuweilen auch auf einer Schicht zerbröckelter

Quest

An implicit sense of ritual also aligns Waanders' project closely with
J. A. Baker's in *The Peregrine*. Yet, where the "agitated, monomaniacal
repetitiveness", of Baker's search, as Robert Macfarlane proposes,
renders "the act of bird-watching" in *The Peregrine* as "sacred ritual",
in Waanders' work, these rites are less solemn and considerably
tempered with an air of rational detachment.[1] Indeed, if, as the writer
and naturalist Helen Macdonald suggests, *The Peregrine* is "one man's
obsessive quest for wild peregrines across the winter landscapes of
East Anglia. An ecological confessions of St Augustine or modern-day
Grail search, [and] the diaries of a soul's journey to grace, a man looking for God", then Waanders' "quest" tests with wry, playful curiosity
the perceived romanticism of such an endeavour.[2]

In this respect, Waanders' "quest" invites fruitful comparison
with the fated project of the Dutch conceptual artist Bas Jan Ader,
In Search of the Miraculous. Ader conceived this multimedia work as
a critique of the solitary, tragic hero and his or her romantic quest
for the sublime. The centerpiece of Ader's project was an ambitious
crossing of the North Atlantic, from Florida to Cornwall, that he
would singlehandedly undertake in his one-man yacht, the Ocean
Wave. Two night wanderings—undertaken by Ader in Los Angeles
and the Netherlands, respectively—were intended to bookend the
crossing. Ader executed the first of these wanderings, *In Search of
the Miraculous (One Night in Los Angeles)*, in 1973. Eighteen black and
white photographs, subtitled with captioned lyrics from the Coasters'
popular song, *Searchin'*, document the artist's walk that begins at
dusk on a highway outside of Los Angeles and concludes at dawn
with him facing out to the ocean. The final walk, however, did not
take place because Ader never crossed the Atlantic. Ten months
after he had set out from Cape Cod, on July 9, 1975, the Ocean Wave
was found adrift and half-submerged off the Irish coast. Presumed
drowned, Ader's body was never recovered.

As the art critic Jan Verwoert explains, Ader's unfinished project
boils down the myth of the solitary romantic hero "to its essential
features: one individual, silent and alone, approaches the limits of
society and culture where the city borders on nature at the coastline,
and goes beyond this limit into the unknown by travelling across
the ocean on a boat by himself".[3] Whereas more effusive strains of
nature writing might re-inscribe this myth of the wild, Ader takes
a more ambivalent approach. Instead of insisting "on the validity

of the romantic idea or deny its erosion like a stubborn traditional-
ist", Verwoert claims, Ader "acknowledges and actively foregrounds
the fact that the motifs through which this idea manifests itself
today are [as the Coasters' song suggests] historical, rhetorical, and
commodified".[4] Ader thus "invokes the grand emotion of romantic
self-experience in a form that is decidedly unemotional and non-sub-
jective":

> By introducing rational distance through the conceptual form of
> his works, he detaches the romantic motifs and emotions from
> their accustomed milieu and thereby makes it possible to approach
> them differently and anew. In particular, it is in the lightness of
> touch and unabashed boldness with which Ader stages these
> motifs that allows them to be looked at, freed from the weight
> of tradition, as simple ideas with great emotional value.[5]

Waanders' quest for *Alcedo atthis* practices a similar sense of
detachment. This sense of disinterest is perhaps most emphatic in
Waanders' claim that his pursuit of the bird "is not an obsession"
but a "coincidence": "It could also have been a green woodpecker.
And my search can be over from one day to the next."[6] Approaching
his subject with detachment and impartiality, Waanders implies
that *Alcedo atthis* is not so much the object of a personal romantic
quest—a private symbol or a coveted grail of irreducible enlight-
enment—as it is an opportunity for probing into the systems and
structures of knowledge itself. In this respect, Waanders recalls what
Thoreau poses in his Journal of 1851: "The question is not what you
look at but how you look & whether you see."[7] Indeed, like Thoreau,
Waanders is concerned with "what finding is [and] what it means
that we are looking for something we have lost".[8] This is as ontological as it is epistemological because, as well as inquiring into the
conditions and procedures of knowledge, as the philosopher Stanley
Cavell suggests, this also "means that we have to find ourselves
where we are, at each present, and accept that finding in our experiment, enter it into the account".[9]

Waanders' "account" is a taxonomic one. If *Alcedo atthis* presented
itself to Waanders as the object of his looking, then, as "a table of
possibilities" that discovers and sequentially arranges phenomena
against "the canonical order of a list", it is the technê of classification that organises how he sees the bird, and, ultimately, himself.[10]
"Dissecting a subject into all of its constituent parts was Hans' way
to search for a more exact knowledge of the object, and an understanding" Karen Davidson suggests, "and by extension, his subject

was as much the self as it was the social and natural environment".[11]

The taxonomic systems that Waanders consults and appropriates in his search for *Alcedo atthis*—particularly field guides, maps,
catalogues, and lists—also inform his concern with *kosmos* and "the
order that reigns in the universe, or entire world".[12] "I find the whole
cosmos in that one bird", Waanders has remarked of *Alcedo atthis*:
"You have to limit yourself as an artist to get a grip on your environment."[13] As a "world-system" or "orderly arrangement", *kosmos* is
a concept that emerges in Presocratic philosophy, the rudiments of
which are reflected in Waanders' attempt to understand his environment by "cataloguing, collecting, classifying, compiling, and
organising data" on *Alcedo atthis*.[14]

The Presocratics' "scientific approach to nature", the historian
Samuel Sambursky writes, "took the form of an attempt to rational-
ise phenomena and explain them within the framework of general
hypotheses":

> The object aimed at was giving general validity to the experience
> obtained from regarding the world as a single orderly unit—a
> cosmos the laws of which can be discovered and expressed in
> scientific terms.[15]

Those same laws were also discoverable within the human who
was considered the microcosm of such world-orderliness. Acquiring
knowledge and understanding about one's environment is therefore,
at the same time, attaining insight into one's own self.

Adopting and adapting seemingly disinterested taxonomic systems
in order to find, in *Alcedo atthis*, "a whole cosmos" invites comparison
with the impersonal serial procedures, repetitions, and constraints
common to the milieu of conceptual art. "Lists, diagrams, measure-
ments, neutral descriptions, and much counting", as Lucy R. Lippard
notes in *Six Years: The Dematerialization of the Art Object from 1966
to 1972*, not only gave artists such as On Kawara, Roman Opalka,
Douglas Huebler, and Hanne Darboven the means for codifying their
"daily life and work routines" within the parameters of their art,
but such rational procedures also allowed for a degree of emotional
detachment and subjective distance.[16]

A similar predisposition for reason and neutrality occurs in
Waanders' use of inventories, records, diagrams, and maps to catalogue and classify *Alcedo atthis* against the larger cosmos it intimates.
One might, for example, compare Waanders' tendency for numbers
and counting to the numerical paintings of the French-born Polish
artist Roman Opalka who, starting at zero, proceeded to systemat-

ically paint a sequential progression of numbers in his horizontal rows across a series of canvases (which Opalka called "details") for the duration of his life. Although potentially limitless in its scope, Opalka's work concluded upon his death in 2011 at number 5,607,249. Like Opalka's search for infinity, the pragmatic methods and methodological documentation that Waanders adopts do not preclude the possibility of metaphysical, spiritual, or emotional resonance, only the effusions of pathos, hyperbole, and hubris that such resonances might prompt. Thus, as much as Waanders' work resists the "spontaneous overflow of powerful feelings" familiar to more Romantic strains of literature and art, he nevertheless tacitly holds to the possibilities afforded by emotional reason and imaginative amplitude.[17]

Waanders' predisposition for "cataloguing", as Alec Finlay notes, "has an obsessive aspect, but one that is redeemed by the generosity and play of the imagination that accompanies it".[18] In this respect, Waanders' approach to his avian subject recalls the writer Jeremy Mynott's conviction that to properly apprehend birds one needs to "be tough-minded and open-minded, to recognise the constraints of science and hard fact but also the insights of literature, art, and the imagination".[19] Linnaean taxonomy and the "taxonomic, aesthetic structure[s]" of collecting and collections (the microcosms of bigger worlds) are perhaps the most salient points of reference for his inclination to catalogue the world and arrange it as cosmos,[20] whereas the imaginative "aery play" of Waanders' work shares certain affinities for the French philosopher Gaston Bachelard's speculative ideas regarding the transformative power of the imagination as it occurs in the poetic object and the poetic reverie.

"The poet lives a daydream that is awake", Bachelard writes in *The Poetics of Space*, "but above all, his daydream remains in the world, facing worldly things. It gathers the universe together around an object".[21] In this spirit, the catalogues, systems, and structures that frame Waanders' quest do not, as one might assume, contain the world but, in the aery daydreams of *Alcedo atthis*, keep it open, dynamic, and fluid.

This aery play also makes the world new and strange. Far from seeing phenomena systematically "in a manner that excludes all uncertainty", as Linnaean taxonomy strives to do, the imagination, "by virtue of its freshness and its own peculiar activity", as Bachelard proposes, "can make what is familiar into what is strange":[22]

> With a single poetic detail, the imagination confronts us with a
> new world. From then on, the detail takes precedence over the

panorama, and a simple image, if it is new, will open up an entire
world. If looked through a thousand windows of fancy, the world
is in a state of constant change.[23]

Instead of simply immobilising the world (naming it, pinning it
down) within a system of classification, Waanders' catalogue sensibilities are, despite their systematic rigour, mobilised by a similar
protean fancy to that described by Bachelard.

"A simple form with shape and colour—usually blue—may", as
Kristine Stiles suggests, "become the emblem for great daydreams":

> One might, perhaps, begin with Waanders' representation of a
> wing. But this appendage for flying is equally a referent for a
> bird, a signifier of flight which, in turn, suggests not only motion
> through air but through liquid since a wing may also be a fin or
> even a rudder. These objects of movement enable change thereby
> destabilizing and transforming form: one thing can quickly
> become something else.[24]

In his enduring search for the secret splendour, the brilliant absence,
of *Alcedo atthis*, the serial rotes of form and repetitive practice not
only objectively posit, as Karen Davidson writes, "the world a stage
of possibility", but also render it mutable, transformative, and
revelatory.[25]

Gewölle, abgelegt. 1—2 Bruten.

Häufigkeit: Besonders im Flachland und an klaren Gebirgsbächen. Durch strenge Winter oft dezimiert und durch den Menschen arg verfolgt, deshalb meist selten, doch kaum über größere Strecken völlig fehlend. Wegen ihrer Seltenheit verdient diese schmucke Vogelgestalt geschützt zu werden!

Nahrung: Krebstiere, Insekten und deren wasserbewohnende Larven, vorwiegend Fische bis etwa 8 cm Größe. Sie werden mit dem Kopf voran ungeteilt verschlungen. Eisvögel, die einen Fisch vom Schwanz her gefaßt haben, wollen die Beute ihren Jungen zutragen.

Род ЗИМОРОДОК — ALCEDO

В фауне Казахстана один вид.

Обыкновенный зимородок — Alcedo atthis L.

Синоним. *Alcedo ispida* L.

Описание. Половой димсрфизм выражен очень слабо. Взрослые самцы и самки сверху синевато-голубые, с более светлыми блестящими участками на спине, снизу коричнезато-охристые. Верх головы покрыт голубыми перьями с бурыми каемками, величина которых изменчива. Этими каемками создается более или менее заметный бурый фон, по которому волнистыми рядами идут голубые пятна. Спина и надхвостье бледно-голубые, крылья сверху и хвост синевато-голубые. Маховые бурые. От клюва через глаз на бока шеи простирается коричневато-охристая полоса, обрамленная снизу почти такой же широкой голубой полосой. Горло беловатое. Грудь, брюхо и подхвостье коричневато-охристые.

Молодые похожи на взрослых, но коричневато-охристые тона на груди у них прикрыты зеленовато-бурыми каймами, создающими общий буроватый окрас всей груди. Это отличие молодых сохраняется еще и следующей весной. Радужина бурая, клюв у взрослых самцов и у молодых черный, у взрослых самок в большинстве случаев надклювье черное, а подклювье светло-коричнееатое, темнеющее к концу. Ноги у взрослых красно-бурые, у молодых темно-бурые.

Размеры: крыло самцов 69—78, у птиц из Казахстана (13) — 70,6—74,7, самок 69—75, из Казахстана (11) — 71—76,5, хвост 33—40, клюв 30—40, цевка 9—11 *мм*.

Вес: самцы, май, Алма-Ата, 27 *г*; июнь, Тарбагатай, 32 *г*; сентябрь, Илек, 32 *г*, самки, май, Маркакуль, 32 *г*; июнь, Калбинский Алтай, 34 *г*.

Птенцы вылупляются голыми.

Яйца шарообразной формы, белые, блестящие, с тонкой мелкозернистой скорлупой. Размеры яиц из Казахстана (низовья Или) по 33 экз. из семи кладок — 20,6—22,6×17,8—19,3, по литературным данным — 21—23,6×17,6—18 *мм*. Вес ненасиженных яиц по кладкам из низовий Или (19 лиц из четырех кладок) 3,5—4 *г*.

MARTIN PESCATORE: *Uccello comunissimo che vive lungo le rive dei fiumi e dei laghi. Si nutre di pesci. Riesce e pescarli grazie al becco acuto che sfiora le acque. Non appena ha la sua preda nel becco, si poggia su una zampa per, tranquillamente, ingoiarla. Nidifica scavando un foro nella parte verticale a precipizio delle rive. Vive in stato endemico in Grecia. Raggiunge la lunghezza di 17 centimetri.*

III. **ALCEDINIDI.**

Bec plus long que la tête, élargi à la base, anguleux, à arète déprimée. Ailes médiocres. Queue ord. courte. Tarses courts. Plumages à couleurs vives, en partie irisées.

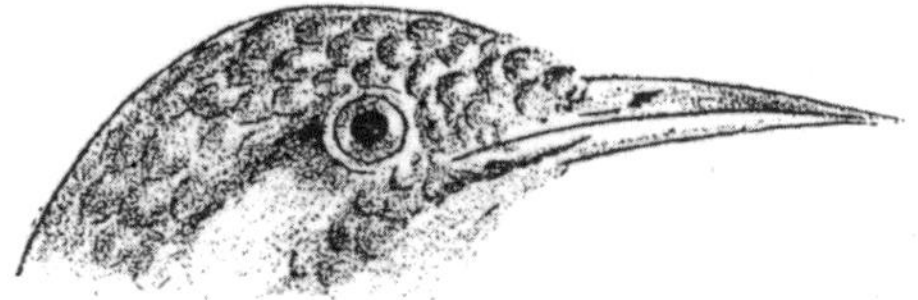

Fig. 337. — Alcedo hispida, *tête*, gr. nat.

1. **ALCEDO** Linné. *Martin-pêcheur.* Fig. 337, 338.

Bec moins large que haut, comprimé, s'atténuant de la base à la pointe ; mandibule supér. à arète arrondie. Narines basilaires, nues, obliques, étroites, linéaires. Ailes courtes, arrondies. Queue courte, en coin ou arrondie. Tarses un peu rejetés en arrière.

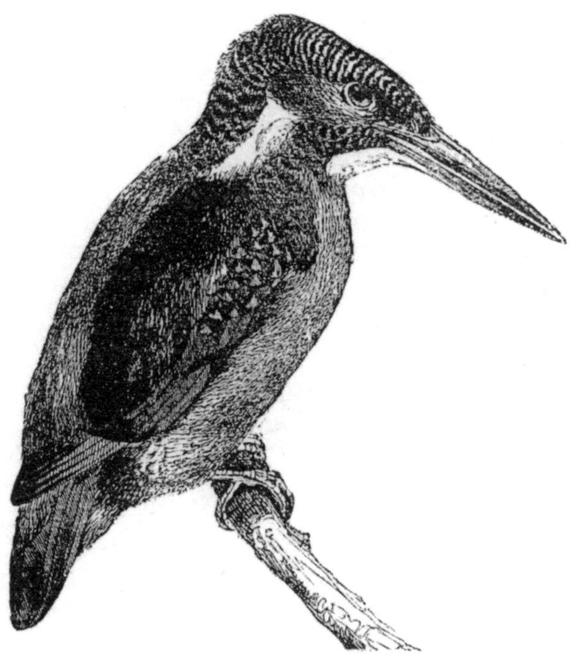

Fig. 338. — Alcedo hispida, presque gr. nat.

Dessus vert bleuâtre ; dessous roux rubigineux ; qques parties bleu d'azur. Lorums noirs. Rémiges brunes, bordées de vert. Bec brun à base rouge. Pieds rougeâtres. Iris brun roux
   hispida L.
Bords des eaux. AC. 0^m,12 sans le bec.

FAMÍLIA: Alcedinídeos
GÉNERO: *Alcedo*
ESPÉCIE: *Alcedo atthis*
COMP.: 17 cm
N.º OVOS: 4-8
INCUBAÇÃO: Pela fêmea e pelo macho

Embaixador único da sua família, o guarda-rios comum possui formas algo desproporcionadas, isto é, é corpulento, com cauda e pescoço curtos, cabeça grande e bico direito e comprido. Assim, é identificável, não só pela sua viva coloração – verde/azul no dorso e patas encarnadas –, como também pelas suas próprias dimensões. Por este último motivo, o guarda-rios, quando pousado, apresenta-se como que encolhido e numa posição vertical, parecendo equilibrar-se apenas deste modo.

O guarda-rios é sedentário, excepto nas regiões em que o gelo sazonal o obriga a afastar-se. Possui um voo veloz e directo, que pratica no seu largo território·lacustre, dentro do qual se mostra deveras activo, não obstante viver solitário. Empoleira-se num ramo saliente sobre a água e espera a aproximação de algum peixe. Quando o avista, mergulha com velocidade e captura-o com o bico.

Chegada a época de criação, o guarda-rios comum junta-se ao seu par e nidifica no fundo de um túnel de 60 cm, que escava num talude arenoso coberto por canas ou juncos, não necessariamente perto da água. O casal procria, em média, duas vezes por ano e choca os ovos conjuntamente.

Os seus ovos são brancos, quase esféricos; 22 x 18 mm. Elípticos curtos.

ЗЕМЕРОДНО РИБАРЧЕ (Alcedo atthis). *ДТ* 16 cm. *РК* 25 cm. *ОП:* има малки полови различия. Възрастните и младите са с ярко синьо-зелено оперение. При ♂ клюнът е черен с червеникава основа в долната част, която при ♀ е почти изцяло червена. *ИЗ:* равно „чрии". *Б:* обитава льосови и земни брегове на реки, езера и блата.

66 LEDŇÁČEK ŘÍČNÍ

(*Alcedo atthis*) Rybárik obyčajný

Od milovníků přírody si ledňáček vysloužil přezdívku „létající drahokam", a to skutečně právem. Jeho peří svítí nejzářivějšími tóny zelené, modré, živě rezavé i bílé barvy. Pokrývá jakoby sraženou postavičku ledňáčka, neboť jeho velká hlava a dlouhý rovný zobák jsou skoro tak dlouhé jako trup.

Obývá téměř celou Evropu a Asii i část severní Afriky, ovšem jen tam, kde protékají řeky nebo potoky. Na těchto místech žije v mnoha rasách, které však patří všechny do čeledi ledňáčkovitých (*Alcedinidae* — rybárikovité).

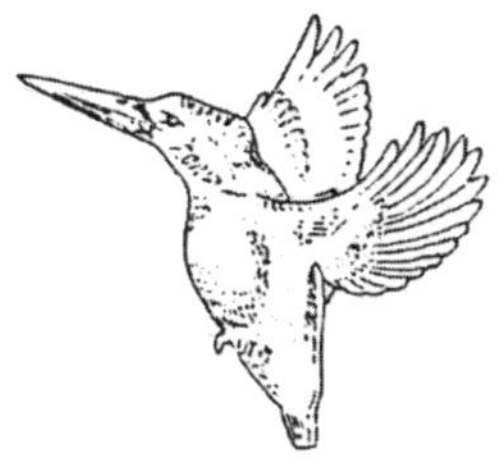

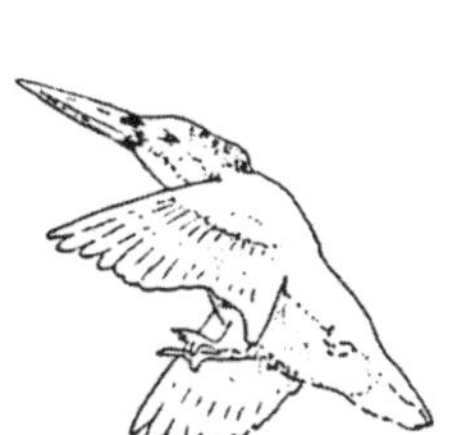

* **Isfuglen,** 18 cm, er den eneste art, som findes i Europa, hvor den forekommer næsten overalt undtagen i de nordligste egne; sydpå når den til Afrika, Indien og Indonesien. Den styrtdykker efter småfisk, vandinsekter og krebsdyr og har rede i åbrinker, hvor den hugger det lange vandrette rederør og reden ud med næbbet. De 6-7 glinsende hvide æg bliver lagt uden underlag omgivet af en krans opgylpede fiskeknogler.

Martín Pescador
Alcedo atthis

Altura:	16 cm
Peso:	♂30-♀45 gr
Ala:	76 mm
Envergadura:	27 cm
Pico:	40 mm
Tarso:	10 mm
Cola:	35 mm

Ave completamente inconfundible por la combinación de verdes azulados en las partes más visibles y, sobre todo, por su comportamiento y biotopo. La cabeza, muy afilada, queda rematada por un fino y agudo pico. La garganta es blanca, así como una mancha en el cuello. Tras los ojos aparece una banda de color canela, el mismo que tiñe todas las zonas ventrales. El obispillo presenta irisaciones muy llamativas. Patas cortísimas y rojas.

翠鳥（翠鳥科）

像女媧補天時，遺落的七彩煉石，顆顆落到凡間化做閃亮的翠鳥。由於女媧的盛情，使這個世界變得更多彩多姿。

翠鳥！當你在野外看到牠時，我敢保證你一定會發出陣陣的讚美感嘆聲。牠那種色彩，美得簡直無法形容，牠在溪邊綻放出不平凡的聲響，給您無限的慕佩。

翠鳥也叫魚狗、跟魚鷹相似也是捕魚高手。但翠鳥比較會選在清澈的溪流邊。因此翡翠水庫附近有許多翠鳥存在。說得也是實在話，翡翠水庫若沒翠鳥，那就失去它的意義了。

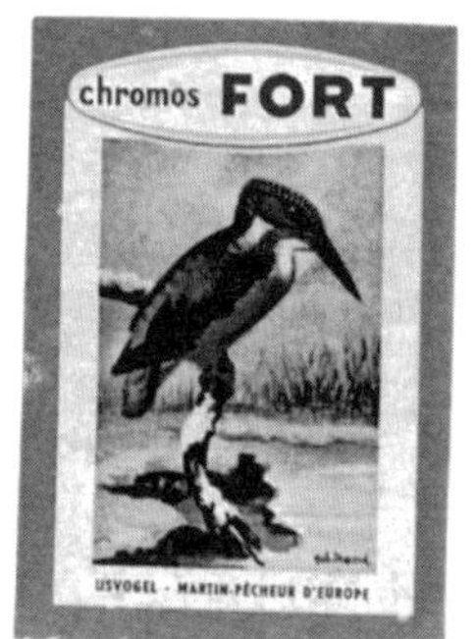

かわせみ〔川蟬・〔翡翠〕・〔魚狗〕〕①ブッポウソウ目カワセミ科の鳥の総称。日本にはカワセミ・アカショウビン・ヤマセミなど数種がいる。②①の一種。全長一七センチ内外。飛ぶと胸腹別色の背が光り、腹面は栗色で美しい。嘴が大きい。水辺にすみ、川魚・カエル・昆虫などを食べる。ユーラシア・アフリカに分布。日本では全国で見られるが、近年、都市化の進行や水域汚染とともに減少した。ヒスイ・ショウビン。圉夏。〔川蟬②〕

Object

....

Bas Jan Ader's conceptual take on the romantic quest and, particularly, his use of the photographic record is adumbrated in a photograph of Waanders, taken in 1994 by Peter Foolen. [*See pages 8–9*] The black and white photograph shows Waanders casually dressed and shading his eyes as he looks out across the Geul river, a tributary of the larger River Maas, in the Geul valley of Limburg. As with Ader's photographs in *In Search of the Miraculous (One Night in Los Angeles)*, Foolen's image might seem a relatively straightforward representation of the romantic artist in the throes of his search. However, this photograph in fact articulates a more nuanced relationship between Waanders and the object of his "quest".

Foolen's photograph depicts Waanders positioned at a prime strategic point for observing kingfishers: at the bend in a river. "Keep special watch where the river widens", the amateur naturalist and photographer David Boag advises in his 1982 book *The Kingfisher*: "on a bend for example, where the water slows down and is often shallower. Fish tend to congregate in these shallows, particularly in the summer, and the kingfisher is not slow to take full advantage of this."[1] Peter Foolen's image, however, suggests happenstance as much as it does foresight. In this respect, Waanders stance recalls a phrase from the book *Birds and Man* by the writer and ornithologist W. H. Hudson, which Waanders uses as the epigraph for *Kingfishers and Related Works*: "A man walking by the water-side sees by chance a kingfisher fly past."[2] Dressed in casual clothes, Waanders' sighting seems all the more fortuitous or spontaneous. Lacking binoculars or any other birdwatching gear, Waanders, it seems, has seen (or is searching for), something that lies beyond the *scope* of the average birder; "a wonderful blue", perhaps, like that seen by Hudson's man by the water-side, "far surpassing in beauty and brilliancy any blue he has ever seen in sky or water, or in flower or stone, or any other thing".[3] Indeed, the way in which Waanders shades his eyes recalls the dazzling brilliancy of the kingfisher. "This gem among birds is so brightly coloured as almost to dazzle the eye in certain lights", S. Vere Benson writes in *The Observer's Book of British Birds*: "I have seen one on the wing looking like a bright blue light rather than anything solid."[4]

The indeterminate (possibly immaterial) object of Waanders' gaze is rendered more enigmatic due to the way the river bank opposite Waanders is cropped from Foolen's image. As well as recalling the absent-presence of *Alcedo atthis* that informs all of Waanders' work, this omission emphasises the ambiguity of the thing that impels his quest. One assumes that *Alcedo atthis* is what Waanders is looking for (or looking at), yet just what it is that holds his attention remains undisclosed and uncertain. Consequently, Foolen's photograph, like Ader's in *In Search of the Miraculous*, implies that the viewer cannot see what the artist sees, but only speculate on what that might be. Indeed, with the artist in the midst of his search, Foolen's photograph is a tacit reminder that Waanders' work is as much about how *Alcedo atthis* has been perceived and represented—its mediations in science, art, literature, and popular culture—as it is about the bird itself.

Foolen's photograph has been used to accompany Thomas A. Clark's laconic tribute to Waanders that was printed as a postcard by the October Foundation in 2001 shortly after Waanders' death. Like Foolen's photograph, Clark memorialises Waanders' seminal encounter with the kingfisher but also acknowledges the indelible impressions that Waanders himself made during his own brief life.

A BRIEF GLIMPSE
A LASTING MEMORY

Clark's epitaph-like tribute not only conjures the title of Ader's conceptual cycle—which, in turn, derives from P. D. Ouspensky's 1949 book *In Search of the Miraculous: Fragments of an Unknown Teaching*— but also recalls the title of a significant book of Waanders' entitled *In Search of Blue* (1988).

One of his earliest books, *In Search of Blue* consists of a series of black ink drawings (photocopied and bound in a large, nondescript black book) of "blue objects, as seen on ships on the river Maas, near the Kingfisherpond".[5] The blue object of Waanders' search is assumedly *Alcedo atthis*. The lack of an article, however, also makes this blue more indefinite, immaterial, and akin to Bachelard's notion of the word, in his *Air and Dreams: An Essay on the Imagination of Movement*, as denoting "emotionality without object" or "sublimation without goal". "The word *blue* designates", Bachelard proposes, "but it does not render".[6] Yet, in both instances, "blue" remains conspicuously absent from Waanders' monochromatic book.

Stiles recognises an indeterminate, immaterial quality in Waanders' work: "water, wings, birds, queens, Kingfishers, and other things", she claims, are the "concrete signs for a space and time between very longing for something and its concrete manifestation in the world of ideas and things".[7] Perhaps like the dematerialised blue of reverie, which, for Bachelard, "unifies the opposite impressions of presence and distance", Waanders' blue forms and shapes intimate "a poetic knowledge of the world [that] precedes rational knowledge of objects".[8]

The ubiquity of blue in Waanders' work has led Thomas A. Clark to compare Waanders' fascination with *Alcedo atthis* to a foundational text of Romanticism: Novalis's unfinished novel, *Heinrich von Ofterdingen: A Romance*, published posthumously in 1802. After learning of the existence of a mysterious blue flower, Novalis's titular character becomes filled with "a strange passion" to behold it:

> It is constantly in my mind, and I can think and compose of
> nothing else. I have never been in such a mood. It seems as if I
> had hitherto been dreaming, or slumbering into another world;
> for in the world, in which hitherto I have lived, who would
> trouble himself about a flower?[9]

Obsessed with the elusive flower, as Maggie Nelson writes in *Bluets*, Heinrich "devotes his life to searching for it: thus begins the adventure, the high romance, the romance of seeking".[10]

As the object of Heinrich's quest, the blue flower would, according to Jeanne Riou, come to symbolise the "Romantics' longing for the absolute".[11] This might appear the very antithesis of the rationale informing Ader's *In Search of the Miraculous* or, indeed, Waanders' own reasoned pursuit of *Alcedo atthis*, yet, according to Gail M. Newman, considering German romantic subjectivity in the context of the British psychoanalyst D. W. Winnicott, "the blue flower is actually a symbol not of a goal that Heinrich has to reach, but of the process of striving itself". The flower "both eludes and intensifies Heinrich's desire, forcing him in effect to continue the search for satisfaction" and, consequently, question the veracity of a sublime *telos*.[12]

Echoing this emphasis on meaningful, instructive travail (rather than gratified attainment), Clark finds in Novalis' novel the rudiments of Romanticism:

> Through the wanderings of Heinrich, Novalis unfolds the
> essential Romantic programme; to raise the question of value
> in an increasingly materialist culture, to suffuse the rational
> with feeling, divert toil into dream, restoring depth, meaning
> and colour to everyday existence.[13]

Like Ader, Waanders does not so much "suffuse the rational with feeling" as use it to discern from the more lofty rhetoric of romanticism the essential, crude ideas and emotions that underpin it. Nevertheless, finding echoes of this "programme" in Waanders' more sober quest,

Clark proposes that Waanders' equivalent to the "blue flower" of the Romantics is "the Kingfisher, at once ideal and real".[14]

Waanders' emerald bird can also be perceived in light of what Bachelard calls the "poetic object". Situating itself "in the center of our imagining being", Bachelard writes in *The Poetics of Reverie*, the object "retains [and] engages us", "infuses us with being" and "which, all by itself, represents the world": "A flower, a fruit or a simple object, suddenly comes to solicit us to think of it, to dream near it, to help raise itself to the companion of man."

When "a poet has chosen his object, the object itself changes its being", Bachelard writes, "It is promoted to the poetic". In this way the poet "put[s] the world under the sign of the object, of a fruit of the world, a flower of the world!".[15] Just as Heinrich puts the world under the sign of the blue flower, Waanders, in his own rational, detached way, puts the world under the sign of *Alcedo atthis*. Thus, this tiny bird compasses the world so that, to quote the title of Waanders' book, "All becomes a kingfisher" (*Alles ijsvogelt*, 1986–89). "A whole world", Jean Poussin suggests in his illuminating essay on Waanders, "exists within a kingfisher, which is a mirror of the universe".[16]

Poussin's sentiment is echoed saliently in one of Waanders' rubber-stamped image of *Alcedo atthis* that depicts the bird, in the throes of flight, carrying the world on its wings [*below*]. Placed under this avian sign, while also being taken-up and transported by it, the world, Waanders' image implies, is experienced more intimately. This particular impression, which occurs frequently in Waanders' work, is a fitting indication of how, as Alec Finlay suggests, Waanders' kingfishers repeatedly invite us "to reflect, in the deepest sense, on what it means to be present in the world"—even if the kingfisher itself remains perennially absent from it.[17]

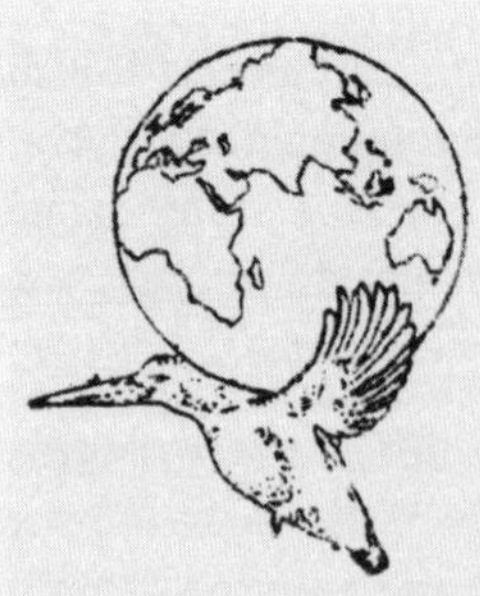

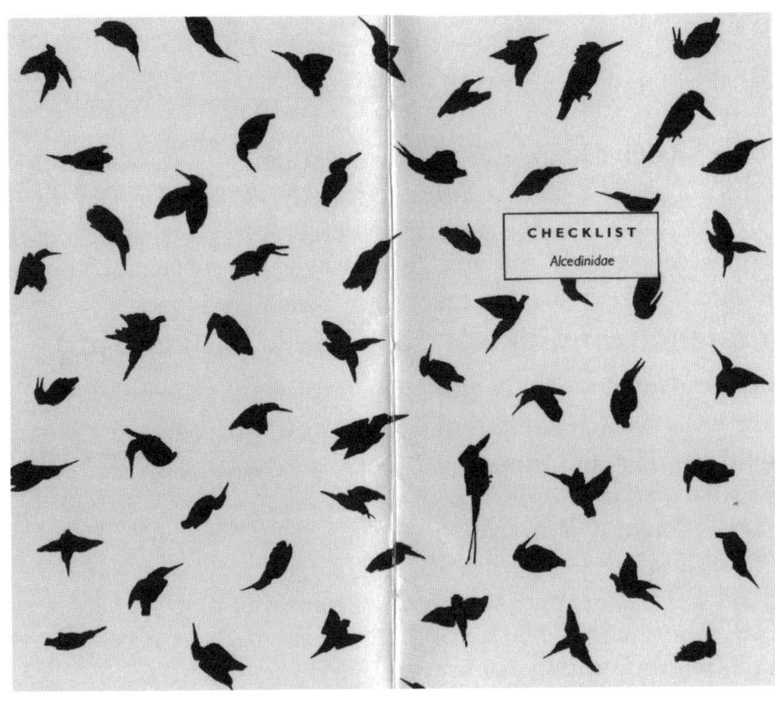

Micronesian Kingfisher
Halcyon cinnamomina
H.c. cinnamomina
H.c. pelewensis
H.c. reichenbachii
H.c. miyakoensis
Mangrove Kingfisher
Halcyon chloris
H.c. chloris
H.c. enigma
H.c. palmeri
H.c. laubmanniana
H.c. chloroptera
H.c. azela
H.c. humii
H.c. armstrongi
H.c. davisoni
H.c. vidali
H.c. occipitalis
H.c. kalbaensis
H.c. abyssinica
H.c. collaris
H.c. teraokai
H.c. orii
H.c. albicilla
H.c. owstoni
H.c. sordida
H.c. pilbara
H.c. colona
H.c. stresemanni
H.c. tristami
H.c. novaehiberniae
H.c. nusae
H.c. matthiae
H.c. bennetti
H.c. alberti
H.c. pavuvu
H.c. mala
H.c. solomonis
H.c. sororum
H.c. amoena
H.c. brachyura
H.c. vicina

H.c. ornata
H.c. utupuae
H.c. melanodera
H.c. torresiana
H.c. santoensis
H.c. juliae
H.c. tannensis
H.c. erromangae
H.c. vitiensis
H.c. marina
H.c. eximia
H.c. sacra
H.c. regina
H.c. pealei
H.c. manuae
Sombre Kingfisher
Halcyon funebris
Mountain Yellow-billed Kingfisher
Halcyon Megarhyncha
H.m. megarhyncha
H.m. sellamontis
H.m. wellsi
Lesser Yellow-billed Kingfisher
Halcyon torotoro
H.t. torotoro
H.t. ochracea
H.t. flavirostris
H.t. tentelare
H.t. brevirostris
H.t. meeki
Chestnut-bellied Kingfisher
Halcyon farquhari
Ultramarine Kingfisher
Halcyon leucopygia
New Britain Kingfisher
Halcyon albonotata
Forest Kingfisher
Halcyon macleayii
H.m. macleayii
H.m. incincta
H.m. elisabeth
H.m. insularis

The flight is low and swift, generally close to the surface of the water'.

Flykten snabb och rak, går tätt över vattnet, — *Maße* von 32 deutschen Brutvögeln: Flügel (27 ♂) 76—80 mm, im Durchschnitt 78,7 mm; (5 ♀) 77—80 mm; It is usually seen perched bolt upright or flying very swiftly and straight low over the surface of the water.

De vlucht is zeer snel en rechtlijnig, veelal vrij laag.

Fluggeschwindigkeit: 16 m/Sek. (58 km/Std.)

rapid steady flight, usually only a foot or two above the water.

Vole très rapidement, généralement au ras de l'eau.

Flight very fast and direct.

Possui um voo veloz e directo.

Flügellänge: 7,5 cm.

During 1942, one OS2U-2 was experimentally fitted with wings of higher aspect ratio with square-cut tips, and a straight-tapered, square-cut tailplane, to check out stability in anticipation of the installation of a larger Wasp engine.

The flight of the kingfisher is not, in fact, very fast, but several factors combine to give the impression of great speed. Considering the size of the bird, the flight is very direct, with no undulations, even over long distances. The flight resembles a bright blue arrow in its speed and colour.

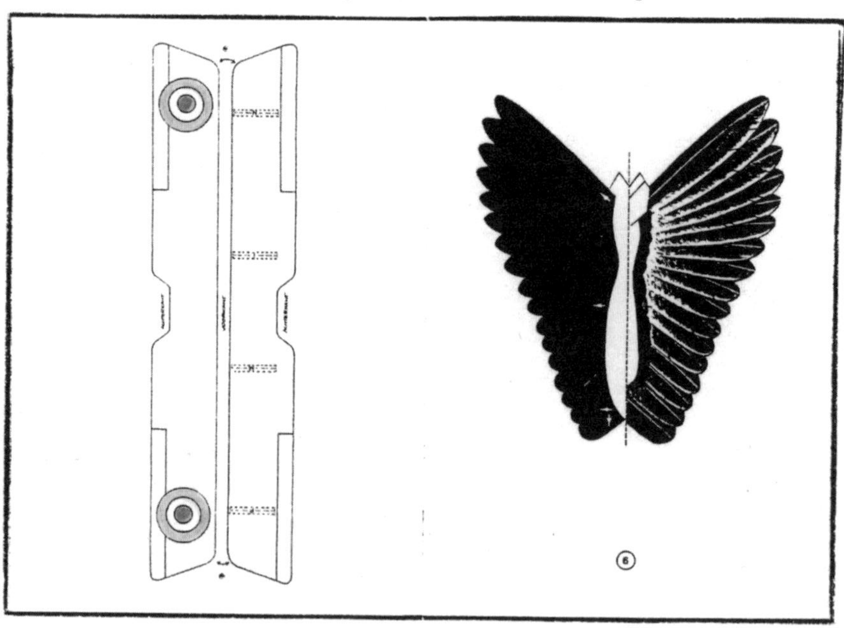

50

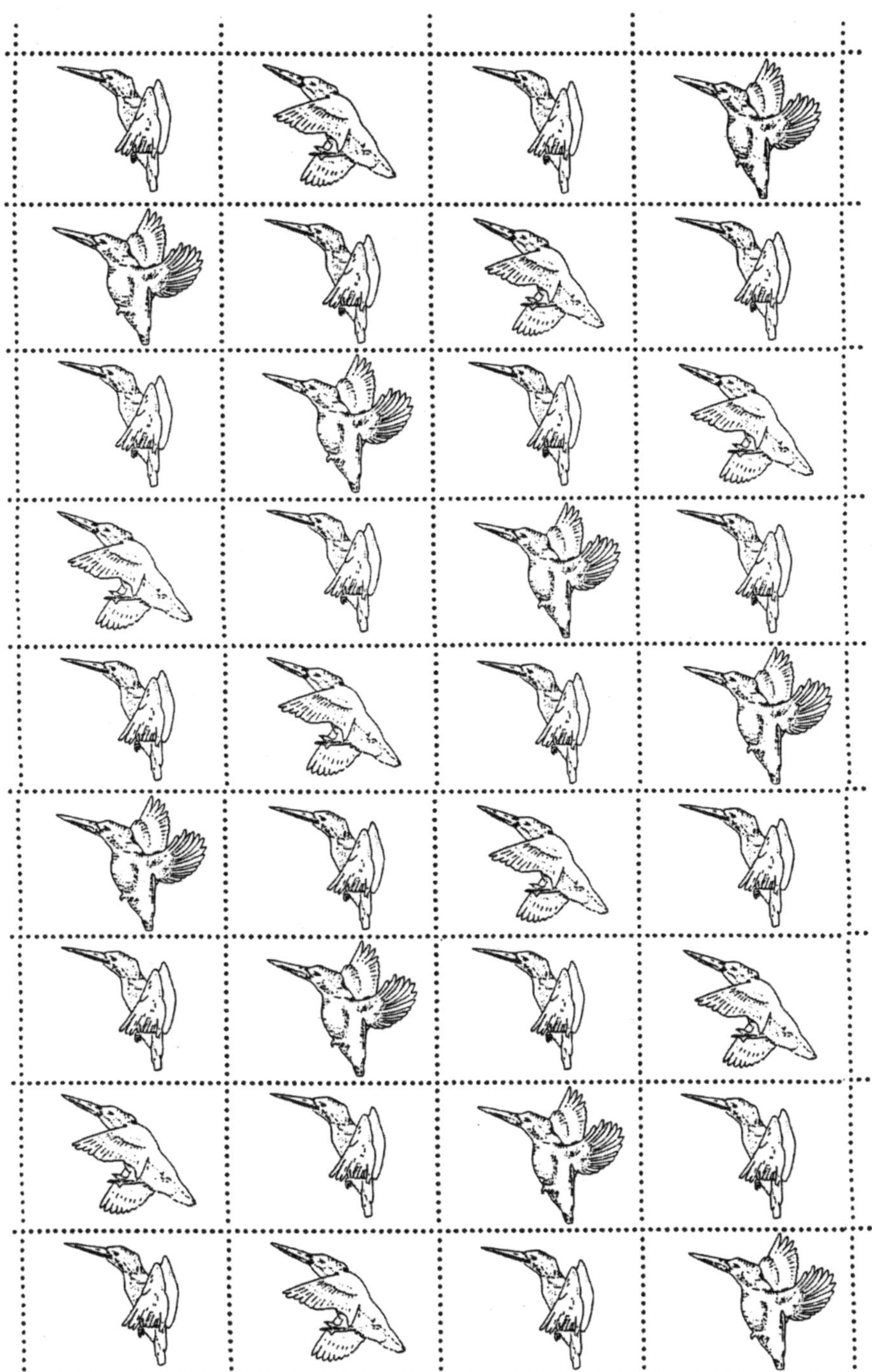

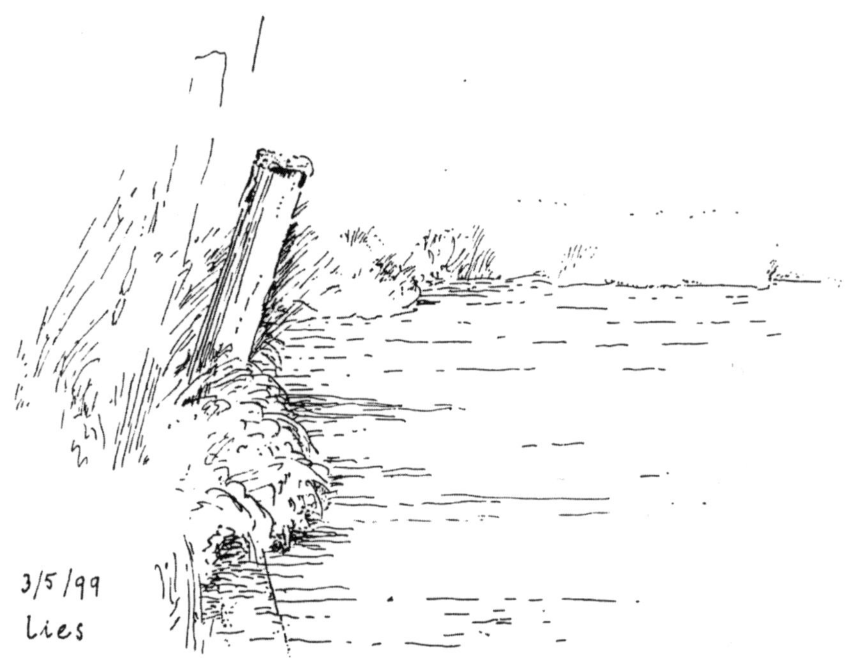

De laatste voorjaarsdatum is 21 april 1955, toen nog een IJsvogel werd
gezien op een paal in een poldervaart bij Lies.

Privation

The kingfisher, Waanders once remarked, "lives near the edge of existence".[1] Waanders' enigmatic statement might be understood in terms of the very real conditions the bird has to contend with in order to survive and exist. Waanders' comment also reflects the fugitive nature of his principal subject, which—"real and ideal", as Thomas A. Clark proposes—haunts his work as an impelling absent-presence. As the galvanising, focusing, organising agent of Waanders' work, *Alcedo atthis* is the elusive, liminal presence that inhabits the edges of experience, memory, and representation.

Not unlike Jacques Derrida's concept of the "trace", which, Derrida claims, "is not a presence but rather [...] the simulacrum of a presence that dislocates, displaces, and refers beyond itself", the sheer potency of the Kingfisher that consolidates every book, print, card, and intervention of Waanders' into a single Work, resides in its very absence.[2] Perhaps like the flower of Mallarmé's 'Crise de vers', the Kingfisher that haunts Waanders' oeuvre is "a pure notion" that is absent from every riverbank, bird guide, description, and account:

> I say: a flower! and outside of the oblivion to which my voice relegates any shape, insofar as it is something other than the calyx, there arises musically, as the very idea and delicate, the one absent from every bouquet.[3]

According to Kristine Stiles, it is in "the repetition of a simple form" that Waanders' "pictures, collages, paintings, and works on paper transport imagination and the sign far from itself while constantly returning to it".[4] Similarly, Jenny Brownrigg identifies the significance of repetition as a form of simulacrum in Waanders' idiom, noting how each of his rubberstamps is the "shadow" and "after-image" of the original bird, as well as a means of marking time until its anticipated reappearance.[5] These repetitive mark-makings and rote impressions of Waanders' therefore perform a dual function. On the one hand, they are a controlling strategy that seeks to recall and preserve the intensity of a past moment and make it present. On the other, and again like Mallarmé's evocation of the flower, the same serial methods compound the very absence that they seek to recall. Consequently, each image in Waanders' work becomes the trace and reminder of what cannot be fully redeemed: pure presence, like Waanders' blue bird, is irrevocably elusive and infinitely displaced.

Derrida's notion of the trace is nominally implicit in the title
of Waanders' early book *Bloody Tracks – Traces Sanglantes* (1987).
Waanders superimposes pale red acrylic prints—the "bloody traces"
(*traces sanglantes*) made and pressed with his own arm—over
photographs and prints of the "tracks" (paths, roads, waterways)
that he had taken in the Netherlands, Portugal, Ireland, and Iceland
in search of the kingfisher. The bird itself is never present in these
images—themselves the traces of irretrievable moments in time and
space—but located elsewhere and beyond. Nevertheless, illuminated like the rufous underparts of *Alcedo atthis*, the traces left by
Waanders' arm prints gesture beyond each desolate image as the
sanguine traces of a force that, as Thomas A. Clark writes, "may
utterly transform the landscape or the life in which it occurs":

> Its flight is a cut in facts. Perhaps it may only be glimpsed out
> of the corner of the eye, or felt as a thrill among the assembled
> forms. Nevertheless the world is redeemed by such an event,
> which ripples back through knowledge as iridescent possibility.
> Now and then, here and there, there may be beauty and vivacity.[6]

Alcedo atthis is, temporally and spatially (now and then, here and
there), a liminal presence, a bird on the edge of existence, just as
Waanders must have at times precariously felt himself to be. Yet the
liminal status of kingfisher—the possibility and promise accentuated
by the bird's conspicuous absence in *Bloody Tracks*—reasserts its
status as a poetic object that puts the world under its sign. Indeed,
it seems especially apposite that Bachelard should intimate a similar
sanguine disposition in his claim that, under the sign of the poetic
object, "we re-enter the world of confidence, the world of the confi-
dent being". Similarly, for Waanders, as *Bloody Tracks* implies, it is the
sanguine trace of the poetic object, the hope and confidence that it
imparts, that "bears witness to a soul which is discovering its world,
the world where it would like to live and where it deserves to live".[7]

According to his own accounts, Waanders would not observe
another kingfisher until 1990. Nevertheless, as the book's title
suggests, the sanguine mood of *Bloody Tracks* expresses an optimisim
and a conviction that further enounters of *Alcedo atthis* are a perennial possibility, with the promise of a sighting, so to speak, always
around the next bend of the river.

Bloody Tracks is characteristic of a number of Waanders' early
books, such as *Island – 15 Places* (1984–86), *Wiel* (Pond) (1988), and
Liedabók (1990), that include photographs or drawings of the places
where he had either seen or searched for the kingfisher. The textural

nature of these and other early works of Waanders' gradually give way to books and other printed forms that are more sparing and restrained in their use of mixed media. By the early 1990s Waanders had introduced his own distinctive handcarved rubberstamps into his work. These stamps, very much the hallmark of Waanders' idiom, are often employed in conjunction with carefully montaged texts and simple images, postage stamps (either official issues or Waanders' own designs), and his own ink drawings.

Waanders employs the latter in *Lies* (1999), one of his many postcards (reproduced in *Kingfishers and Related Works*), which depicts a location where someone other than Waanders had sighted a kingfisher perched on a pole somewhere along the Poldevaart canal, near Lies, on April 21st 1955. [*See page 52*] "Although the presence of a number of birds in the distance is indicated by small dots", Tjeu Teeuwen notes, "the image shows no kingfisher at all. Still you closely observe the bushes, hopefully study the stumps and poles".[8] Waanders' card implicitly asserts the location of this sighting as the scene of something extraordinary: the site, perhaps, of a miracle, revelation, or healing. An otherwise nondescript place has been hallowed by the fleeting presence of the exceptional there. The fact that the identity of the witness remains undisclosed emphasises the significance of the occurrence itself.* Although the title of the postcard refers to the place of this sighting, for the English speaker it also suggests false statement and belief. We do not need to know who saw the bird, only accept that they did.

Hallowed observation is also implicit in *In Search of Blue* and the blue objects that Waanders draws from the ships he observed on the river Maas. The title and the content of Waanders' book together recall how the word "object" can refer to the end to which effort is directed (the thing sought or aimed for in a quest or search) as well as a tangible thing that can be seen and touched. Both meanings are applicable to *In Search of Blue*, yet the presumed blue object of its search remains a fecund absent-presence in the spirit of *Bloody Tracks* and *Lies*.

Each of the book's objects only reiterates this deficiency and lack. Divorced from their originating environment, these abstract shapes and forms obliquely resemble the field guide's "decontextualised ways of seeing" and representing birds.[9] Ever since the acclaimed naturalist and ornithologist Roger Tory Peterson innovated the form in his seminal *A Field Guide to the Birds*, first published in 1934, field guides have tended to depict the "readily noticeable visual impressions" of birds

* The witness may possibly be Waanders's father who was a birdwatcher. See Embrechts, 'Leven op de rand van het bestaan', online.

(their "field marks") rather than their singular "technical features".[10] These "trademarks of nature", as Peterson dubs them, include a species' size, shape, and colour, all of which mark and differentiate it from other species in the field.[11] "Field marks", the literary academic Spencer Schaffner suggests, "make bird identification possible with the help of a visual guide, thus ensuring the perpetuation of the guides themselves".[12] These in turn, "describe and illustrate only those features of a species a birdwatcher needs to know to distinguish one species from another", Spencer Schaeffer writes: "No more is needed."[13] As John Law and Michael Lynch elaborate:

> Each manual, and its novice user, operates on a set of commitments: that bird species exist in nature; that they can be identified and indexed on the basis of sensory (mainly visual, but also audible) evidences; that separate species can be identified and named; and that species can be represented in paradigmatic illustrations and described in texts.[14]

Thus, every field guide, Law and Lynch write, "employs a tacit 'picture theory' of representation: an idealisation of the potential correspondence between a representation in the text and the 'bird in the field'".[15] Simplified, paradigmatic illustration becomes another key taxonomical tool for indexing a world of unruly phenomena. Every unique bird is measured against a Platonic-like Ideal or archetype.

To impress these avian blueprints most emphatically, contour, shape, form, colour, and pattern are accentuated at the expense of detail and context. In these paradigmatic illustrations, birds are removed from the environments they normally inhabit. "All distractions were banished", the environmental historian Thomas R. Dunlap notes of Peterson's seminal drawings in *A Field Guide to the Birds*:

> Peterson stood quail and pheasant on the page without a blade of grass or a bit of ground under them; his ducks and geese floated on invisible ponds, their bodies ending at a ruler-straight waterline; woodpeckers perched on tree stumps of ectoplasm; and warblers curled their feet around the barest suggestion of a twig.[16]

Not only does a similar removal occur in *In Search of Blue*, with each shape floating free of any identifiable context, but Waanders tacitly indicates how "the Peterson system", as it is commonly known, might be comparable to the nonfigurative rationales of twentieth-century geometric abstract painting. Just as painters such as Mondrian, Theo Van Doesburg, or Max Bill considered geometric forms more pure than forms copied from nature, the modern field guide jettisons mimesis in favour of gestalt recognition so that the observer may see more clearly, more "purely", free of distraction.

The rudiments of the field guide's binocular vision are implicit in *In Search of Blue*, which inverts its basic assumptions about descriptive seeing in order to re-present and re-cast a series of obscure objects in new light. Like Thoreau, Waanders' series of drawing invite the reader to see where before he or she may have only looked. The comparison that Jean Poussin draws between Waanders and Leibniz elaborates on this emphasis on seeing. Noting how Leibniz "suggests that the disorder we see (e.g. unkempt weeds and grasses growing on the banks of the River Maas) is due not to an error of nature but to lack of intelligence on our part", Poussin implies that to see is also to read and understand.[17]

This idea of intelligent seeing is echoed in Jeremy Mynott's suggestions for observing birds. "We can only see what the mind is prepared to believe", Mynott contends. This requires "ambition of imagination", a mode of observation that "marshals, integrates, and then finally transcends" two other types of observation: "active attention"— the "means by which we concentrate in a selective way on specific features of the world"—and "informed expectation", which refines the observer's focus "on the basis of what [they] already know about the preferences and behavior of certain species".[18] With the descriptive organisation of the field guide as primer, the observer apprehends the world schematically in reference to specific, predetermined criteria.

A similar "ambition of imagination"—of focused, clear, discriminate seeing—informs *In Search of Blue*. Each object recorded by Waanders is essentially the consequence of "active attention" in anticipation of *Alcedo atthis*. The book's assimilating "ambition of imagination", however, might also be conceived as Waanders' own take on the Book of Nature, a proto-scientific concept wherein nature is conceived as script that can be read for gaining knowledge, insight, and understanding of larger truths. A popular trope of romanticism, Ralph Waldo Emerson evokes the Book of Nature in his essay 'The Poet' when he conceives the world as "a temple whose walls are covered with emblems, pictures, and commandments of the Deity".[19] The visible world invites being read hermeneutically so that its most supreme verities will de disclosed.

The blue objects of *In Search of Blue* can be considered as the ciphers, hieroglyphs, symbols, or signs of their absent avian referent. One might, for example, "read" the various triangular forms that recur throughout the book as the ciphers of the kingfisher's distinctive profile. Likewise, the various long, tapered shapes that Waanders

presents might recall the bird's distinctive dagger-like bill. If "the
kingfisher is the cause and explanation of innumerable phenomena",
as Jean Poussin asserts, then such portentous assumptions might
not seem so incredulous. "Follow its beak and you will understand
everything", Poussin proposes: "The kingfisher is the beating heart of
the universe. The kingfisher *is* the universe" (emphasis added).[20]

Poussin's reasoning is not too far removed from the enfolded
"episteme of resemblance" that, according to Michel Foucault, was
the dominant mode of epistemological inquiry in pre-Enlightenment
Western science and philosophy. It was "resemblance that organised the play of symbols, made possible knowledge of things visible
and invisible, and controlled the art of representing them", Foucault
writes: "The universe was folded in upon itself: the earth echoing the
sky, faces seeing themselves reflected in the stars, and plants holding
within their stems the secrets that were of use to man."[21]

If one looks carefully enough, or interprets its symbols appro-
priately, a universe "folded in upon itself" may come to resemble
a kingfisher, or vice versa. The oppressive implications of this are
echoed in Poussin's suggestion that Waanders' work can be "stifling
in its single mindedness". In his search for order among the "apparent absurdity of this world", Waanders' kingfisher "can be seen
everywhere, in every imaginable circumstance, like a malevolent
spirit looking over man's shoulder throughout history".[22] Poignards
resemble the bird's bill, aircraft approximate its anatomy, compasses
evoke its legends, and cosmonauts mirror its flight and existence.
Likewise, twigs, branches, riverbanks (even shop signs) spell out the
immanence of a species whose anticipated yet deferred appearance
"is divine in nature".[23] Even in those territories where the bird is not
commonly found, such as Iceland, a mere coincidence in nomenclature could lead Waanders to seek the *ijsvogel* (ice-bird) there, or be
compelled by a butterfly's name: the *Kleiner Eijsvogel* (Little Kingfisher)
Limenitis camilla.* Thus, the dictionary might, as William H. Gass
writes in *On Being Blue*, be "as disturbing as the world, full of teasing
parallels and misleading coincidence", but such misdirection can, as
Waanders' work intimates, also serendipitously lead the searcher
down new, unexpected paths of knowledge and experience.[24] The
object of such pursuits may still remain as fugitive as ever, but like
Heinrich's quest, the journey brings its own rewards and discoveries.

---

* The single edition of *Island – 15 Places* (1984–1986), Waanders's first book, is a mixed media
"report of a journey on Iceland, in search of the kingfisher all over the country", *Field Guide to
the Books of Hans Waanders*, item no.1, n.p.

DISTRIBUTION GÉOGRAPHIQUE.

Générale : Europe généralement du milieu de la Scandinavie et de la Russie, à partir de la latitude de Petrograd, à la Méditerranée. Les limites de propagation vers l'est sont encore incertaines. Accidentellement à Madère. Remplacé par des formes très voisines dans le nord de l'Afrique et en Asie.

Widely distributed from Europe and Asia to the Solomon Islands. In New Guinea known to occur only in the east, extending west to the Sepik River in the north and the Aroa River in the south. Probably has a more extensive range on the north coast than presently known. Also occurs eastern satellite islands (recorded Goodenough, Fergusson, Samarai, Misima and Woodlark Islands), many islands of the Bismarck Archipelago (Long, Tolokiwa, Umboi, Sakar, New Britain, Watom, Duke of York, New Ireland, New Hanover, Tabar, Lihir, Tanga, Feni, Mussau, Emira), the Admiralty Islands (Manus), Nissan, Buka and Bougainville.

Verbreiding buiten Nederland en geographische vormen: Het verbreidingsgebied omvat Europa, noordelijk vanaf Zuid-Scandinavië en Noord-Rusland. Subspecies zijn beschreven van Noordwest-Afrika, Azië en den Indischen archipel.

Breeding of *A. atthis* in New Guinea does not yet appear to have been recorded but reliable local informants state that it tunnels into banks.

Two records only—a pair at Aksaray, 20–21 April 1946, and a single bird at Lake Mohan 25 April 1946.

Extralimital. Western Siberia and Transcaspia to Iran, Afghanistan and Turkestan.

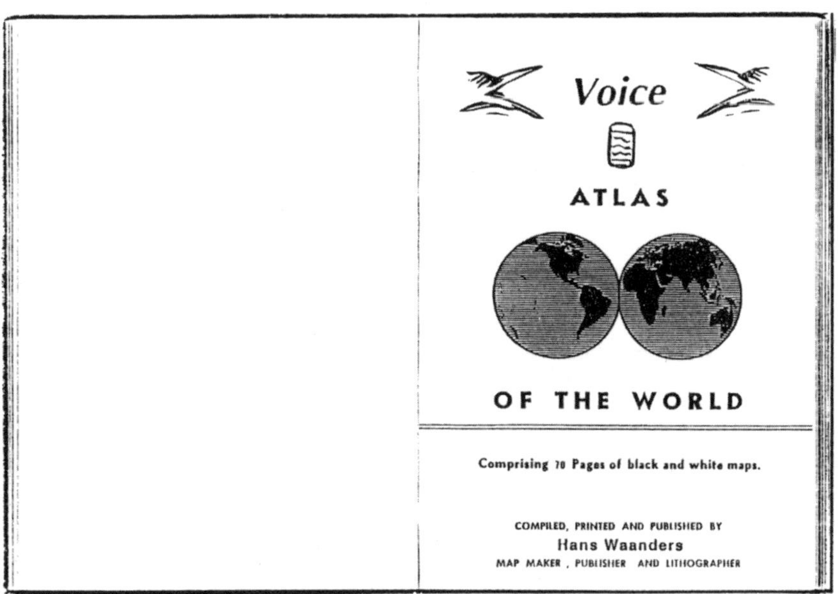

Fauna-element: van de Oude Wereld. – *Verspreiding:* palearctisch, oriëntaal, Australisch en ethiopisch, in alle klimaatgebieden met uitzondering van die van toendra's en woestijnen. De noordgrens reikt tot aan de juli-isothermen van 12–14 °C. De IJsvogel heeft in het palearctische gebied geen nauwe verwanten. Er kan daar dus ook geen soort-concurrentie optreden, hetgeen wel in de tropische gebieden het geval is. In de Nieuwe Wereld heeft de IJsvogel geen directe verwant. De geïsoleerde broedgebieden op het Zuidelijk Halfrond, nl. Afrika, oostelijk Indonesië en het Oostpapoease gebied, worden bewoond door populaties met blauwe in plaats van bruine oordekveren; zij vertegenwoordigen waarschijnlijk het oorspronkelijke kleurtype van de IJsvogel.

Южная и умеренная зоны Европы и Азии, Япония, Индонезия, Северная Африка.

Common, especially at the Amyro Marsh.

RANGE Europe to New Guinea and Solomon Islands.

SUBSPECIES IN NEW GUINEA One, *hispidoides* (Lesson); Celebes and Moluccas, western Papuan Islands (Misol and Salawati), north-eastern New Guinea (Astrolabe Bay and China Straits), D'Entrecasteaux and Louisiade Archipelagos, and Bismarck Archipelago, and Admiralty Islands.

Throughout South Vietnam, including some coastal islands.

January to June, earlier in the South of India than in the North.

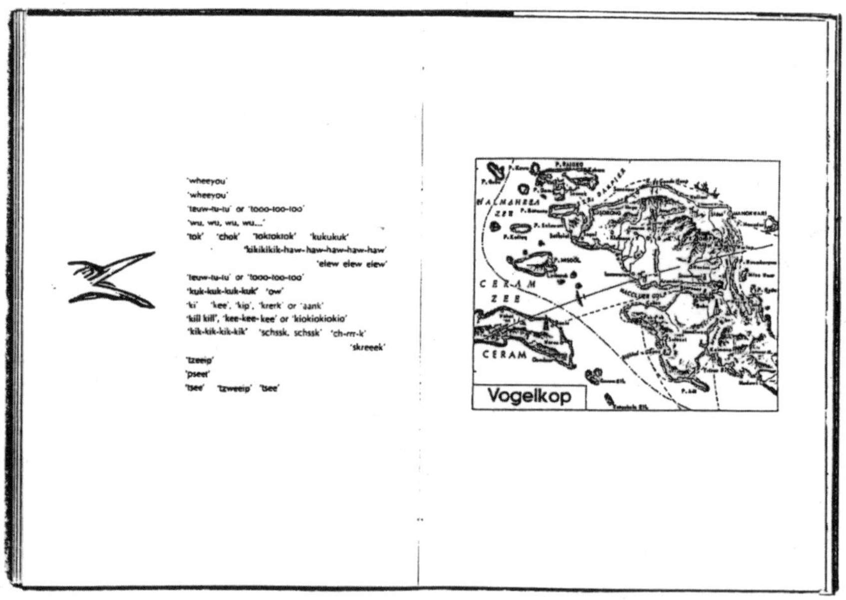

China; Hainan; Taiwan; Philippines and Sundas to New Guinea and Solomons.
SE Asia: common resident up to 6,000 ft.

영국에서 일본까지, 북쪽은 북위 60°까지의 구세계. 아프리카, 동남
아시아. Generally common throughout the British Isles,
but rare in northern Scotland.

Występowanie:

Występuje na całym obszarze Małopolski. Liczniejszy w dolinach większych rzek jak
Wisła, Górna Warta, San. Rozpowszechniony jest też na rzekach Pogórzy: Zachodniobe-
skidzkiego (513.3) i Środkowobeskidzkiego (513.6). Najwyżej został stwierdzony do 600
m n.p.m. w Beskidzie Żywieckim (513.51), Bieszczadach (522.12) i w Pieninach (514.12)
(Bocheński1960). Jest gatunkiem zmniejszającym swoją liczebność w związku z odlesia-
niem brzegów i zanieczyszczaniem chemicznym wód (Tomiałojć 1990). northern
Syria and possibly in northern Lebanon.

The central group of the Solomon Islands, Gizo, Rendova, and presumably also
New Georgia, are inhabited by a beautiful, very blue and brightly coloured race of
Kingfishers. Three males, including adult and immature birds, were
obtained by Mr. Teraoka on Tsushima, on Oct. 2, 4, 10.

The subspecies *salomonensis* Rothschild and Hartert
is found throughout the Solomon Isls. from Bougainville and
Mono to Malaita and San Cristobal.

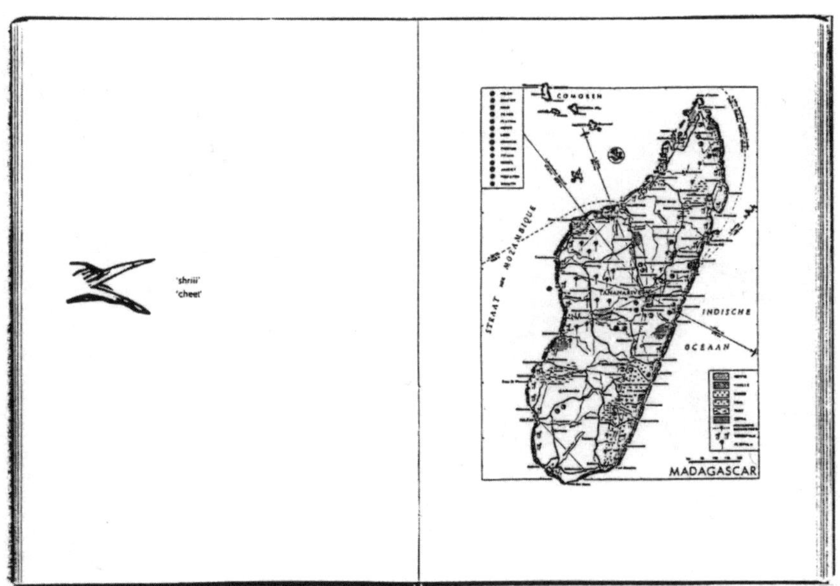

Zeldzame jaarvogel. Neemt in de wintermaanden wat in aantal toe. Is na de winter van 1962—1963 zeer zeldzaam geworden.
Is waargenomen in de Duinplassen, bij de reservoirs van het Pompstation, in de omgeving van het landgoed Groot Hasebroek, in de Raaphorst, Clingendaal, Haagse Bos, Waterpartij, Sorghvliet, Meer en Bos, Ockenburg, Zuiderpark en Te Werve.
Broedvogel: tot 1963 broedend op de Raaphorst en in de omgeving van Groot Hasebroek. Heeft ook gebroed in het Haagse Bos, Clingendaal en Oostduin, Sorghvliet, Meer en Bos, Ockenburg en Zuiderpark.

Slo   **BH** (— Herc)   **Srb** (— SE Srb, — Kos ?)
Cro Slav C Cro Kotar   Mtg   Mak

A. a. atthis (L.) 1758: 109, Egypt.
                            BH Herc   **Srb SE Srb Kos ?**
Cro Istra Qu Dalm   **Mtg**   **Mak**
Scarce in Northern Scotland, and absent as a breeder from the Shetlands, Orkneys, and Outer Hebrides; also scarce in Ireland.

Virtually throughout China.

Breeds virtually throughout China west to Shansi, s Shensi, southeasternmost Kansu, Szechwan, and s Tibet, and south to Kwangtung, Kwangsi, s Yunnan, and Hainan (*bengalensis*). Breeds in w Sinkiang in the valleys of the Ili and Tekes rivers (*atthis*). [N Africa, Eurasia to India, Malaya, New Guinea, and the Solomon Is.]

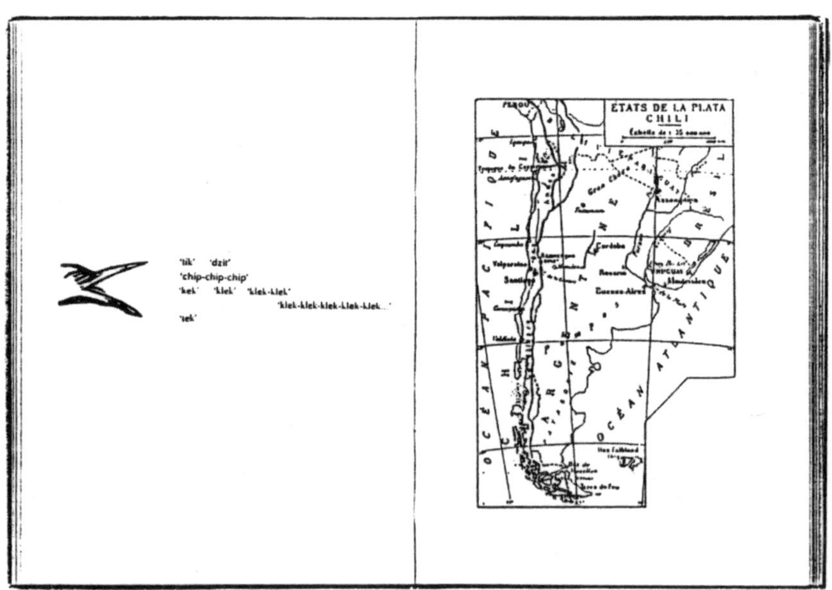

Melancholy

In Search of Blue reiterates an implicit melancholy tone that is intrinsically part of the themes of loss and privation that haunt Waanders' work. In *In Search of Blue* this further accentuated by reproducing its blue objects in black ink. "A colour is continuously, insistently, indivisibly present in what it is", William H. Gass proposes. Colour, he suggests, "is a completed presence in the world, a recognizable being apart from any object, while a few odd lines (since a line is only an artificial edge), a few odd lines are [...] nothing" unless "matched against colour".[1] One might note a similar discrepancy between this notion of pure colour and the Aristotelian forms (the "simple outline[s] on a white background") that *In Search of Blue* documents.[2] Waanders' black line drawings lack the indivisible presence they seek to re-present with each form being diminished in its monochromatic reproduction. Like the dark muted landscapes in *Bloody Tracks* that are illuminated by the sanguine traces (the afterimages) of sighting *Alcedo atthis*, it is the kingfisher's absence in *In Search of Blue*'s that make its forms *blue*: blue with longing and desire but also, more vicariously, blue with augury and portent; the emblems and the ciphers of a Blue world.

The melancholy tone that pervades Waanders' work can be considered in light of what Richard Stamelman, in the context of modern French poetry, conceives as a poetics of loss, absence, and death. "From the moment we take notice of the world and become aware of our place in it", Stamelman suggests, "we become painfully conscious of the loss that shadows all human activity". Waanders' fleeting *ijsvogelwiel* experience makes this sense of loss all the more acute. With this transient moment precipitating all of the work that follows it, Waanders' project, as *In Search of Blue* intimates, is a perennial endeavour "to overcome loss by naming it, by representing it, and by finding new forms and images through which to retell, recall, remember, and resuscitate what has disappeared".[3]

In this poetics of loss, Stamelman suggests, absence and presence "coexist in a stubborn confrontation, neither giving ground to the other" and offering "no synthesis of or resolution to their antagonism". Yet, as Stamelman notes, this antagonism is as generative as it is melancholic, provoking work that "exists in order to make present certain formal and aesthetic realities (words, images, colours, forms), whose existence is possible only because what they designate is absent". *In Search of Blue*, like many of Waanders' books, might be considered from this perspective; "enveloped in the coincidence of absence-presence" Waanders' blue shapes oscillate between a "faith in the recuperative power of art and language to recall what has vanished" and an acceptance of "the reality of the lack upon which all representation rests".[5] Indeed, perhaps like Heinrich's own blue search, Waanders' search restores depth and meaning to the everyday by not finding or realising the thing it seeks beyond it. "Dispossession makes possible the creation of images", Stamelman suggests, "and negativity, as embodied in absence, death, and loss, animates the quest of writing and other forms of figuration". Thus, if, as Stamelman proposes, "representation involves images and traces, not origins", then its inability to fully recover or repossess presence also "fuels the fires of artifice" and incites the possible.[5]

The evocative absence of *Alcedo atthis* in *In Search of Blue*—and the new perception it encourages—is especially poignant in several later books and booklets of Waanders' including *Fishing Perches* (1999) and *Perches* (2001). These books collect photographs of the perches that Waanders made as lures for the resident kingfishers in the various locations (including Scotland, France, and the Netherlands) that he visited. The literary linguist Nigel Fabb considers these discreet interventions "a comment on two aspects of birdwatching: its scopophilic aspects (particularly the desire to see the kingfisher, one of the most beautiful birds in Europe), and the fact of absence". "For birdwatchers, most of the time, the bird is absent", Fabb suggests, "the play of absence and presence is part of the pleasure of the pursuit (which is why birders do not go to the zoo)".[6]

Devoid of birds, Waanders' photographs of these perches enigmatically complicate this play of absence and presence by simultaneously evoking the promise of arrival and the regret of departure. As a result, the bird is impressed more poignantly, haunting both the environment and the viewer's imagination by its conspicuous absence. Each perch that Waanders makes from the sticks and branches he collected not only becomes a measure of this absence, but, like his earlier "bloody tracks", is also the trace or vestige of the artist's own transitory presence in the landscape, and perhaps, the world. Again, like *Bloody Tracks*, these fragile, impermanent installations are also affirmative, sanguine gestures—gestures of faith and optimism, possibility and encounter—that Waanders' work is steadfastly commited to and resolutely invested in. The Kingfisher, each stick or branch quietly affirms, *will* return.

perch (2) *n* pole or bar for birds to roost on; branch *etc* on which a bird rests; seat, *esp* in high position; secure resting-place.

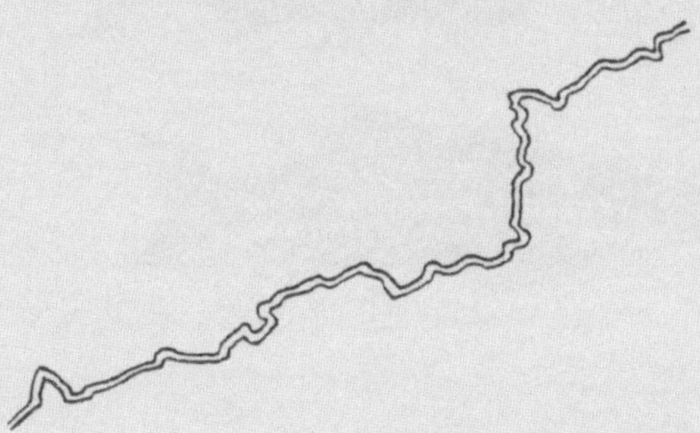

border [*bawrder*] *n* edge, side, margin, boundary, frontier; narrow strip of ground forming an edging plot usually planted with flowers; edging to a piece of material; **The B.** boundary between England and Scotland and the country adjacent.

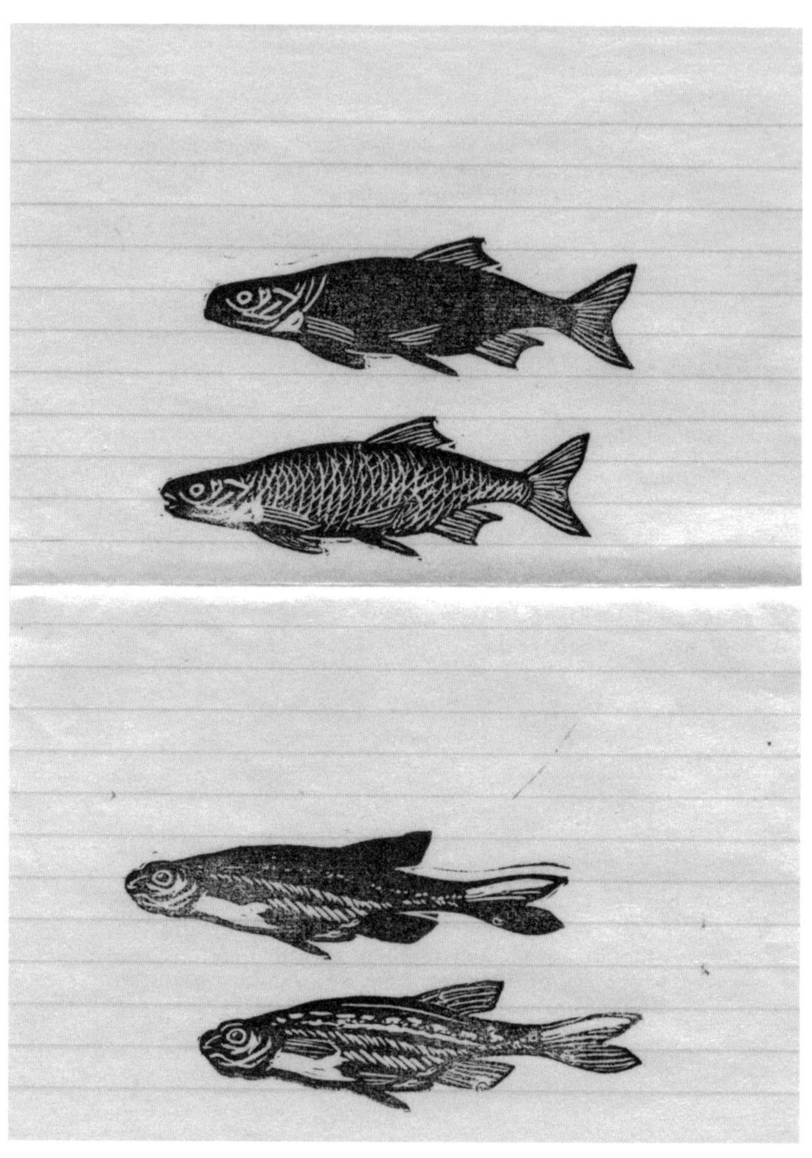

Doliny rzek i strumieni z urwistymi brzegami zarośnięte krzewami i drzewami, zbiorniki wodne i stawy rybne z miejscami dogodnymi do lęgów.

Voorkomen: De ijsvogel is voor zijn levensonderhoud afhankelijk van schoon, helder water. Bij voorkeur houdt hij zich op bij beken en vijvers, waar aan de oevers struiken of bomen met overhangende takken groeien.   The common kingfisher frequents fresh water of every description, including forest streams, and occasionally wanders to tidal creeks and the coast. Er hält sich gern an den mit Gebüsch bestandenen Ufern fließender Gewässer auf; vom Oktober bis März ist er genötigt, als Strichvogel. eisfreie Gewässer aufzusuchen.

Habitat.— absent from swift-flowing streams, preferring slow-flowing rivers and brooks with mud banks.

Biotoop : Oevers van beken, rivieren of vijvers met helder en visrijk water, bij voorkeur waar er steile zandige afgravingen zijn. Ook in vochtig loofbos, met omgevallen bomen, of kasteelparken met vijvers. In bergstreken talrijk tot 600 m. (Alpen).

Habitat: Fréquente le bord des eaux douces pas trop polluées : ruisseaux, étangs, lacs, rivières, fleuves dont les berges sont garnies de buissons ou d'arbres qui lui servent de perchoir.

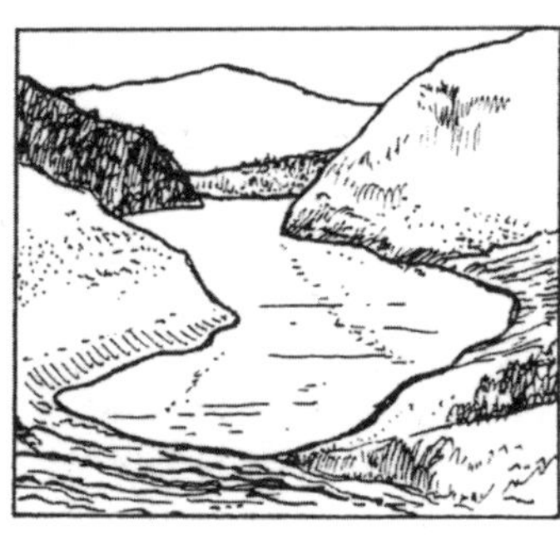 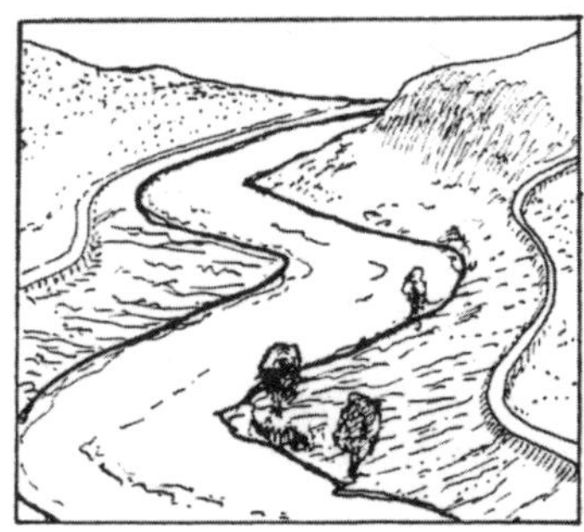

sø	flod	**Danmark**
See	Fluss	**Deutschland**
lake	river	**Great Britain**
lago	río	**España**
lac	fleuve	**France**
límnē	potamós	**Hellás**
lago	fiume	**Itàlia**
meer	rivier	**Nederland**
sjø	elv	**Norge**
jezioro	rzeka	**Polska**
ozero	reka	**Sovetskij Sojuz**
lago	rio	**Portugal**
järvi	joki	**Suomi**
sjö	flod	**Sverige**
buhairah	nahr	**'Arabiyah**
telaga	sungai	**Indonesia**
jhīl	nadī	**Bhārat, Pākistān**
kosui	kawa	**Nippon**
hu	he	**Zhongguo**
göl	nehir	**Türkiye**

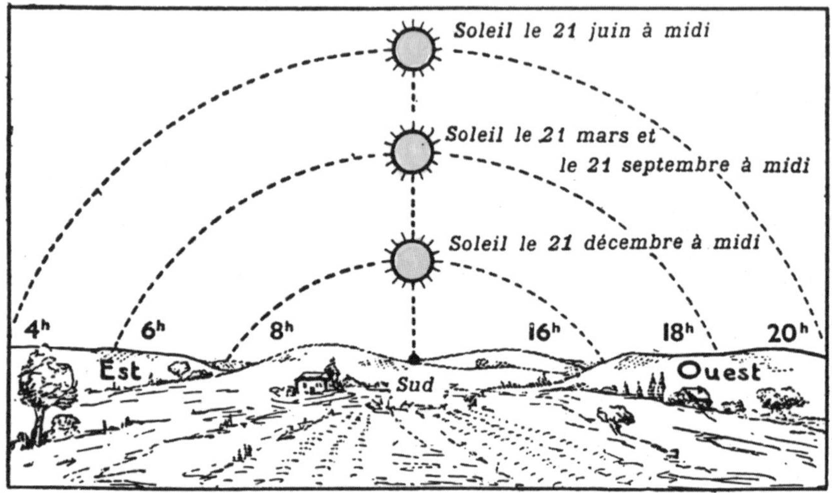

— **Variations de la trajectoire du Soleil à diverses époques de l'année**

And these days are calm when it so happens that
southerly winds blow at the solstice, after the Pleiad
has been northerly.

Depuis l'Antiquité, le Martin-pêcheur est le héros de beau-
coup de fables et de légendes.

ALKYóNE of HALKYóNE. (*Alcyŏne.*) (Grieksch), de dochter van
Aiŏlos en *Enarëte* leefde in eenen gelukkigen echt met *Keyx*. Daar
zij zich echter door hunnen trots lieten verleiden om elkander
Hera en *Zeus* te noemen, werden zij door dezen veranderd, zij
in een ijsvogel, hij in een zeemeeuw. — Volgens een ander ver-
haal stortte zij zich, toen haar echtgenoot bij eene schipbreuk
was omgekomen, uit liefde voor hem in zee, en beiden werden
in ijsvogels veranderd. —

"Expect St. Martin's summer, halcyon days."

perque dies placidos hiberno tempore septem
incubat Alcyone pendentibus aequore nidis.

Halcyon

Situated between absence and presence, retrospection and expectation, the melancholy that imbues and impels Waanders' work quietly reclaims the kingfisher's old appellation, "halcyon". According to Rosemary Eastman, the word "comes from the Greek ἀλς, the sea, and κυών, to brood", and relates to the fabled bird that was believed to breed during the winter solstice on a floating seaborne nest.[1] Consequently, the bird was believed to possess the powers to bring the wind and waves to a state of calm during this brief fourteen-day period known as "halcyon days".

In Greek mythology, Halcyone or Alcyone (from which the genus name *Alcedo* derives) was also the daughter of the god Aeolus and possessed the power to control the winds. As the variant versions of Hesiod, Pseudo-Apollodorus, Ovid, Gaius Julius Hyginus, and Virgil recount, when Alcyone's husband perished after his ship was struck by a thunderbolt thrown by Zeus, Alcyone, out of grief, threw herself into the sea and drowned. As an act of compassion, the gods transformed the couple into birds. Many accounts claim that at least one of these two birds was a kingfisher. "The power that sailors attributed to Alcyone", as David Boag explains, was then "passed on to the Halcyon bird, or kingfisher, which was credited with protecting sailors and calming storms".

Aspects of this legend are also evident in the folklore surrounding the bird. "The ancient Greeks", according to Boag, "thought that the dried body of a kingfisher, if hung up, would protect from lightning"—a notion that would persist in the belief that "just one blue feather on a thread around the neck [could] provide protection from lightning". The significance of the halcyon for sailors would also endure in the idea that the bills of dead hanging kingfishers could serve as compasses because they "would always point into the wind" or, as others have maintained, to the North.[2]

Waanders alludes to this latter piece of folklore in *Kingfishers and Related Works* by way of Christopher Marlowe's play, *The Jew of Malta*, quoting the merchant Barabas:

> But now how stands the wind?
> Into what corner peers my halcyon's bill?
> Ha! to the east? yes. See how stand the vanes—

Like a weathervane, the orientation of the bird's bill, along with the inclination of its feathers ("vanes"), gives Barbaras sufficient cause to hope that his trade ships are making safe passage and already "gotten up by Nilus' winding banks".[3]

Another of Waanders' work that draws on the navigational associations of the kingfisher is his stampwork installation, *Compass* (1993). Printed on a wall of the Van Abbemuseum in Eindhoven, *Compass* consists of stamped forms of the bird's beak pointing to the four cardinal points. The installation not only recalls the bird's associations with navigation (as revealed in Marlowe's play) but it also conveys how *Alcedo atthis* was Waanders' own way of navigating the world and orienting his work within it. Echoes of such a sentiment can be traced back to earlier works of Waanders', including *A Travel Survival Kit* (1989–1990)—Waanders' "guide to survive anywhere in the world"—which equips the reader "with maps, surveys, images, and the kingfisher's name in over fifty languages".[4]

As a consequence of its poetic appellations, 'halcyon' is now more synonymous with tranquility and peace than it is navigation and seafaring. Phil Robinson, in his 1883 book *The Poets' Birds*, notes how "the halcyon, by way of heraldry, became a stock image of poetry. In the days of emblazoned shields and tournament devices", Robinson suggests, "the halcyon was one of the most popular of crests. From the heralds the poets received it, and as they received it, transferred the sea-calming, wind-foretelling bird to their verse."[5] For William Shenstone, William Hayley, Shelley, Keats, and, of course, for Tennyson, *Alcedo atthis* became, as Robinson sardonically remarks, "the pet of the poets, the dainty halcyon", of eighteenth and nineteenth-century verse.[6] Jeremiah Holmes Wiffen, to take a less familiar example, evokes the "brilliant halcyons" in his poem 'Aspley Wood' (1819), describing how the birds "seek the shades, / And fluttering upon azure wings, appear / Loveliest above secluded waters."[7]

Notwithstanding Gerard Manley Hopkins's later evocation of the bird's brilliant iridescence in the opening line of his eponymous poem "As kingfishers catch fire, dragonflies dráw fláme", Wiffen seems to be the anomaly in Robinson's skeptical question: "Is there no poetry in the contemporary kingfisher that it should be anything but the 'brooding halcyon' of the past?"[8] "A mythical charm is universally popular, a natural one seldom", Robinson asserts: "How often is the kingfisher's beauty referred to? and yet what interminable references there are to the 'halcyon' tranquilizing the waves!"[9] "Of the real bird", Robinson comments, "they seem to have known nothing—except that (sometimes) it was 'blue,' 'very blue,' 'sapphire,' and that it fished".[10]

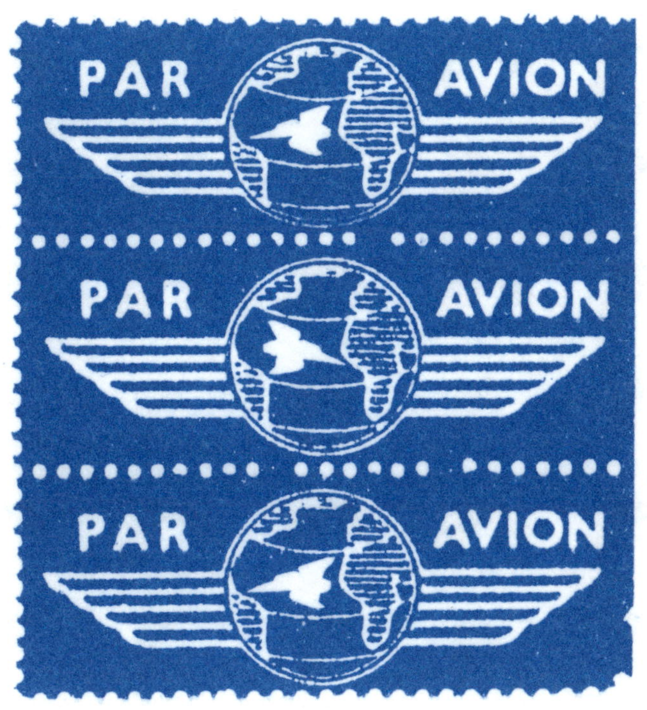

PAR
AVION
PAR
AVION
PAR
AVION

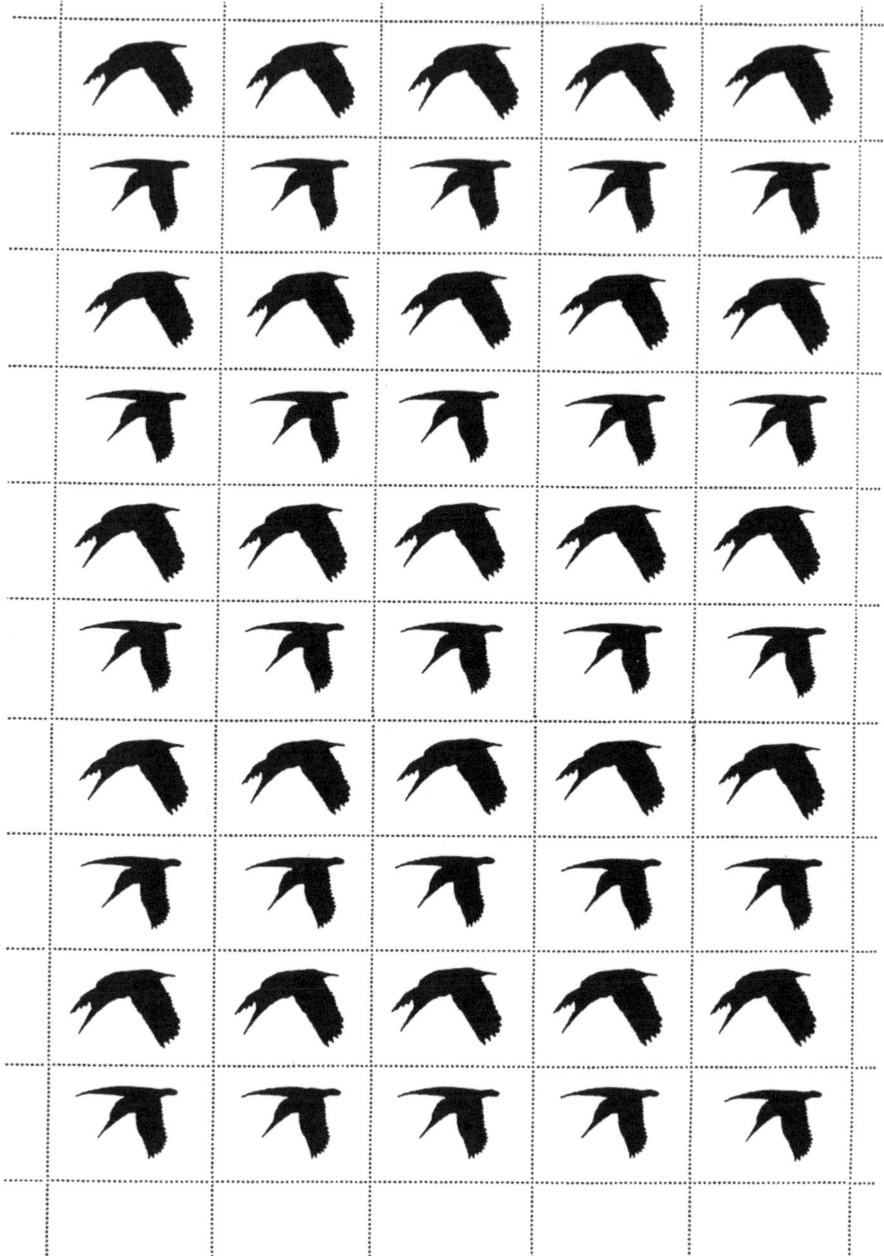

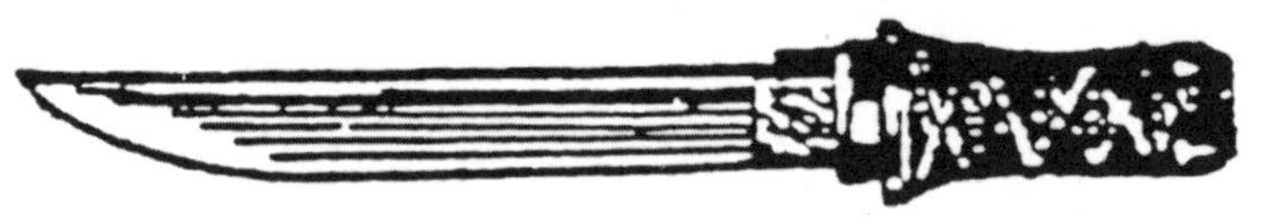

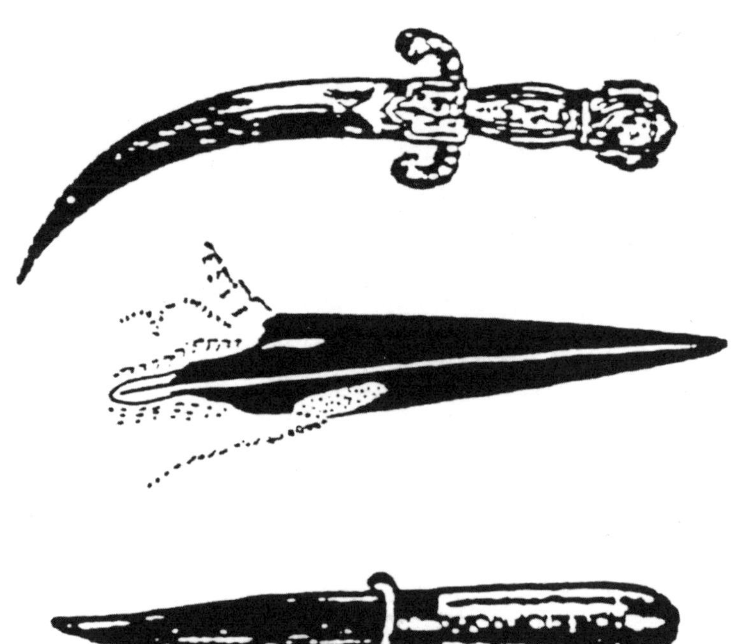

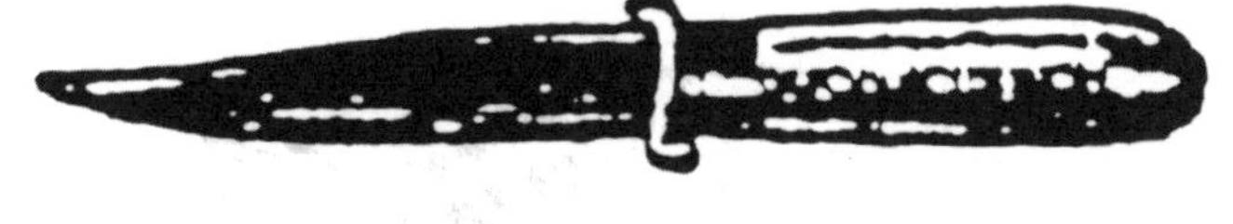

POIGNARD

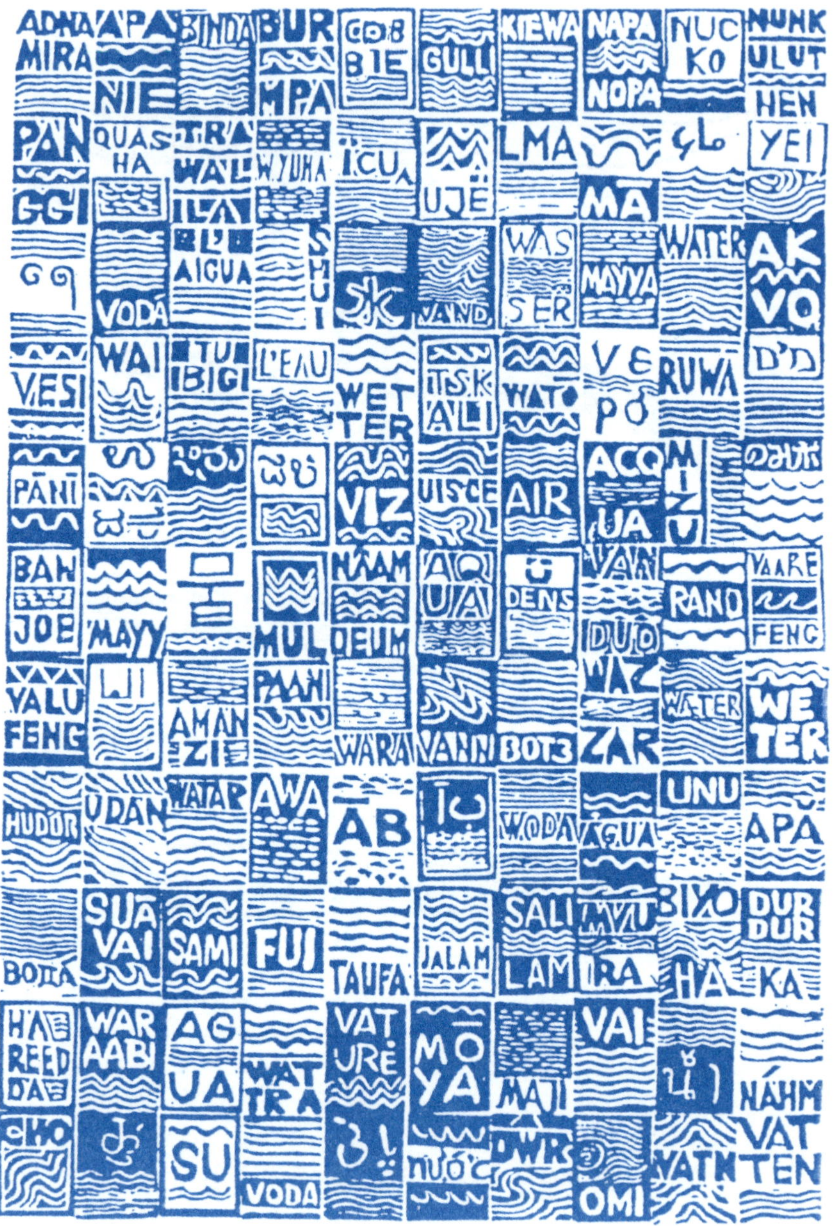

Reverie

In twentieth-century poetry, T. S. Eliot makes brief allusion to the halcyon legend and the kingfisher in his *Four Quartets* (1941), finding in the light reflected on the bird's wing an "answer" to the halcyon-like "still point of the turning world".[1] Eliot's is perhaps a more subtle example of how the kingfisher has, as Kristine Stiles writes become "the symbol for the ways in which humanity has accounted for the momentary suspension of struggle—the halcyon days of life".

Stiles finds in Waanders' work a "deep and unpretentious" equivalent of this halcyon reprieve and suspension. Although Waanders eschews the apophatic asceticism of Eliot or the poeticisms of eighteenth and nineteenth century verse, his work, in its own way, "represents a hiatus amidst the struggle for life and death, a blue halcyon moment that is both full of hope and nostalgia".[2] Such a sentiment is echoes by Jean Poussin who finds Waanders' work a sustained reflection of "the kingfisher-blue depths of his dreams".[3] Although such dreaming carries with it the pejorative associations of distraction and fantasy, in the context of Waanders' work this term is more suggestive of the "wide-awake diurnal" dreaming that Gaston Bachelard calls "poetic reverie".[4]

Poetic reverie, the archaeologist and classicist Eva T. H. Brann writes, "is the purest state of the imagination, sheer fluid, dynamic inwardness in which the boundaries between the subject and object are truly lost".[5] When these boundaries dissolve, Gaston Bachelard writes, the "duality of subject and object [becomes] iridescent, shimmering, unceasingly active in its inversions".[6] The germ of poetic reverie is "the poetic image" which, according to Bachelard, is "the most fleeting activity of [the creative] consciousness".[7] Bachelard uses "poetic image" interchangeably with the term "poetic object".

> Suddenly an image situates itself in the center of our imagining being. It retains us; it engages us. It infuses us with being. The *cogito* is conquered through an object of the world, an object which, all by itself, represents the world. The imagined detail is a sharp point which penetrates the dreamer: it excites in him a concrete meditation.[8]

The imagined detail that engages occurs when one's attention is fully absorbed on a specific task. "At times when we believe we are studying something", he suggests, "we are only being receptive to a kind of day-dreaming".

Despite being absorbed by an object of the world, reverie constitutes "a state of mind" that, in possessing "a sort of stability or
tranquility", "helps us escape time" and situates the dreamer "in
a world and not in a society".[9]

> A world takes form in our reverie and this world is ours. The
> dreamed world teaches us the possibilities for expanding our
> being within the universe. There is futurism in any dreamed
> universe.[10]

Even reveries based on the past contain futurism, Bachelard reasons,
because "the dead past has a future, the future of its living images,
the reverie future which opens before any rediscovered image": "In
reverie we re-enter into contact with possibilities which destiny has
not been able to make use of".[11] It is in this respect that the dreamer
escapes time and envisions a possible future-past that exists beyond,
or at the edge, of those temporal boundaries. After all, Bachelard
reasons, "Isn't dreaming upon an origin going beyond it?".[12]

To the familiar associations of daydreaming Bachelard gives ontological depth and well-being. The meditative detachment experienced
while lost in hopeful thoughts puts the dreamer in a more fulfilling
relationship with the world, "opening all the prisons of the being so
that the human possesses all becomings". In this sanguine renewal
of the past, in imaginatively feeling "a past of what could have been",
melancholy might be meaningfully accommodated:

> Sad memories take on at least the peace of melancholy. And even
> that indicates a difference between dream and reverie. The dream
> remains overburdened with the badly lived passions of daytime
> life. Solitude in the nocturnal dream is always a hostility. It is
> strange.[13]

In contrast to the nocturnal dream, the diurnal dream of reverie
establishes what Bachelard calls "well-being" by stabilising the badly
lived passions of daytime life and keeping "the human psyche on the
fringe of all the brutality of a hostile and foreign non-self". In this
way, "a whole universe comes to contribute to our happiness when
reverie comes to accentuate our repose". Thus, like Waanders' oneiric
reprieves from an otherwise relentless struggle for life and death,
"the images of the poet's reverie dig life deeper, enlarge the depths
of life".[14]

Bachelard's reverie makes it possible to see how the blue halcyon
state of Waanders' work renews the word's tired poeticisms: sleep,
tranquility, peace of mind, quiet times, youth. Waanders' blue

daydreams re-imbue these clichés with a salience that reaches back to what might be called the "still point" of his work: the *ijsvogelwiel* experience of 1982. Like Bachelard's reverie, which, "is always more or less centred on one object", Waanders' memory forms the basis of a reverie that is "both monotonous and brilliant" in its nuanced recurrences and repetitions.[15]

Yet, if the halcyon state of Waanders' work suggests a release or a respite from the world's dichotomies, contraries, and opposites, it does so without completely evading or transcending them. As Kristine Stiles suggests, there is a "quiet heart storm below the work" of Waanders'—"an urgency at the foundation of this otherwise serene, apparently delighted art"—is stirred by a deep longing for an ineffable something that evades apprehension. Thus, rather than "the brooding" halcyon of the past, it is perhaps the kingfisher perched in momentary repose "on the edge of existence"—between deficiency and plenitude, loss and recuperation, futurition and retrospection—which conveys the halcyon-like daydreaming of Waanders' work most forcefully.

Habitat: Lowland rivers where it perches on stones, riverbank vegetation, logs or stranded debris.

Vrij zeldzame broedvogel aan niet te snel stromend water.

Típicamente se les encuentra posados en las orillas de ríos, quebradas y lagunas.

on slow-flowing streams, often moving to coasts in autumn and severe weather. not uncommon along open water, and by ditches and ponds in open country, but rarely seen on forest streams. In the Kelabit uplands it frequents the irrigated padi fields.

Vit au bord des eaux douces et en déplacements hivernaux parfois au bord de la mer, car en cette saison il devient erratique. Found not only on rivers, but also along the sea-coast, wherever the action of the waves has produced steep banks. Lakes, streams; also mangroves in winter.

Habits: Lives near water feeding on fish and aquatic insects. Usually has a favourite fishing place from which it plunges on its prey, returning to its perch each time. Er hält sich gern an den mit Gebüsch bestandenen Ufern fließender Gewässer auf; vom Oktober bis März ist er genötigt, als Strichvogel eisfreie Gewässer aufzusuchen.

Habitat. River beds, especially of large lowland rivers.

Elinympäristö: vesistöt, mielellään purot ja joet, joilla pensaat kaartuvat veden yli. Talvisin avoimina pysyvät vesistöt ja merenrannikot. This little Kingfisher is seen on small streams, lakes, rivers and pools.

At water in creeks, on sea coast, in wadis, pools, where it is usually solitary and most active at dusk. calls with a thin distinctive whistle, *chee*, *see* or *chikee*.

Bei Verschmutzung bleibt er den Gewässern fern.

Hij houdt zich bij open water steeds aan het zoete water op; bij dichtgevroren binnenwater vertoonen enkele voorwerpen zich ook aan de oevers van de zeegaten en de daarin uitmondende wateren. They generally frequent streams in forest as well as in open country, preferring water with low banks.

Se trouve partout où il y a de l'eau.

commonly found along the banks of rivers and lakes

De vogel houdt van helder water, waar hij in stootduik zijn prooi (vis) vangt.

Habitat: waterways, marshes, mangroves; mostly in *open* country.

Frequents freshwater habitats and mangrove in open country.

HABITS AND FOOD. The common kingfisher frequents fresh water of every description, including forest streams, and occasionally wanders to tidal creeks and the coast.

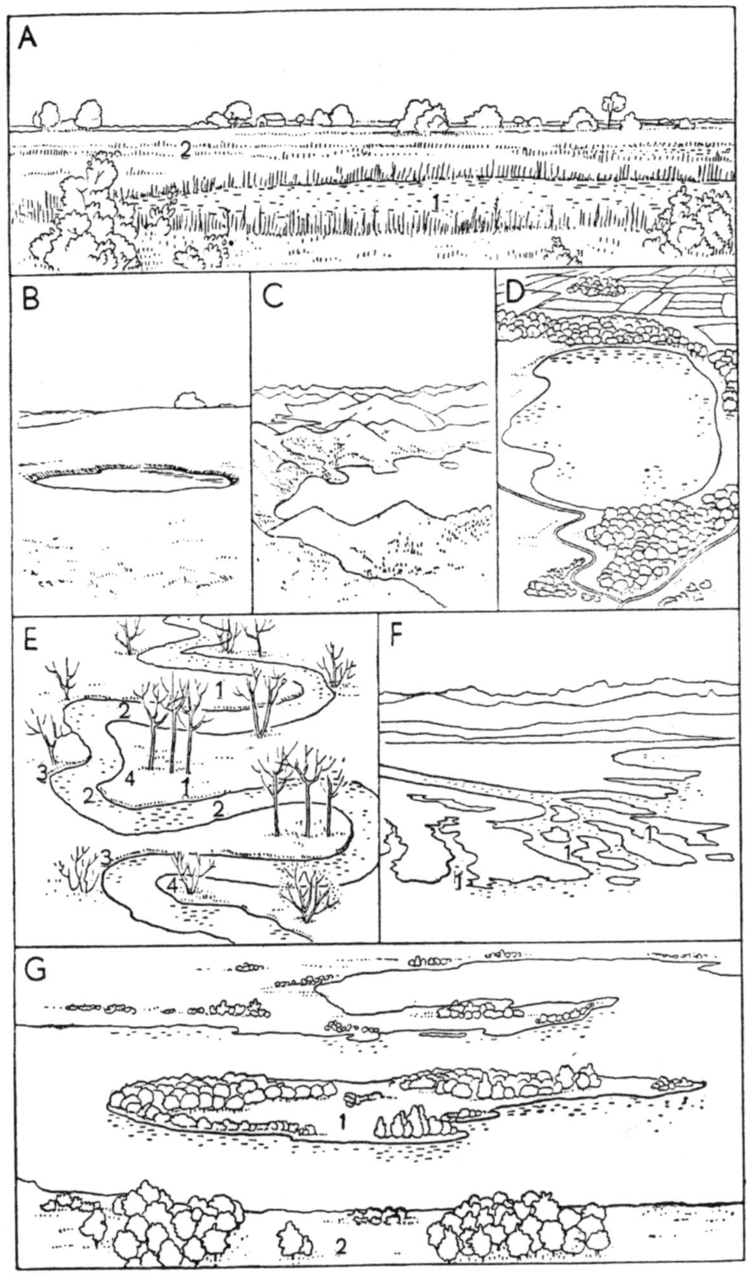

Frequents freshwater habitats and mangrove in open country. Perches on rocks or overhanging branches and plunges into the water to catch fish.

Il niche au bord des ruisseaux et des rivières, dans des creux de racine ou des trous d'écrevisse, qu'il aménage à son gré.

Lever vid vatten, sitter vanl. på en utväxande gren el. flyger med snabba vingslag tätt över vattenytan. **vivanta ĉe riveroj**

agrémente les rives des cours d'eau.

Bij strenge koude veel bij zout water.

Beside water; inland in the summer, on the coast in winter.

Frequents the lower reaches and mouths of rivers and creeks, mangrove creeks, coastlines and, locally or occasionally, ponds and small swamps in subcoastal savanna and gardens.

Aufenthalt: Ufer von Bächen, Strömen und stehenden Gewässern, selten an Seeküste. Hij houdt zich bij open water steeds aan het zoete water op; bij dicht-gevroren binnenwater vertoonen enkele voorwerpen zich ook aan de oevers van de zeegaten en de daarin uitmondende wateren. Affects streams, canals, rush-fringed tributary channels, ponds, roadside ditches, etc.

HABITS AND FOOD. The common kingfisher frequents fresh water of every description, including forest streams, and occasionally wanders to tidal creeks and the coast. Habitat restricted perforce by nature of its food, but, given water, bird is found in diverse situations, streams, canals, lakes, fen-drains, and, particularly in winter, tidal estuaries, gutters on salt marshes, and rock-pools on coast.

Beehler (1978) considered the habitat in northern New Guinea to be 'along streams in forest' but other evidence is much to the contrary. At Lae during 1970–71, except for one occurrence at the Botanic Gardens, I found it only along the sea-shore, particularly where there were high banks, and at river-mouths. Elsewhere I have seen it along low cliffs of dead coral, feeding in tidal pools, at river-mouths and once (Bell 1970c) in mangroves. Reports in the Papua New Guinea Bird Society Newsletter describe habitat in northern New Guinea as river-mouths and coastlines, but in southern New Guinea records are from ponds, sewerage works and wide streams with gravel bars.

It is purely an aquatic species feeding along streams and rivers,

De IJsvogels zijn goede duikers, voeden zich met visschen en waterinsecten, waarom zij in de nabijheid van rivieren en meren wonen.

– Vorkommen: An den Oberläufen der Bäche und Flüsse und an Teichen. Im Winter in die Ebene und ans Meer kommend. – St und TZ. –

Er liebt klare Bäche und stehende Gewässer.

Beside water; inland in the summer, on the coast in winter.

Typically perches close to or low over water.

It is usually seen perched bolt upright. The bird is generally seen on a willow branch with concentrated look on the water. It darts like an arrow and catches its prey and then perches on the branch again.

Zit vaak stil (op loerpost). normally perching low down on exposed roots or on overhanging branches and fronds, its posture typical of the group, with head and neck hunched into the shoulders and plumage relaxed.

zittend op zijn uitkijkplaats. Perches almost motionless above some stretch of water then suddenly swoops obliquely after its prey, returning to its original perch.

Kingfishers saw service as catapult-launched reconnaissance aircraft at sea

often sits on some exposed perch sitzt stundenlang unbeweglich auf einem Pfahl, Felsenstein oder weit hinausragenden Ast zum Beutespähen.

The Kingfisher catches its prey of bullheads and sticklebacks by diving from a branch like an arrow (the whole process takes only a fraction of a second). Nach Nahrung späht er an irgendeinem verstecten Sitzplätzchen am einsamen Ufergelände.

rests on a high bank or post. sur une branche de la rive ou posé au sommet d'un bout de bois émergeant de l'eau. **in den regel vanaf over** hangenden tak, boomstomp, paal, **van een landhek etc.** . fißt auf einem Aft direkt über dem halbvereiften Bach und späht aufmerkfam ins Waffer. plenty of low perches

Habits Like other kingfishers, this one perches 1-2 m above the water, on sedges, posts, twigs or riverbanks, looking stumpy, large-headed, short-tailed and short-legged, bill and tail pointing down as the bird sits intently for long periods. Now and then it turns around, briefly cocks the tail and, the better to gauge distance, bobs its head and body when food is detected.

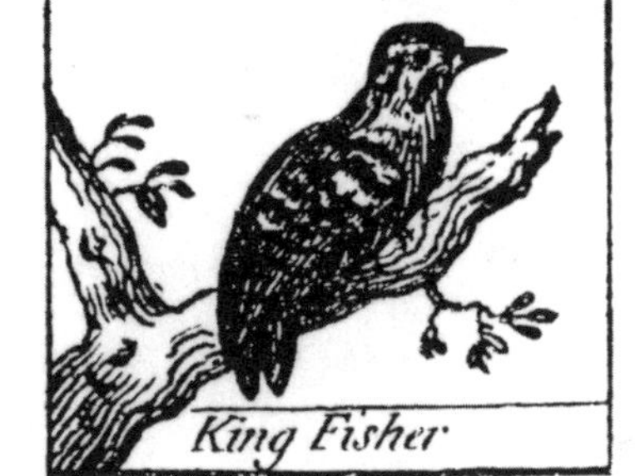

Meistens fliegt er eine bestimmte vor der Röhre liegende Warte an, oft eine Wurzel, einen Zweig oder einen größeren Stein,

you can recognize a Kingfisher's 'execution block' by its glistening cover of fish scales. fonft aber auf einem Pfahl oder einem über das Waffer reichen den Afte nach Beute späht.

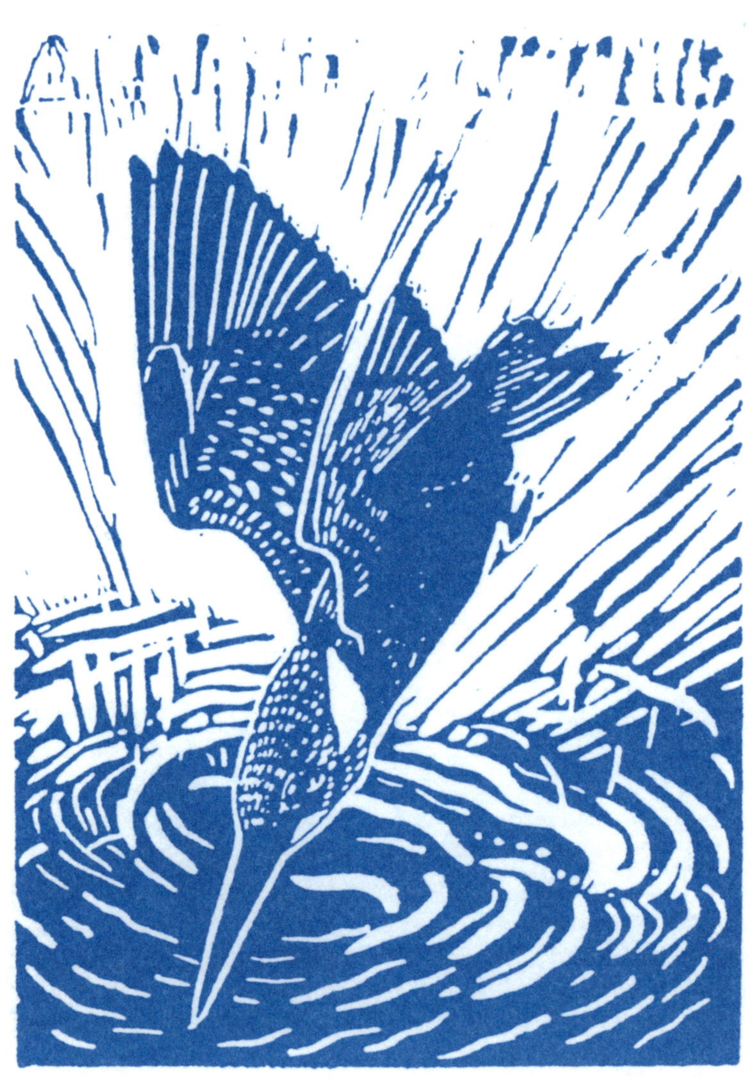

Collection

For all their meditative respite, the blue halcyon moments of Waanders' work are borne of monotonous, unassuming, and prosaic practices and activities that have more in common with the enthusiasms of the hobbyist than the "still point" of the ascetic. "Though it's a hallmark of the artist, or scientist for that matter, enthusiasm is, at century's end, considered 'uncool'", the poet Ronald Johnson writes: "It is one of those fiery words which have come steadily down in the world. Originally it meant 'to be inspired by a god'".[1]

One domain where enthusiasm still holds sway is the amateur one of the hobbyist. Indeed, with its roots in the Latin *amāre* (to love), the pastime pursuits and specialised endeavors of the amateur recall how hobbies are borne of the passion and enthusiasm for specialised interests and, in the case of collecting, specific desiderata. Be it bird watching or collecting stamps, cigarette cards, or books, to be lost in one's love, Waanders' work repeatedly implies, is to experience a blue halcyon moment. Like Gaston Bachelard's poetic reverie, the halcyon moments of the hobbyist manifest in the psychological space "between what concentrates and what exalts".[2]

One might compare "the quiet heart storm" of Waanders' work —its confluence of repose and urgency—to what Jean Baudrillard calls the collector's "passionate pursuit of possession", where "the everyday prose of objects is transformed into poetry".[3] "Every passion borders on the chaotic", Walter Benjamin similarly claims, and in every collector there exists "a dialectical tension between the poles of order and disorder": "For what else is [a] collection but a disorder to which habit has accommodated itself to such an extent that is can appear as order?"[4] Echoing Benjamin's sentiments, Baudrillard deems collecting to be "a measured, diffuse, regulating passion" that ultimately *collects* the collector.[5] As much as it is the "cause or subject of a passion", the coveted object, when sanctioned and organised by the collection, establishes within the collector a "vital equilibrium", even if, as Baudrillard argues, "the balance thus achieved is a neurotic one".[6]

Whereas for Baudrillard collecting implies "a closed synchronicity [that] may certainly be deemed denial of reality and flight" (particularly flight from human relationships), in Waanders' case, the intrinsic systems and serial arrangements of collecting provide the means for reconnecting with the world more emphatically. In this respect, Waanders work recalls cultural historian Susan M. Pierce's conception of the collection as a metaphor for its own singular conception of reality. Despite the material links that the objects of a collection might retain with "the 'real' world", they are, Pierce suggests, simultaneously "endowed with a life of their own which bears the most intimate relationship to that of their collector".[7] In this way, Pierce writes, the collection becomes "a metaphor for this 'reality,' a dream, an inscription on the world".[8]

Literature professor Susan Stewart makes a similar claim in her book *On Longing* (1984), suggesting that the collection "seeks a form of self-enclosure" which is made possible because of its "ahistoricism":

> The collection replaces history with *classification*, with order beyond the realm of temporality. In the collection, time is not something to be restored to an origin; rather, all time is made simultaneous or synchronous with the collection's world.[9]

A series of questions aimed at the stamp collector from an old stamp catalogue, reproduced by Waanders in his *Standard Catalogue* (1991), gives an indication of how such classification might work in constructing and regulating a collection:

> Do you collect Foreign countries?
> Do you prefer Unused or Used?
> To what face value do you collect?
> Do you specialise? If so, in what countries, groups or period?
> Please send me a selection of the following...[10]

As this list of questions suggests, the taxonomic, aesthetic structure of a collection is determined by pre-set criteria and personal preference: be it topic, country, condition, provenance, denomination, or some other specific interest. Underpinning this process is a keen sense of differentiation where, as Stewart notes, "the objects of hobbyist's collection have significance only in relation to one another and to the seriality that such a relation implies".[11] Nevertheless, the multiple ways in which the same object might be understood and appreciated—by topic, condition, country, and so forth—parallels what Gaston Bachelard suggests about the world: "If looked through a thousand windows of fancy, the world is in a state of constant change." Conceivably, the multifaceted appeal of a single stamp can also open up an entire world.

As an amasser of knowledge, the artists' books collector Henk Woudsma writes, Waanders "organised the world according to available material about the kingfisher".[12] The multilingual nature

of the material that he collected and its extensive temporal scope
(from ancient myth to contemporary science)—makes Waanders'
"collections" both spatially and temporally synchronous. Yet, unlike
the "closed synchronicity" that Baudrillard conceives, these collections
construct systems of belief in relation to, rather than in denial of,
the world. Each individual book and catalogue of Waanders'—
even his biographical life lists—fit within his work's larger, more
encompassing system of classification (of order and arrangement)
that, in breadth and scope, "restores meaning to everyday existence"
as a corollary of the real.[13]

Waanders' own propensity for collecting goes back to his childhood
collections of matchboxes, stamps, globes, and cigar bands. Perhaps
in acknowledgement of this fact, Waanders pastes a coloured photo-
copy reproduction of a Henri Wintermans cigar band—originally
included in his books *Gagarin* (1992) and *Boctok* (1998)—in each copy
of *Kingfishers and Related Works*. Placed adjacently to a multilingual
cento of texts relating to the distribution of the kingfisher [*See pages
59–62*], this cigar band, which displays the image of a globe, intimates
the global scope and reach of Waanders' bird in a world enfolded by
Alcedo atthis.

Situated in the midst of the vast amount of material that Waanders
collected on the kingfisher, the Wintermans cigar band also functions
as a kind of microcosm of *Kingfishers and Related Works*, tacitly reas-
serting collecting as a defining idiom and formative sensibility of the
larger work in which it appears. The introduction of the cigar band
has been credited to the cigar maker Gustav Bock in the mid-nineteenth century, whose cigars bore paper rings with their maker's
signature.[14] The collected cigar band, as a trace or vestige of the
absent cigar, might be considered analogous of the brilliant absence
underpinning Waanders' work. This dialectical tension is rendered
more poignantly by the way such absence, as the Wintermans cigar
band intimates, is defined by the plenitude of the circumambient
world it enfolds. In both instances—cigar band and bird—signature
impressions are made in reference to an object that is no longer
present.

This absent-presence implies a kind of nostalgia, which, for Susan
Stewart, "is a sadness without an object, a sadness which creates a
longing that of necessity is inauthentic because it does not partake in
lived experience" but "remains behind and before that experience".
Echoing Bachelard's *reverie future*, Stewart suggests that nostalgia
"wears a distinctly utopian face, a face that turns toward a future-
past, a past which has only ideological reality". Thus, the past that

nostalgia seeks is a past that "has never existed", is "always absent", and which "continuously threatens to reproduce itself as a felt lack". This absence is also "the very generating mechanism of desire", she proposes, the "longing for absolute presence" that impels the dialectical tensions of absence and presence at play in any collection.[15]

With a typical collection (like the cigar band) tending "to centre around its absent term", this notion of nostalgia becomes pronounced. According to Baudrillard, the absent object, "defined by its final position and hence creating the illusion that it embodies a particular goal or end", becomes the "symbolic distillation" of the collection: "The object is the symbol not of some external agency or value but first and foremost of the whole series of objects of which it is the (final) term." Waanders' kingfisher (real and ideal, as Thomas A. Clark suggests) is similarly conceivable as the symbol and "simple signifier" that holds his work together. Like Richard Stamelman's poetics of absence and loss this "final term" of Waanders' encyclopedic collection "attains exceptional value only by virtue of its absence".[16]

ASCENSION

British colony in Africa.   An island attached to St. Helena.

AUSTRALIA

British colony.   Capital—Canberra.

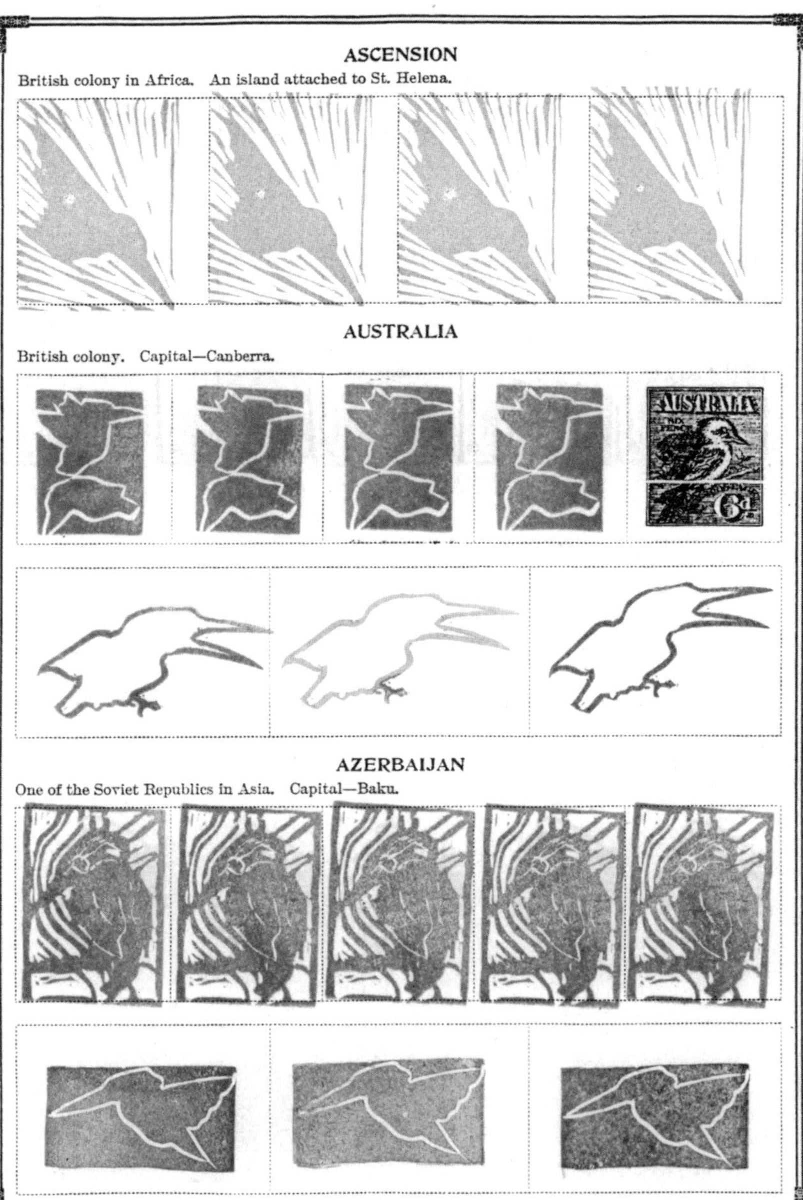

AZERBAIJAN

One of the Soviet Republics in Asia.   Capital—Baku.

NORTHERN NIGERIA

British colony in Africa.

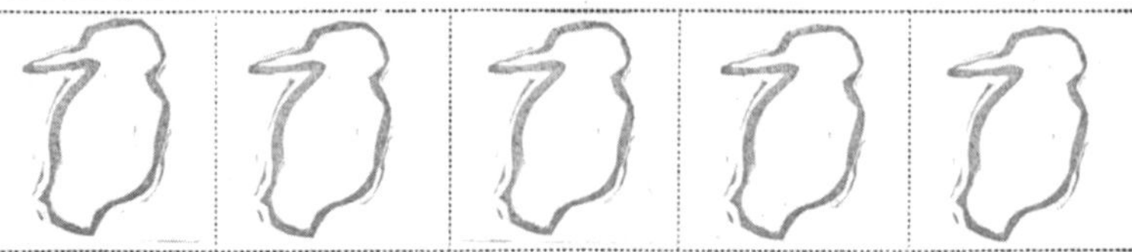

NORTHERN RHODESIA

British colony in Africa.

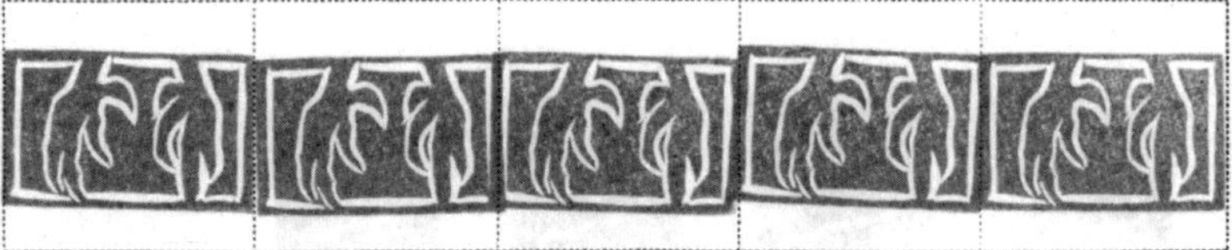

NORTH INGERMANLAND

A Baltic port belonging to Finland.

NOSSI BE

French colony in Africa.   Chief town—Hellville.

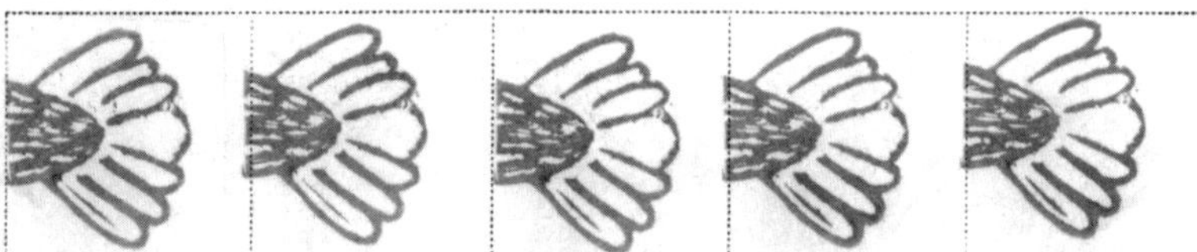

NYASALAND PROTECTORATE

British protectorate in Africa along the Southern and Western shores of Lake Nyassa.

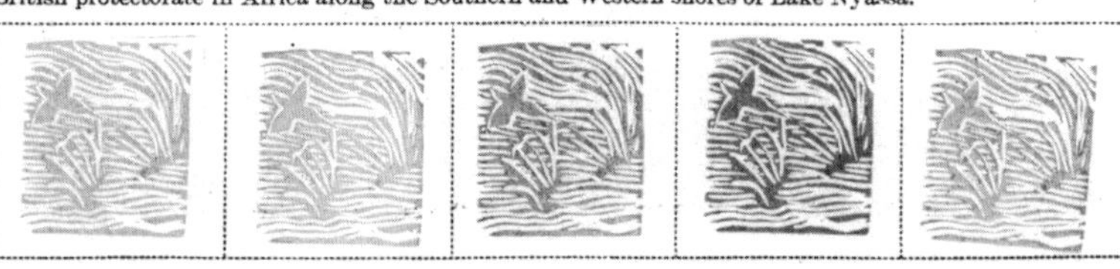

TONGA

Kingdom under British protection.   Capital—Nukuolofa.

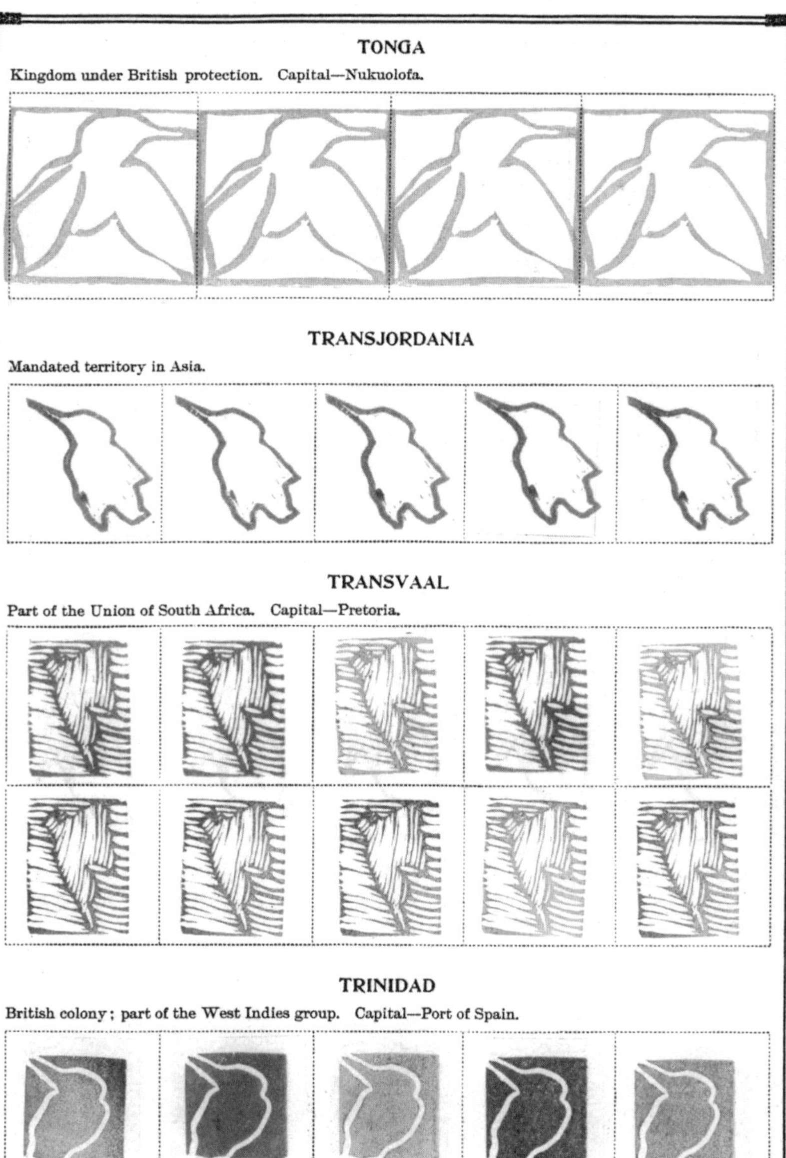

TRANSJORDANIA

Mandated territory in Asia.

TRANSVAAL

Part of the Union of South Africa.   Capital—Pretoria.

TRINIDAD

British colony; part of the West Indies group.   Capital—Port of Spain.

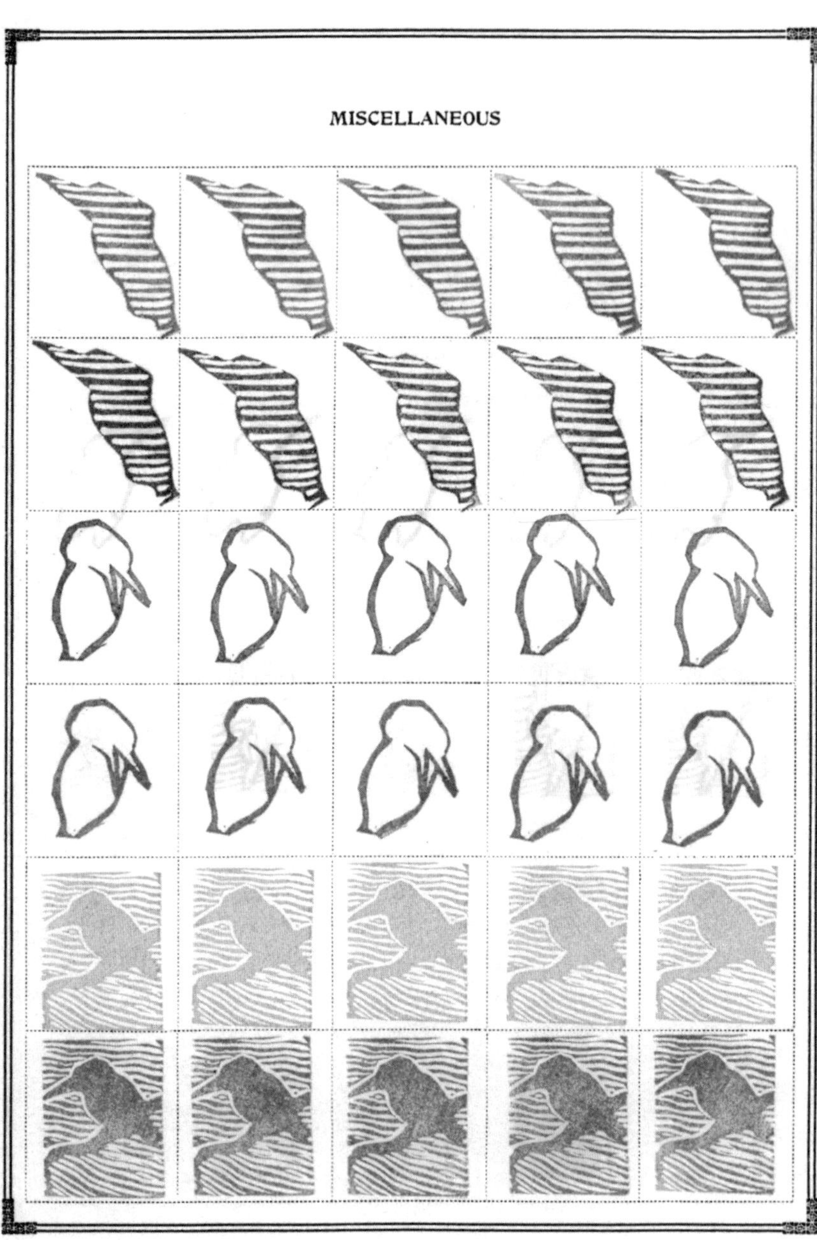

Blue

The tacit suggestions of *Alcedo atthis* in the popular appellation of stamp collecting as "the king of hobbies and the hobby of kings" makes this form of collecting especially salient for a body of work preoccupied with the *king*fisher.[1] Yet, the significance of the postage stamp for Waanders rests as much on its function and symbol of communication as it does its status as a collectible object. As a long distance mediator or relayer of information, the postage stamp is imbued with the future-past of reverie and nostalgia as well as the dialectical tensions of absence and presence that shape such dynamics.

Distance defines and determines the essential purpose of the postage stamp and is the very thing that the postage stamp seeks to overcome in order to deliver and present. Nevertheless, if the function of the postage stamp is *to make present*, that presence, as the implicit puns in *post* and *post-age* suggest, is always deferred or delayed. The postage stamp's relation to distance is equally ambivalent. Although, as Norie Neumark suggests, "the technologies of penny post may have fundamentally altered the specificities of the geographical distances that envelopes [and stamps] travelled", geographical distance retained significance "both on its own and in its articulation with an emotional and temporal distance". In seeking to dissolve remoteness, Neumark proposes, postal technology paradoxically "reasserted distance (as it waits and needs to be dissolved)".[2]

A similar reassertion of distance informs the German writer Gustav Schenk's account of the burgeoning hobby of stamp collecting in Europe during the mid-nineteenth century. As Schenk notes, the appeal of the postage stamp was not simply to make the far away more present but to also cultivate distance as reverie. The attraction of these tiny pieces of postal bureaucracy, Shenck writes, "seemed to originate from the aura of distance" they imparted as a consequence of global exploration, colonisation, and a popular fascination with the exotic:

> The stamp became symbolic of the fabulous, of long and successful voyages; in the hands of children and excitable men and women plagued by secret desires and a nostalgia for far-away places it was the seal of a boundless world.[3]

In Waanders' work, the postage stamp assumes similar significance by marking distance. In the limbo of transit, located somewhere

between sender and receiver, Waanders' stamps—and the stationary
they mobilise—are precariously errant signifiers exiled from their
place of origin. Furthermore, Waanders' postage stamps incite nostalgia (from the Greek *nostos*, "homecoming" or "homeward journey")
by always questioning the possibility of such arrival. The "Postal
System", as Ulises Carrión notes, "seems rather slow, unsafe, complicated, awkward, inefficient, [and] uncontrollable".[4] Prone to becoming
lost, misdirected, or damaged en route, the postage stamp (and the
mail art that appropriates it) is a pertinent corollary of Waanders'
kingfisher that exists equally precariously on the edge of existence.
"Newsworthy sightings of the little bird" in works of Waanders
such as his silkscreen prints *Lighthouse* and *Lightboat* (1997), Karen
Davidson observes, "include tragic run-ins with lighthouses and
lightships".[5] [*See pages 96 & 97*]

Rebecca Solnit's speculations on the blue of distance in her book
A Field Guide to Getting Lost reflect usefully on the implicit nostalgia of the postage stamp and postal communication as it occurs in
Waanders' work. "Some things we have only as long as they remain
lost", Solnit suggests, "some things are not lost only so long as they
are distant".[6] Blue, according to Solnit, is the colour that signifies
these sentiments most emphatically. Inadvertently recalling the
marginal existence of Waanders' kingfisher, Solnit proposes: "The
world is blue at its edges and in its depths. This blue is the light that
got lost."[7] Solnit could as well be outlining the contours of Waanders'
work:

> The blue of distance comes with time, with the discovery of
> melancholy, of loss, the texture of longing, of the complexity of
> the terrain we traverse, and with the years of travel. If sorrow
> and beauty are all tied up together, then perhaps maturity brings
> with it […] an aesthetic sense that partially redeems the losses
> time brings and finds beauty in the faraway.[8]

This aesthetic sense is conditioned by the emotional connotations
of blue as "the colour of solitude and desire, the colour of there seen
from here, the colour of where you are not" and "the colour of longing for distances you never arrive in, for the blue world".[9]

The "sense of beauty, yearning, and mortality" that Alec Finlay
finds so pervasive in Waanders' work is defined by a similar aesthetic
sense of blue—a blue which is illuminated brilliantly, but fleetingly,
by a bird quickly lost to sight.[10] For Solnit, it is Yves Klein who best
exemplifies this aesthetic sense of blue; what Klein himself dubbed
"the immaterialisation of blue".[11] Waanders shares a number of

similarities with Klein, the most obvious of which is his mutual preoccupation with blue. Indeed, to paraphrase Klein, one might say that the blood of both artists' sensibilities is blue.* For Klein, Solnit writes, blue "is the colour that represents the spirit, the sky, and water, the immaterial and the remote, so that however tactile and close-up it is, it is always about distance and disembodiment".[12] Klein would find belated affirmation of his blue sensibilities—his obsession "with flight, levitation, and immateriality as well as the sky and the colour blue that signified it"—in the writings of Bachelard, particularly *Air and Dreams*, which he refers to extensively in the lecture he delivered at the Sorbonne in 1958.[13]

A year before he delivered this lecture, in 1957, Klein painted a globe entirely in his characteristic blue. It was Klein's way of promoting a world without borders, divisions, or territories and a gesture —a "reverie in the presence of a blue", as Bachelard might say—that made it seem "as though the earth itself had become sky, as though looking down was looking up".[14] Four years later, in 1961, Klein's own blue reveries "of a world without divisions", the art historian Hannah Weitemeier writes, found a measure of affirmation in the figure of Yuri Gagarin: "After the first manned space flight in 1961, when the Russian cosmonaut Yuri Gagarin reported that, from space, the earth looked like a deep blue ball, Klein was profoundly impressed, and felt his vision had been confirmed."[15]

1957 was also the year that Klein issued his own postage stamp, the first, according to John Held Jr, to be "created by a fine artist in an artistic context".[16] Initially these small scale, perforated equivalents of his blue monochrome paintings were affixed on the mailings promoting two of Klein's exhibitions in Paris in 1957. However, Klein would repeat this practice for several later shows, including *The Specialization of Sensitivity in the State of Prime Matter as Stabilized Pictorial Sensitivity* (also known as *Le Vide*, 'The Void') that opened at Gallerie Iris Clert in April 1958. The stamps used in the promotion of *Le Vide* would in their own subtle way become small pertinent iterations of it. Klein was keen to ensure that the postal authorities franked his stamps in order to authenticate their status. These cancellation marks (from the French "obliteration")—what Walter Benjamin refers to as "the occult part of the stamp"—assumed a performative role in Klein's issue.[17] At the same time as validating Klein's stamps,

* In his lecture, 'The Evolution of Art Towards the Material'. delivered at the Sorbonne in 1959, Klein remarks: "*The blood of sensibility is blue*, says Shelley, and that is exactly my opinion." Yves Klein, 'The Evolution of Art Towards the Material', in *Yves Klein: Air Architecture*, eds. Peter Noever and François Perrin (Berlin: Hatje Canz, 2005), p.36.

this bureaucratic mark also annulled them in order to prevent
them being re-used. Klein's microcosms of blue, therefore, not only
commemorated *Le Vide*, they themselves became Void. Thus, like the
mail art that proceeds them, Klein's stamps "travelled not as vehicles,
but as meaningful cultural and artistic objects" in their own right.[18]

Waanders makes more overt use of the postal cancellation mark
in *Blue Queens*, a small red postage stamp booklet that he made in
an edition of seventeen copies in 1992. Each copy collects standard
British postage stamps of Queen Elizabeth II in a variety of colours.
Every postage stamp that is not blue is cancelled or defaced with
a blue circular mark bearing the legend: BLUE. While *Blue Queens*
recalls the theme of one of Waanders' earliest books, *Kingfishers and
Queens* (1987)—a colourful mixed media book that explores the links
between the kingfisher and English queens—it also anticipates the
kingfisher rubberstamps that Waanders would later impress upon on
a range field guides, books, postcards, cigarette cards, cigar bands,
and postage stamps. Like these later interventions, the obliterated
stamps in *Blue Queens* invoke their absent Other—the Blue King,
Alcedo atthis. An old, obscure meaning of "deface" seems especially
salient in this respect. Meaning, "to outshine by contrast, cast in the
shade", each of Waanders' obliterations renders the brilliant absence
of his blue bird all the more vividly.

Postage stamps and defacement are also the principal themes of
the series of *Blue catalogues* that Waanders began making in 1991.
These single, unique editions are original postage stamp catalogues
for various countries, including South Africa, Indonesia, Japan, and
the Soviet Union, that date from the 1950s up to the 1980s. Each
catalogue is painted over entirely with a blue ink wash, with the
exception of the word "blue" (or its equivalent) wherever it occurs.
Thus, in these *Blue catalogues* Waanders takes the "rule-governed"
classification of collecting to an extreme that borders on monomania. Yet, whether obsession or reverie, like Klein's blue globe, the
obliterating blue of Waanders' *Blue catalogues* collapse borders and
divisions in the name of a blue sensibility and a blue Ideal.

Closely related to the *Blue catalogues* is *Ruimtevaart 1963–1964*
("space travel"), which Waanders' made as an edition of just five
copies in 1992. Following the format and methods of the blue
Catalogues, in *Ruimtevaart* Waanders uses preexisting postage stamp
catalogues that he systematically blots out with blue ink. In the
case of this particular title, however, as well as preserving the word
"blauw", Waanders also retains the name and image of Yuri Gagarin
wherever it occurs.

Waanders made several works based on the cosmonaut who died (Icarus-like) in 1968 when the MiG15 jet he was travelling in crashed during a training flight. Indeed, Waanders' own interest in Gagarin is as much about his fall as it is about his more feted flight.* Gagarin, Teeuwen suggests, represents "an extension of the concept of the kingfisher" as it occurs in Waanders' work.[19] Thus, in the life of Gagarin, the themes and motifs that Waanders identifies in *Alcedo atthis*—survival, flight, fall, and, perhaps, the pushing of frontiers—are recapitulated. This is apparent in a late book of Waanders', published in 2001 entitled *Kocmoc* (cosmos), which takes Gagarin's seminal flight into space as its subject. Commemorating the 40th anniversary of Gagarin's space voyage in the form of a series of rubberstamp prints, Waanders includes one that depicts the blue profiles of two kingfishers in conjunction with the Russian names Kingfisher (зимородек) and Gagarin (гагарина). This particular stamp depicts bird and cosmonaut as complementary, interdependent opposites. Like Ying and Yang, they are corollaries of the same aerial dynamic and carry within them their own counterparts. As much as flight and ascension, there is the possibility of fall and descent.

In addition to his death, one particular incident in Gagarin's life that reflects this duality of flight and fall concerns the cosmonaut jumping from a second floor balcony. Either as a result of intoxication or in order to escape the scene of an adulterous liaison, Gagarin's leap resulted in an unsuccessful landing that left him hospitalised with facial trauma.[20] Waanders may very well be evoking this incident in his book *Gagarin* (1992)—the fall to *Kocmoc*'s flight.** Taking "Gagarin's last minute: memories, associations, emotions", as its subject Waanders includes Klein's iconic *Saut dans le vide* (*Leap into the Void*, 1960) in its countdown of Gagarin's last mortal minute. A composite of two photographs taken by Harry Shunk and Jean Kender in the month of October, *Saut dans le vide* shows Klein suspended in mid-flight, or levitation, moments after leaping from a second story window located on a quiet Paris street. Coincidence or correspondence: on the edge of existence, at the threshold of the void, suspended between flight and fall, it is possible to see in this image of Klein not only an echo of Gagarin but of *Alcedo atthis* itself, and, perhaps, Waanders.

* Russian space travel held a broader appeal for Waanders, no doubt because the first artificial satellite, *Prosteyshiy Sputnik–1*, was launched into space on October 4th 1957—the same day that Waanders, twenty-five years later, would see *Alcedo atthis*.

** In the same year, 1992, Waanders also made a single edition book, *Icarus*, which explores "The Icare theme of flying & falling on 20 large pages with collections, associations and kingfishers", *Field Guide to the Books of Hans Waanders*, item no.29, n.p.

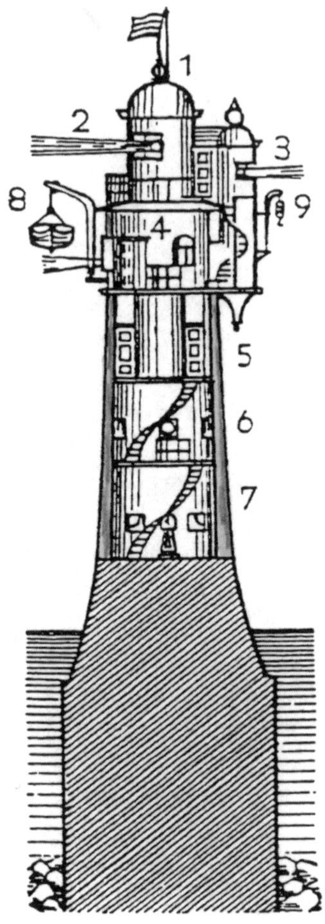

Kingfisher reported dead on Bull Rock Lighthouse (Ireland) September, 1904.
Kingfisher reported dead Orfordness Lighthouse (Suffolk), March, 1884, with another mainland record of the same date.

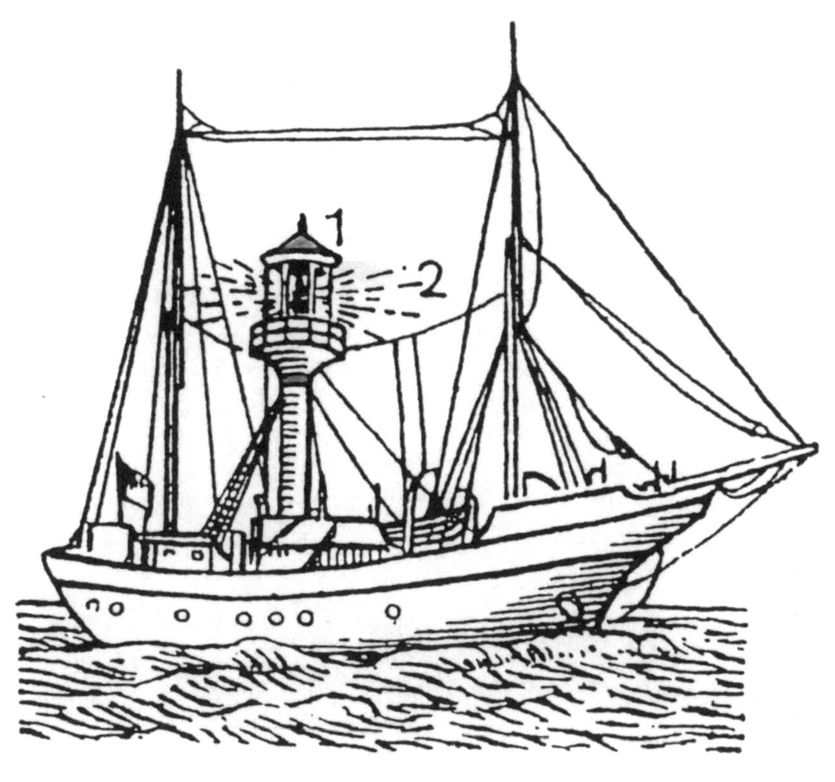

Kingfisher reported dead on Blackwater Bank Lightship (Ireland) July, 1904.
Kingfisher reported dead on Leman and Ower Lightship (Norfolk) October, 1909.
Kingfisher reported dead on Kentish Knock Lightship, March, 1904.

Flight. Exceedingly swift and straight.

Even at a distance and when colours are not evident, short shuttle-shaped form and direct and rapid flight close to surface of water are unmistakable.

Pfeilt oft im Tiefflug den Wasserläufen entlang.

il file comme une flèche de saphir entre l'eau

Verhalten. I. allg. tagaktiv. Geradliniger Streckenflug mit sehr raschen Flügelschlägen (10–20 m/s) niedrig über dem Wasser; über Land meist höher über Grund. Auf fester Unterlage nur Trip-

Maximum speed, 164 (172) *m.p.h. at* 5,500 *ft.*, 157 (165) *m.p.h. at sea level; economical cruising speed*, 119 (125) *m.p.h. at* 5,000 *ft.; time to* 5,000 *ft.*, 12.1 (7.4) *min., to* 10,000 *ft.*, 29.1 (17.1) *min.; service ceiling*, 13,000 (15,500) *ft.; normal range*, 805 (910) *mls. at* 119 (125) *m.p.h.; maximum range with* 172 (201) *Imp. gal.*, 1,155 (1,480) *mls.*

This is a race of the European Kingfisher, and like that bird is usually seen as a bright flash of brilliant blue travelling close above the water of a small stream. It does not even glide when about to settle on a branch, but flies directly at it, then, at the last possible moment, almost stalls in mid-air and fans its wings back and forth horizontally before landing. With its deep breastbone and heavy flight muscles, the kingfisher is built for strong flapping flight, not for gliding.

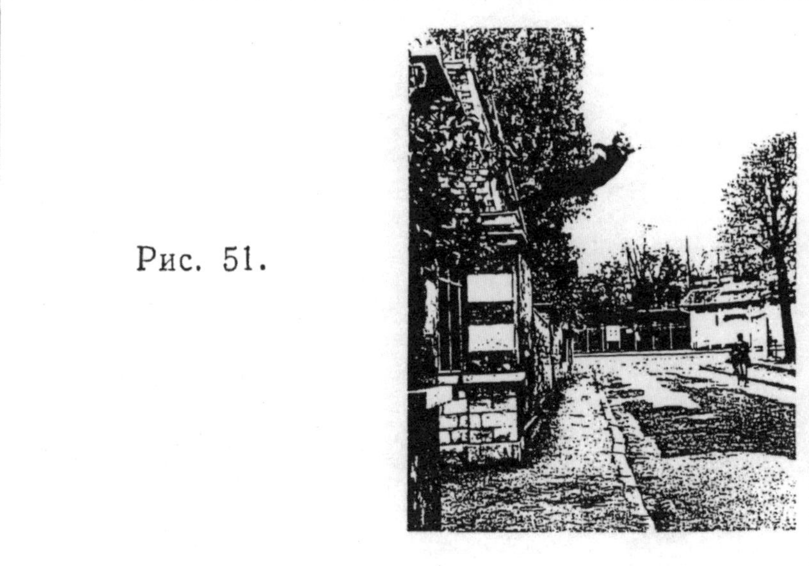

Рис. 51.

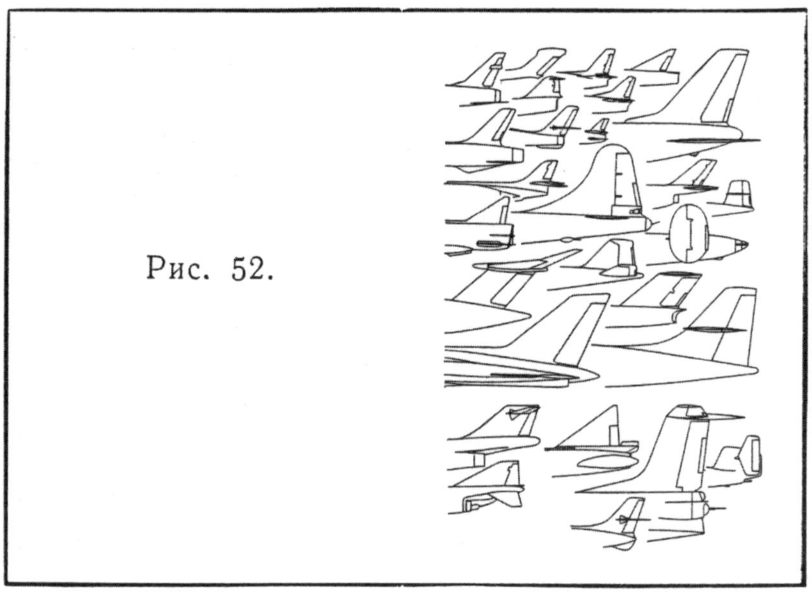

Рис. 52.

At 9:07 A.M., Moscow time, the countdown ended. When he heard the lift-off command, the cosmonaut radioed: "Off we go. Everything is normal."

In orbit now, Gagarin was weightless, the first man to experience that sensation for more than a few seconds at a time.

Seventy seconds after lift-off, Gagarin was radioing: "I feel well. Am continuing flight. The g-forces are increasing. Everything is all right." He recalled later that he could hardly move his hands and feet and he felt as though an "uncompromising force" was riveting him to his seat.

At 9:52 A.M., Moscow time, Vostok 1 was over South America. "The flight is proceeding normally. I feel well. The on-board apparatus is working faultlessly," the cosmonaut radioed. He reported that he was eating and drinking at the scheduled times, although he was neither hungry nor thirsty.

From high over Africa at 10:15 A.M. the cosmonaut sent the reassuring message: "Flight proceeding normally, am feeling no ill effects from weightlessness."

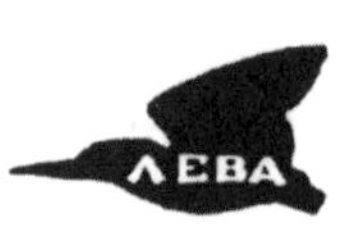
ЛЕВА

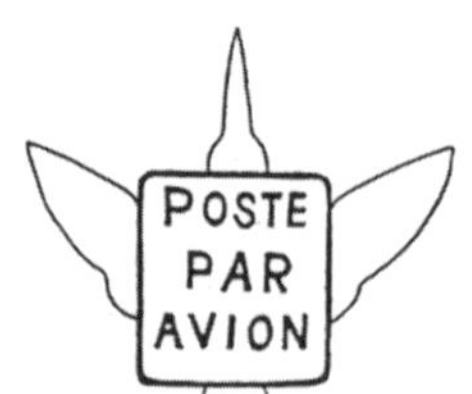
POSTE
PAR
AVION

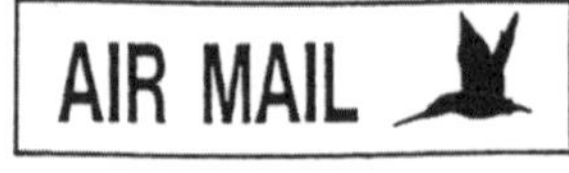
AIR MAIL

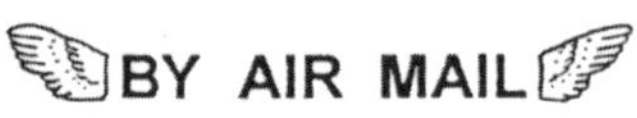
BY AIR MAIL

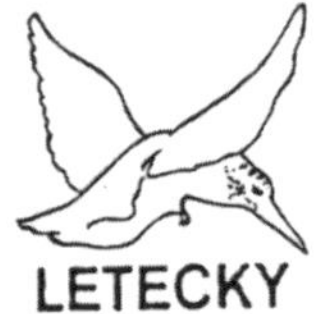
LETECKY

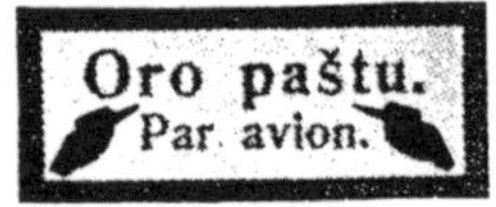
Oro paštu.
Par. avion.

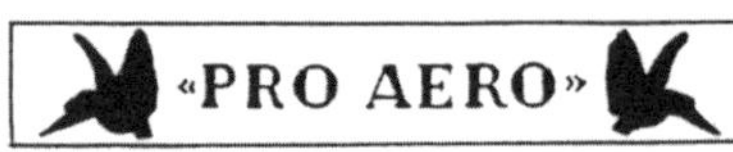
«PRO AERO»

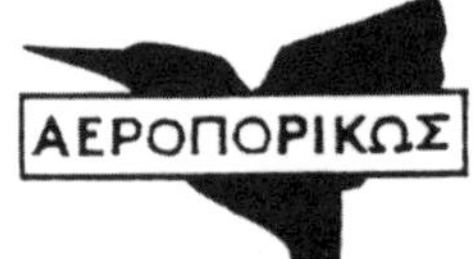
ΑΕΡΟΠΟΡΙΚΩΣ

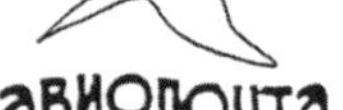
авиопочта

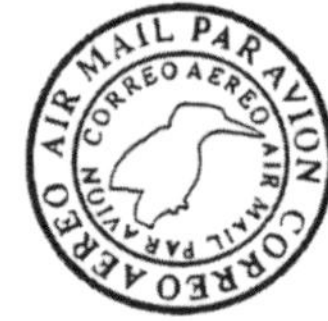
AIR MAIL PAR AVION
CORREO AEREO
AIR MAIL PAR AVION
CORREO AEREO

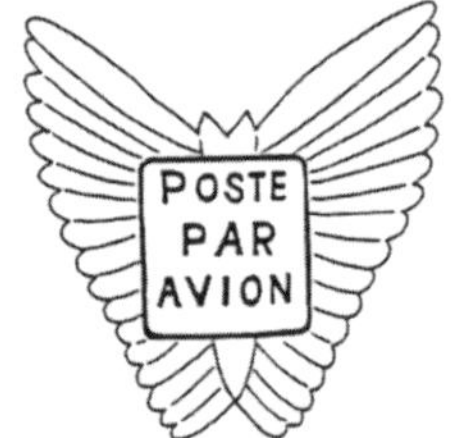
POSTE
PAR
AVION

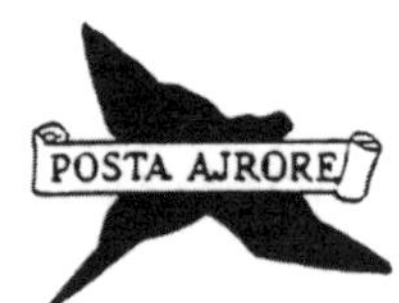
POSTA AJRORE

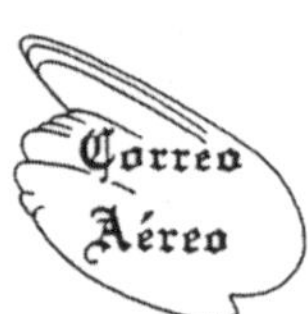
Correo
Aéreo

FLYGPOST·PAR AVION

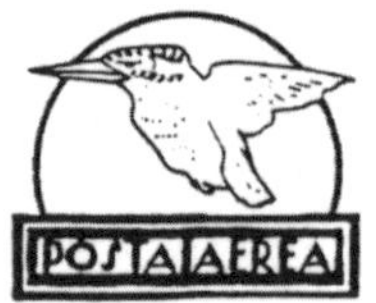
POSTA AEREA

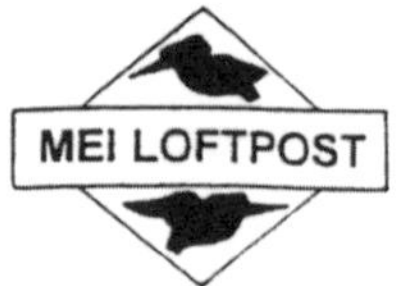
MEI LOFTPOST

Space

Waanders' "constant use of blue", Kristine Stiles believes, communicates "ethereal and atmospheric transcendence as well as sorrow, longing, and sadness".[1] Intrinsic to these blue qualities are the perspectives of distance and desire that they elicit. On the one hand, blue signals a desire for transcendence: the distance it covers in passing over, or going beyond, prescribed limits. On the other, blue is expressive desire and the need to dissolve distance and the sense of separation, exile, and removal it creates. Recalling similar dichotomies of blue, Rebecca Solnit suggests that the blue of longing is its own resolve:

> We treat desire as a problem to be solved, address what its for and focus on that something and how to acquire it rather than on the nature and the sensation of desire, though often it is the distance between us and the object of desire that fills the space in between with the blue of longing.[2]

Such longing can "only be relocated, not assuaged, by acquisition and arrival", Solnit adds.[3] And, like Heinrich's quest for the blue flower, this is perhaps where the real meaning and value of longing and desire can be found.

As a collectible object and as a relay of communication, both of these terms, "acquisition and arrival", as well as Solnit's suggestion of relocation, recall the postage stamp. The stamp's function as a symbol of long-distance communication in Waanders' work finds renewed potency in the deferral of such acquisition and arrival. Each postage stamp, like the other blue forms in his work, might, therefore, be considered the traces of the absent bird and metaphors (the carryings-over) for the nostalgic blue distances and sanguine horizons where the kingfisher has been seen or sought.

Just as stamps have the ability to travel freely and widely, Waanders' avian subject is both a partaker in, and the facilitator of, global dialogue. This point is reiterated in *A Conversation / Een Gesprek* (1998), an audio project and book that Waanders made in collaboration with the American artist Lauri Twitchell. As the title suggests, *A Conversation / Een Gesprek*, is based on a short conversation between two species of kingfishers: the North American Belted Kingfisher (*Megaceryle alcyon*) and *Alcedo atthis*. From April 25th to June 18th, 1998, Waanders and Twitchell constructed an audio conversation from recordings of the respective birds' calls that were sent back and forth across the North Atlantic. The "conversation", which lasted several months, takes the form of a recording lasting little more than three minutes. A CD of the recording is included in the book that Waanders and Twitchell made to document the project. Twitchell recorded the sounds of *Megaceryle alcyon* on a shotgun microphone while she was living near a marsh in Portland, Maine: "I processed the sound with a digital sound program called Sound Edit which produced a waveform", Twitchell explains: "I emailed the waveform across the ocean to Hans and to *Alcedo atthis*."[4] Waanders would reply in kind with a call of *Alcedo atthis*, although pauses of up to two months might punctuate this call-and-response exchange.

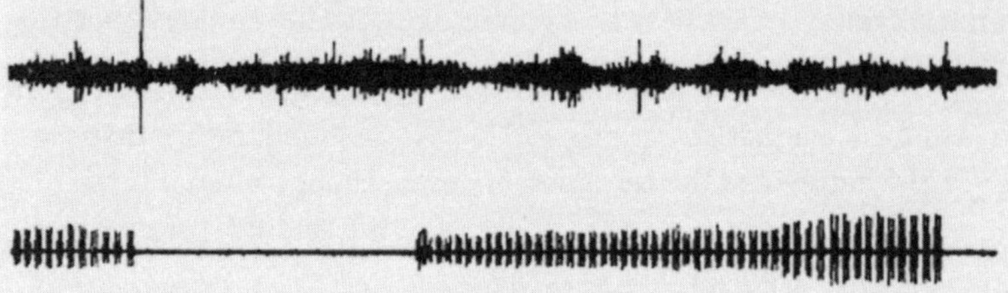

Fourteen of the birds' waveform diagrams are included in *A Conversation*, with the vertical lines "recording amplitude or loudness" and "the thickness of the [horizontal] line" depicting pitch.[5] Visually, these horizontal and vertical lines also suggest the kingfishers' habitats: the former suggesting calm, still stretches of water, upon which are reflected the vertical profiles of trees, marsh grasses, rushes, and reeds. In the waveforms of *A Conversation* therefore is a tacit reiteration of Waanders' tendency to depict the habitats and topographies of *Alcedo atthis* devoid of the bird itself. In this particular instance, however, the bird and the landscape are inextricably one and the same thing: the bird calls its world into existence.

A Conversation also reiterates the implicit episteme of resemblance of *In Search of Blue*. In this instance, the old hermetic adage "as above, so below" is implicitly conveyed in the way that earth and sky are reflected in the "water" of these waveforms. Consequently, and not unlike Yves Klein's blue globe, looking down becomes looking up. "Conversation" recalls its close etymological links with "conversion" and seeing becomes hearing (and hearing, seeing). The perceived distance between things—between subject and object, here and there—are diminished as the universe folds in on itself. Old World and New World, momentarily, find a measure of correspondence and accord that brings them into closer spatial and temporal proximity.

The international scope of *Alcedo atthis* is also apparent in Waanders' adoption of telegraphic modes of communication in work such as the postcard *Halycon* (1999), which spells out the word "halcyon" using semaphore flags. These flags follow the system of the International Code of Signals, the purpose of which is "to provide ways and means of communication in situations related essentially to safety of navigation and persons, especially when language difficulties arise".[6] As well as playfully acknowledging the halcyon's associations with calm seas and safe navigation, Waanders' allusion to this international semaphore system implicates *Alcedo atthis* as the transmitter of a universal code capable of bridging the distances of time and place. By tacitly aligning the cosmopolitan distribution of the *Alcedinidae* family with a communication technology that also extends across most of the globe, Waanders' postcard posits the kingfisher as a citizen and subject of the world.

The cosmopolitan nature of *Alcedo atthis* is also implicit in a series of books, including *504 Air Mail*, *1408 Air Mail*, *448 Luftpost*, *1008 Per Luchtpost* and *Correo Aereo 864* that Waanders made in 1997 around the theme of airmail. Each of these titles consists of Waanders' own airmail stamps (also known as "etiquettes"), with the numerical figures indicating the quantity included in each title. Each of Waanders' stamps depicts a kingfisher, or an aspect of its anatomy, along with the legend "airmail" in English, German, Dutch, or Spanish. In 1997, Alec Finlay's Morning Star press published *Correo Aereo*, a small sampler of these and similar rubberstamped designs, and Waanders produced the silkscreen print, *Proposals*, which also presents a selection of his global airmail designs. [*See page 100*]

Like the postage stamp's symbolic status as the "seal of a boundless world", Waanders' small airmail stamps are the germinal points of departure for aerial reveries and daydreams. These small prints imply the kind of freedom often projected onto birds, those "beautiful vagabonds", as the American naturalist John Burroughs describes them, "masters of all climes and knowing no bounds" in their "free, holiday lives".[7] In this avian spirit, evoking travel, exploration, and encounter, each print becomes the signifier of, and invitation to, imaginative flight and transport. Waanders' reference to A. Y. Campbell's poem 'There Are Still Kingfishers' is especially notable in this context. As well as anticipating his own sighting of *Alcedo atthis* at the *ijsvogelwiel* in 1982, Campbell's description of a solitary encounter on Wren Bridge in Cambridge also inadvertently asserts the figurative power of postal communication: "But with joy, peace, and faith my spirit is mailed / Since on Wren's bridge at noon,

unseen, unhailed, / I, all alone, saw the kingfisher fly".[8] Waanders
playfully compounds these suggestions of spiritual and postal
delivery by reproducing Campbell's lines on a postcard format—
a communication medium designed expressly for being mailed.

Kristine Stiles has suggested that, "the metaphor of travel, travel
as it is impressed in the sign of the postage stamp, emblem of
movement", communicates "the places of the mind and heart to be
discovered in Waanders' work".[9] In this context of travel and movement, Waanders' airmail stamps might be read similarly as a renewal
of the kingfisher's ancient navigational folklore. If, as Jean Poussin
suggests, Waanders' "kingfishers guide us through the world with
their beaks" and, with their dagger-like bills carve out "new horizons", then they do so in the modern milieu of global air travel.[10]

First 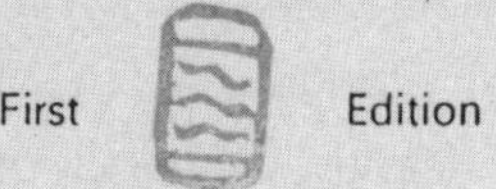 Edition

STANDARD
CATALOGUE

SOIXANTE-DIXIÈME ANNÉE

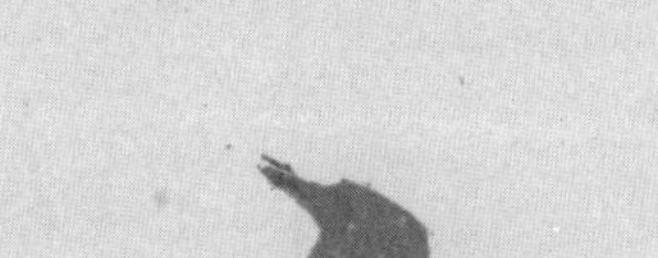

One Hundred and Twelfth Edition

Unsere Kataloge sind in fast allen Briefmarken-, Buch-
und Papierwaren-Handlungen zu haben.

Book as Art

We offer you 50 years of experience and a sterling reputation,
qualified experts in all departments, deluxe illustrated catalogues.

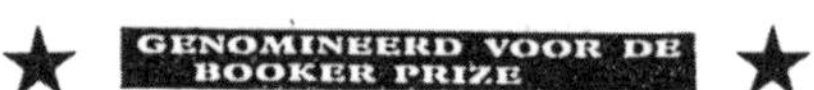

- A Catalogue number in every space.
- Hundreds of illustrations.
- Pages of heavy grade paper.
- Hinged-post binder covered in dark green Fabrikoid. Room for extra pages and interleaving.
- Supplements published annually.

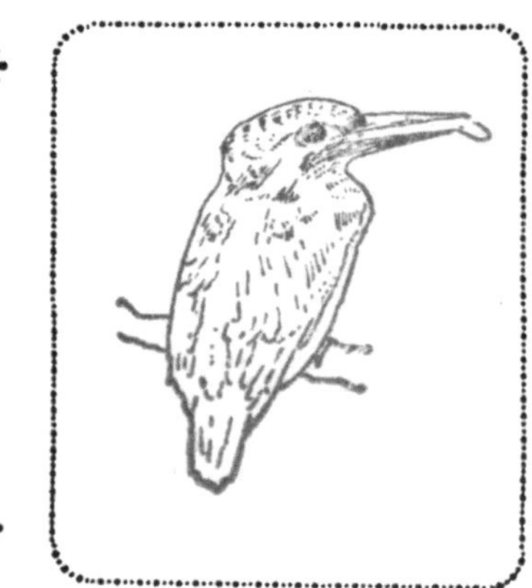

Instruction pour l'usage du catalogue.

Explications des signes.

▣ = *dentelé*	✳ = *neuf*	✕ = *oblitéré à la plume*
▢ = *non-dentelé*	⊙ = *oblitéré*	◯ = *percé d'un trou*
▢ = *percé*		

Abréviations employées pour les couleurs.

bl' = *bleu*	g'n = *vert*	or' = *orange*	s' oder schw. = *noir*	
br' = *brun*	h' = *claire*	p' = *pourpre*	u' oder ultr. = *outremer*	
d' = *foncé*	k' = *carmin*	r' = *rouge*	v' = *violet*	
f' = *pâle*	l' = *lilas*	sdm = *chamois*	z'rot = *rouge brique*	
g' = *jaune*	o' ou ol' = *olive*	sch' = *ardoise*	zl' = *rouge vermillon*	
gr' = *gris*				

Exemple:

br'karmin = *carmin-brun*		g'braun = *brun-jaune*	
d'grün = *vert-foncé*		s'violett = *violet-noir*	

The booklets before 1960 have another numbering (deviation).

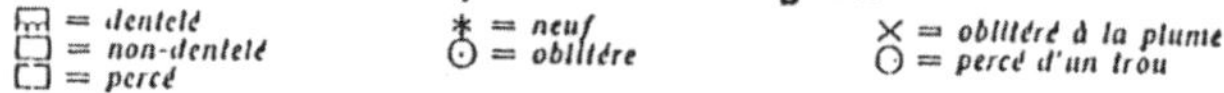 Commandez en indiquant le nombre et le mot de commande

*

3. "Kingfishers & Queens" (first version)
   1986 / 34 X 51,5cm, / 18pp. / gebonden, in doos / opl. 1
   collage, foto, inkt, aquarel, stempel.
   mixed media / bound, in box / ed. 1
 * overeenkomsten en verschillen tussen ijsvogels en koninginnen.
 * *different kinds of links between kingfishers and queens.*

*

4. "Alles ijsvogelt", *All becomes a kingfisher*
   1986-1987 / 23 X 32cm. / 10pp. / gebonden, in foedraal / opl. 5
   collage, foto, inkt, aquarel, stempel.
   mixed media,/ bound, in case / ed. 5
 * diverse soorten afbeeldingen van vogels, die allen via een
   stempel omgevormd worden tot ijsvogels.
 * *images of numerous birds, all transformed with a*
   kingfisher stamp.

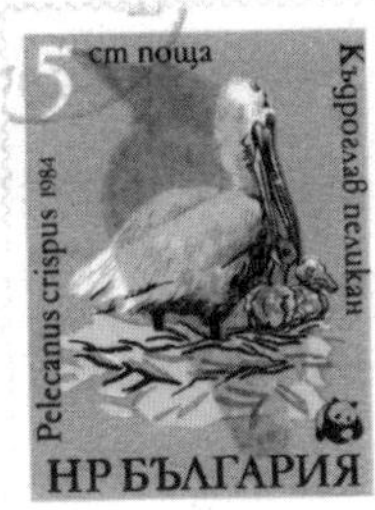

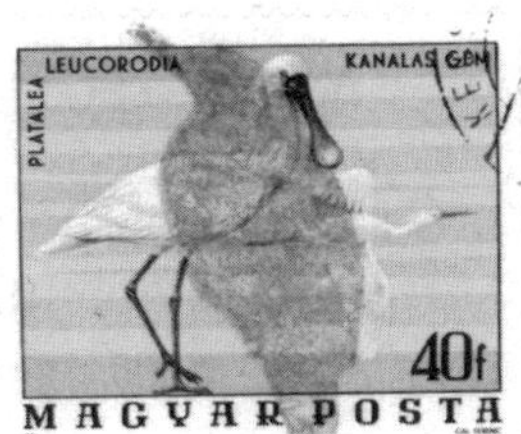

*

5. "Diesseits - Jenseits"
   1986-1987 / 33,5 X 51cm./ 10pp. / gebonden, in doos / opl. 1
   collage, foto, inkt, stempel.
   mixed media / bound, in box / ed. 1
 * een wandeling rond het IJsvogelwiel, een verslag in foto en
   schilderwerk: associaties en observaties.
 * *report of a walk around the Kingfisherpond, with photographs and*
   paintings: associations and observations.

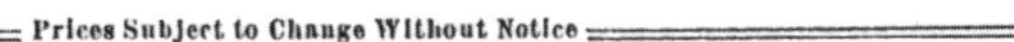

Boeken   **BOOKS**

---------------------------------- ✳ ----------------------------------

23. "Kingfisher Album"- The parts"
24. "Kingfisher Album"- Water"
25. "Kingfisher Album - Lines & Silhouettes"
    1991 / 22 X 28cm. / 28pp. / gebonden / opl. 15 (per boek)
    stempel op geperforeerd papier
    stamp on perforated paper / bound / ed. 15 (each)
  * een trilogie van drie postzegelboeken: elk boek bevat een serie van
    12 zelfontworpen en met de hand gedrukte zegels
  * *a trilogy of three postage stamp albums: each book contains twelve
    self designed and hand printed postage stamps.*

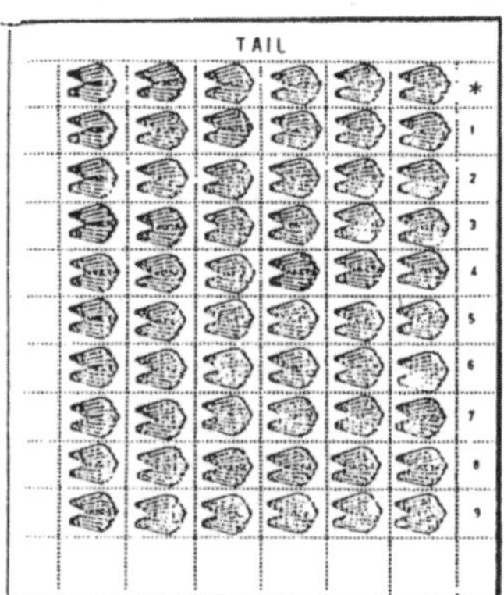

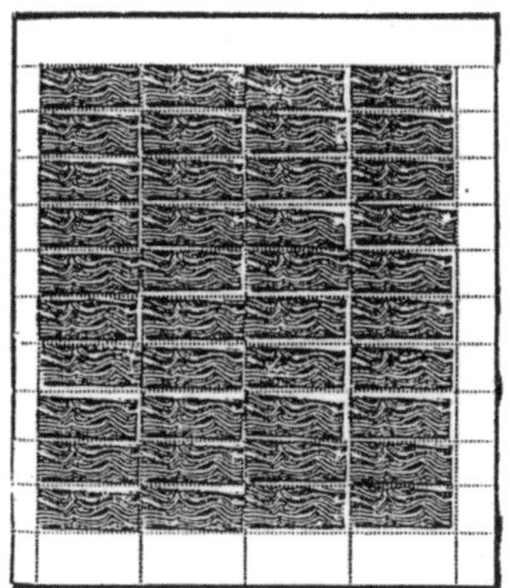

26. "Blauer Katalog"
    1991 / 11,5 X 16,8cm. / 312pp. / gebonden / opl. 1
    inkt op papier
    ink on paper / bound / ed. 1
  * een duitstalige postzegelcatalogus, blauw ingeïnkt met uitzondering
    van het gedrukte woord "blau".
  * *a german postage stamp album, painted with blue ink, with the
    exception of the word "blau".*

Catalogue

Waanders' airmail stamps are essentially a variation of the artist's postage stamp. Michael Bidner, a pioneer of the form and avid philatelist, describes these stamps as a "medium or form to explore, exploit, and house expression. Any or all aspects of a real stamp may be noted or ignored."[1] Whereas postage stamps are "authorised by governments", Chuck Welch stresses, "it is the realm of imagination that governs the unorthodox, ephemeral aesthetic of artistamps created by mail artists".[2] Waanders' own postage stamps, like his airmail prints, have tended to take the form of rubberstamped impressions of *Alcedo atthis*—silhouetted in profile or depicting an anatomical part—on small perforated squares.

While, like the mail artist, Waanders would often paste his own stamps alongside official postage stamps on his correspondence, his stamps also provide the content of books such as *Alcedo atthis I* and *Alcedo atthis II* (1990), *Album Martin Pescador* (1991) and his trilogy of *Kingfisher* albums (1991), all of which assume the form of a philatelist's stamp album or stockbook. It is not surprising therefore that these titles, as Waanders wryly remarks, are "often mistaken for an ordinary postage stamp album by the beginner".[3] By being taken out of circulation and conserved between the glassine interleaves of the stamp album, Waanders' postage stamps are as evocative of philately and stamp collecting, as they are the "ephemeral aesthetic" of mail art. Indeed, the *Kingfisher* albums or *Album Martin Pescador* would suggest that, as much as the postage stamps themselves, it is the mindset and the apparatus of the collector, along with the "rule-governed", "taxonomic, aesthetic structure" of collecting, that appeals to Waanders' sensibility.[4]

A prime example of the collector's mindset is *Standard Catalogue*. Printed in 1991 at the peak of his working with the postage stamp medium, *Standard Catalogue* is essentially a playful catalogue raisonné of Waanders' books that (as the prior example of a collector's questionnaire suggets) parodies the cultures of philately and stamp collecting. All of Waanders' books, up to 1991, are listed and described amidst a busy montage of visual and textual material sourced from a number of stamp catalogues from the 1950s and 1960s. [*See pages 105–108*] Sewn in cerulean blue boards, the catalogue's pages (some of which are also blue) are full of manicules and other typographic symbols that indicate, or jostle against, images of philately paraphernalia such as stamp prongs, albums, advertisements, announcements, and glossaries. Enhancing the rich visual quality of the catalogue's pages are Waanders' own rubber-stamped images and postage stamp designs, used postage stamps, and small reproduced images of his books. The result is as playfully idiosyncratic as the collaged booklet that Harry Smith—a compulsive collector of various subjects, from commercially recorded American vernacular music to paper airplanes and Ukrainian Easter eggs—includes in his 1952 *Anthology of American Folk Music*.

Like Smith's *Anthology* booklet, *Standard Catalogue* treads a fine line between order and disorder, with the striking visual exuberance of the catalogue's pages belying the scrupulous taxonomies they frame. "Every passion borders on the chaotic", Walter Benjamin has suggested, "but the collector's passion borders on the chaos of memories".[5] For the collector of books, Benjamin's main example, the "confusion of a library" is counterbalanced by the "order of its catalogue".[6] As Waanders' title, *Standard Catalogue*, implies, the lists and inventories of the catalogue impose standards (measures and criteria) that not only order a collection but also regulate the less ruly passions that impel it and which it in turn provokes.

Waanders' own systematic methods of collecting and organising data about his subject, as Karen Davidson suggests, are governed "not so much [by] a demand for right thinking as for right prac-tice".[7] Thus, the way that Waanders gives taxonomic structure to his findings on *Alcedo atthis*, the way he orders and arranges it, is as important as the data itself. As well as the rule-governed systems of the collection, it is perhaps the impassioned systems of birdwatch-ing that reflect most pertinently the "right practice" of Waanders' own methods.

In contrast to the material objects that comprise, for example, stamp or cigar band collections, birdwatching is essentially the immaterial collection of observations and facts. As "the rational arrangement and exposition of all that is known of birds, and the logical inference of much that is not known", ornithology places emphasis on rational and lucid systems of taxonomy in the form of lists, diagrams, statistics, maps, and field guides.[8]

In consistency and continuity of application it is perhaps above all the taxonomical system of classification innovated by the Swiss botanist Carolus Linnaeus that remains the foundational system for the science of ornithology and its amateur cousin, birdwatching. For Linnaeus, the science historian Paul Lawrence Farber writes, "natu-ral history's goal was to construct the catalog of life".[9] Linnaeus's seminal work in this area, *System Naturæ* (first published in 1735), establishes a "system of identities and [an] order of differences existing between natural entities".[10] Michel Foucault summarises this system as "a *description of the visible*" which "reduces the whole area of the visible to a system of variables all of whose values can be designated, if not by a quantity, at least by a perfectly clear and always finite description".[11] Like a collection, the efficiency of Linnaeus's system rests on it arbitrarily selecting a finite and limited group of characteristics by which to classify and organise species. "To observe, then", Foucault writes, "is to be content with seeing—with seeing a few things systematically": "With seeing what, in the rather confused wealth of representation, can be analysed, recognised by all, and thus given a name that everyone will be able to understand."[12]

Where "God created, Linnaeus organised", the botanist is reputed to have boasted.[13] Underpinning this audacious claim is the idea that the taxonomist approximates the Adam of Genesis. "Classification precedes collection", the art historians John Elsner and Roger Cardinal claim: "Adam classified the creatures that God had made; on the basis of his nomenclature, Noah could recollect those creatures in order to preserve them." Yet, if classification makes collecting possible, collecting, in its turn, "hastens the need to classify". "Collecting is", according to Elsner and Cardinal, "classification lived" and "the narrative of how human beings have striven to accommodate, to appropriate and to extend the taxonomies and systems of knowledge they have inherited".[14]

Within the respective domains of ornithology and birdwatching, Linnaean taxonomy serves slightly different purposes. Whereas the ornithologist applies its principles in "the laboratory", Thomas R. Dunlap writes, the birders' use of systematic classification is concerned primarily with developing "the craft knowledge of identification" out in the field. In the late-nineteenth and early twentieth century, according to Dunlap, ornithologists "used taxonomy as an analytical tool to organise birds", while amateur birdwatchers, who "followed the professionals in their passing of differences down to the level of subspecies", did so "only to get the right name for the checklist".[15]

The systematic logic of taxonomy is not, however, restricted to the pursuits of biologists and the "expert amateur knowledge" of the birder, but extends to the more "personal responses to nature" where "the pleasure of looking closely, and the sense of revelation in small things closely attended to [...] takes an equal or almost equal place with the facts themselves".[16] Although, as Spencer Schaffner suggests, "romanticism, transcendentalism, aestheticism, and anthropomorphism may inform bird-watching encounters", they only do so "after the first act of identification, based on taxonomies of distinguishing traits, has been established".[17]

Waanders, in the series of 'Field Guides' that he made as aids to identifying and (as with his earlier *Standard Catalogue*) cataloguing his own books, frames his own taxonomical sensibilities in the context of amateur bird watching. These 'Field Guides' appropriate the key tenets of the taxonomical systems of the amateur field manual. Each book of Waanders' is listed and rendered identifiable by "description", "field characters", "distribution", and "general notes" and are often cross-referenced with other "species". [*See pages 116–119*] In comparison to the visual montages of *Standard Catalogue*, the 'Field Guides' are more minimal and less textural in their design and use Waanders' own simple black pen drawings to illustrate each entry. Cathy Courtney describes the book as a "parody of a guidebook on birds" which is at once "both self-sufficient and a documentation of Waanders' past book works". By "documenting each title's availability as if it were (as it is) a rare species to be found only in occasional habitats", Waanders' books, as Courtney suggests, are shown as being as elusive and difficult to spot and identify as the species of bird that they are primarily committed to.[18]

Waanders structures his book like a typical amateur field guide, supplying plentiful illustrations of "booktraps", "book baths", and useful "Book watching vantage points" for the observer. [*See page 119*] In parody of the standard practice of field guides to include a simple diagram of a bird's topography, Waanders provides a topography of the book. Where one would normally be presented with a diagrammatic index of a bird's rudimentary anatomical parts—feather groups, wing structures, head and facial features—Waanders maps the standout features of the codex—pages, spine, covers—for quick and easy identification. In the spirit of the field guide, Waanders also includes a number of otherwise blank pages headed "notes" and, in Russian, "для заметок" ("for notes"), placed intermittently throughout the book, for the user to compile his or her personal lists of the books/species they have spotted.

In addition to evoking the design and function of field guides, Waanders also mimics their enthusiastic didactic tone. By sleight-of-tweezer, Waanders steadfastly substitutes the word "book" for "bird" in a series of texts lifted from a multilingual range of field guides and birdwatching books. In their allusions to beginners, non-specialists, hobbies, and leisure activities, these doctored reflections on the merits of birdwatching frame the activity of "bookwatching" as an

amateur one that can potentially transform the way the neophyte
sees and experiences the world.

A particularly salient example occurs in Waanders' repurposing of
Roger Tory Peterson's preface to his book *How to Know the Birds* (1949):

> Books can fly where they want to when they want to. So it seems
> to us, who are earthbound. They symbolise a degree of freedom
> that we would nearly give our souls to have. Perhaps this is why
> book watching has almost become a national hobby in Britain and
> is rapidly becoming one here. It is an antidote for the disillusion-
> ment of today's world, a world beset by pressures it has never
> before known. Many men in business and the professions find in
> books a much-needed balance, a retreat from their highly complex
> affairs and the artificiality of the city. Housewives find in them a
> pleasant relief from the routine of the home, and children enjoy
> their pursuit for the release it gives their abundant energies. Boys
> in their teens make the keenest book recorders for once they fall
> under the spell of the "lure of the list", they play the game for all
> its worth.[19]

Providing "balance", "retreat", and "relief"—as well as feelings of
freedom and release—birdwatching, Peterson's original text implies,
can restore equilibrium and constitute a restorative experience. Not
unlike the reverie or daydream, this pastime has the ability to take
the enthusiast out of his or her daily routines and provide them a
measure of wellbeing and happiness. Yet, as Peterson's concluding
sentence indicates, the "lure of the list" presupposes the passion of
the collector. As much as it might be for the thrill of the chase, this
passion is also directed toward the satisfaction of compiling and
completing data.

The "lure of the list" also situates the birder in the category of the
"spotter". Inadvertently recalling Waanders' *Lies* postcard, John Bevis,
in his essay 'The Observer', suggests that the "triumphant observation" of spotting "is more an article of faith, a collection of sightings
which are unwitnessed and unprovable, of moments which shine in
the memory with the greater or lesser intensity of stars".

> It is collecting at its most existential, free of the sentiment,
> fetishism or acquisitiveness which can taint the accumulation of
> objects. The end product, a bland list of names or numbers, has
> no decorative or marketable value, and even in an information-
> driven age, a very small cache of meaning.[20]

Such unverifiable lists, Bevis implies, are the traces or afterlives of

transient, irretrievable sightings in time and space. The "spotter"
may, therefore, very well agree with the proposition set out by
Ludwig Wittgenstein in his *Tractatus Logico-Philosophicus*: "The world
is the totality of facts, not of things" (1.1).[21] In this respect, this form
of collecting saliently adumbrates the dematerialisiation of objects
proposed by Lucy R. Lippard and John Chandler in their defining
essay on conceptual art, 'The Dematerialization of Art', first published
in *Art International* in February 1968.*

A prime example of this dematerialization is the serial procedures
and practices that the American conceptual artist, Mel Bochner, in his
seminal 1967 essay, 'Serial Art, Systems, Solipsism', dubs "systematic
thinking":

> Systems are characterised by regularity, thoroughness, and repeti-
> tion in execution. They are methodical. It is their consistency and
> continuity of application that characterises them.[22]

Bochner compares the regular, methodical nature of systematic
thinking to solipsism, suggesting that the art that practices such
consistency and continuity aligns itself closely with "the self-enclosed
confines" of the solipsist's mind. "Serial art", Bochner suggests, "in
its highly abstract and ordered manipulation of thought is likewise
self-contained and nonreferential" and, like the solipsist's "boundaries of thought" make "the random dimensions of reality lose their
qualities of extension".[23]

Elaborating on Bochner's claims, Johanna Burton in her essay on
open systems art, 'Mystics Rather than Rationalists', suggests that
the artist-solipsist's "objects, procedures and ideologies express
discrete self-generated (and self-generating) systems used to
navigate—rather than mirror—the world". [24] Rather than appropriating "systems culled from outside him or herself", the solipsist
constructs their own systems that are "seemingly strange or illog-
ical, not grounded in collective experience but in individual tactics
of negation".[25] One might compare these "tactics" to those that
Jean Baudrillard attributes to the collector and his or her desire to
resolve "real time into a systematic dimension" (*pastime*) by means
of collected objects that "together make up a system through which
the subject strives to construct a world, a private totality".[26] John

* In 'The Dematerialization of Art', Lippard and Chandler, addressing the growth of "ultra-
conceptual art that emphasises the thinking process almost exclusively" at the expense of
"the physical evolution of the work of art", suggest that such "a profound dematerialization
of art [...] may result in the object's becoming wholly obsolete". Lucy R. Lippard and John
Chandler, cited in Lippard, *Six Years: The Dematerialization of the Art Object from 1966 to 1972*
(Berkeley & Los Angeles: University of California Press, 1997), pp.42–43.

Bevis's "bland list" of the spotter is also echoed in such solipsistic art practices, particularly the way in which the spotter's disinterested record of a passionate pursuit functions "as a means of bringing order to a personal sense of disorder, of taming the psychological Wild West".[27]

A conceptual equivalent of such "existential" listing occurs in the serial, process-based works that the Japanese conceptual artist On Kawara undertook to document his daily existence. Kawara's *I Met* series, for example, documents in single-column typed lists (stamped with the date and arranged chronologically in binders) the people that he conversed with each day between 1968 and 1979. During the same period, Kawara also undertook a serial mail art project. Each day, from May 10th, 1968 to September 17th, 1979, Kawara sent to two different friends or associates a tourist picture postcard of the location where he happened to be at that particular moment in time. Kawara would uniformly stamp each card with the exact time that he arose on that day and rubberstamp his and his recipients' addresses. Kawara never signed his postcards or included any handwritten information.

"The fascination exerted by Kawara's obsessive and precise notations of *his* place in the world (time and location)", Lippard writes, imply a kind of self-reassurance that the artist does, in fact, exist".[28] Kawara's practice foresees Waanders' similarly solitary tabulations. The implicit solipsism (from the Latin *solus*, "alone", and *ipse*, "self") of Kawara's projects is teased out further by Lippard when she notes how, "without pathos, their objectivity establish[es] the self-imposed isolation which marks his way of life as well as his art".[29] Yet, like the spotter's list, Kawara's *I Got Up* series is essentially "an article of faith". One might be able to cross reference the time and location recorded on the postal cancellation marks with the landmarks pictured on the postcards, but the constraints of Kawara's practice and his accounts of getting up cannot be verified. Furthermore, as Jonathan Watkins notes in his monograph on the artist, Kawara's "announcement of the exact time, to the minute, gives the work a quasi-scientific tone that raises the question of who actually cares?".[30]

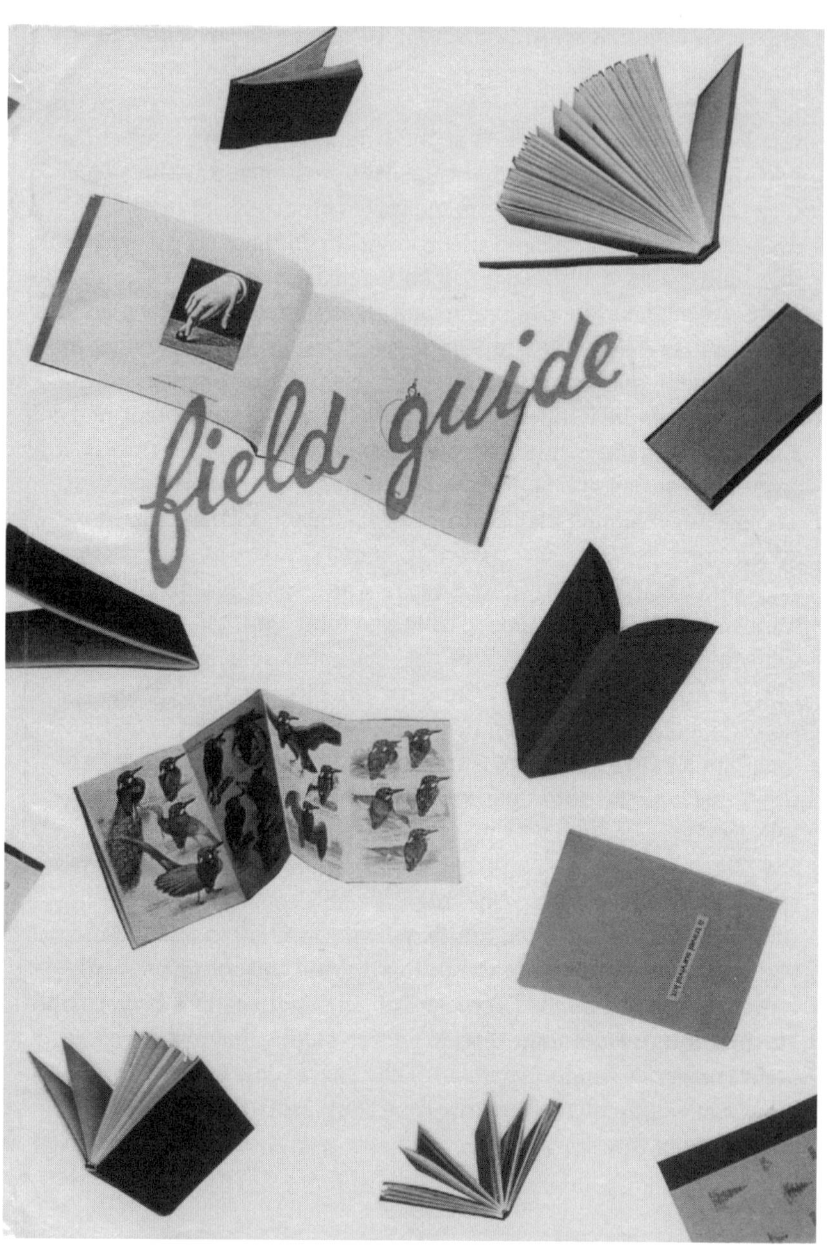
field guide

41. AN ALBUM OF CIGARETTE CARDS

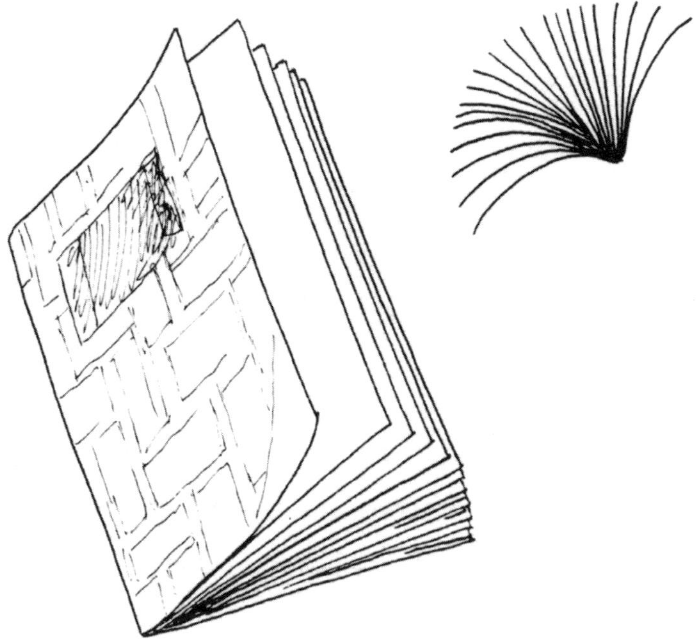

Description: Medium. 19,8 X 27 cm. 48 pages. Soft cover.
1994. Signed.
Field characters: Soon recognized by its colourful cover. Thin.
Many pasted-in pictures inside, covered with blue stamps.
Distribution: Formery widespread and common, now this
book is nowhere common. Only 1. Extremely rare.
General notes: A remake of an old Album of Cigarette Cards.
All birds in this album are transformed into kingfishers.

42. ZO LEER JE VOGELS KENNEN [How to know birds]

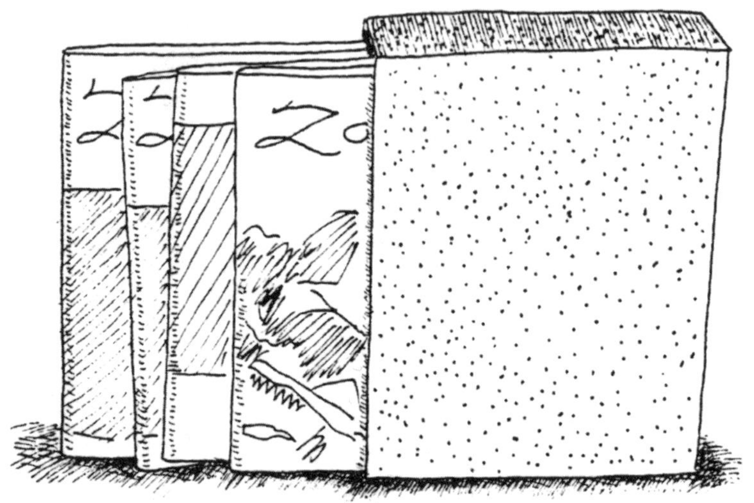

Description: Medium. 17,5 X 25,5 cm. 48 pages [4 X]. Soft
cover. 1995. Signed and numbered.
Field characters: Covers are colourful [with photographs of
birds]. They are mostly hidden in a greenish case. Inside, many
pasted-in pictures of birds, all covered with a blue stamp.
These albums have a restricted distribution, but are said to be
not uncommon within their range.
Distribution: Formerly resident and widespread, but these
subspecies is quite rare. [5] Thinly and locally distributed.
General notes: A set of four, closely related books with 200
bird-pictures. 199 are transformed into kingfishers.

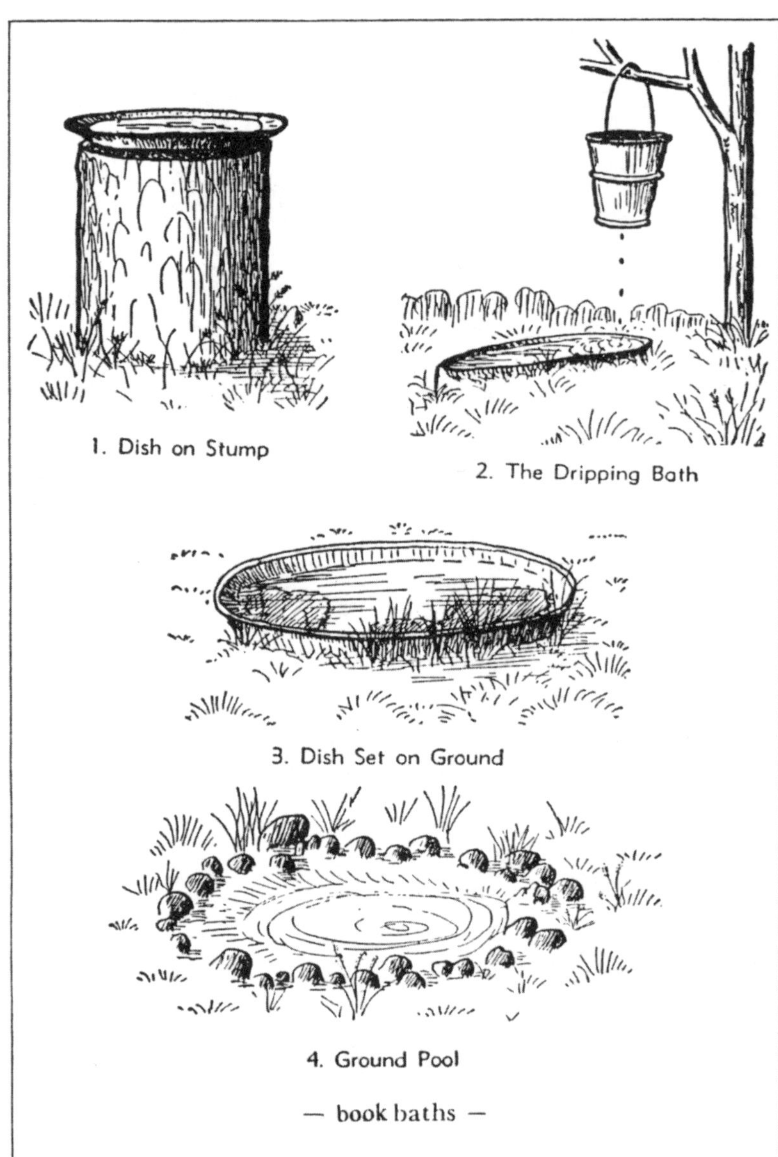

1. Dish on Stump
2. The Dripping Bath
3. Dish Set on Ground
4. Ground Pool
— book baths —

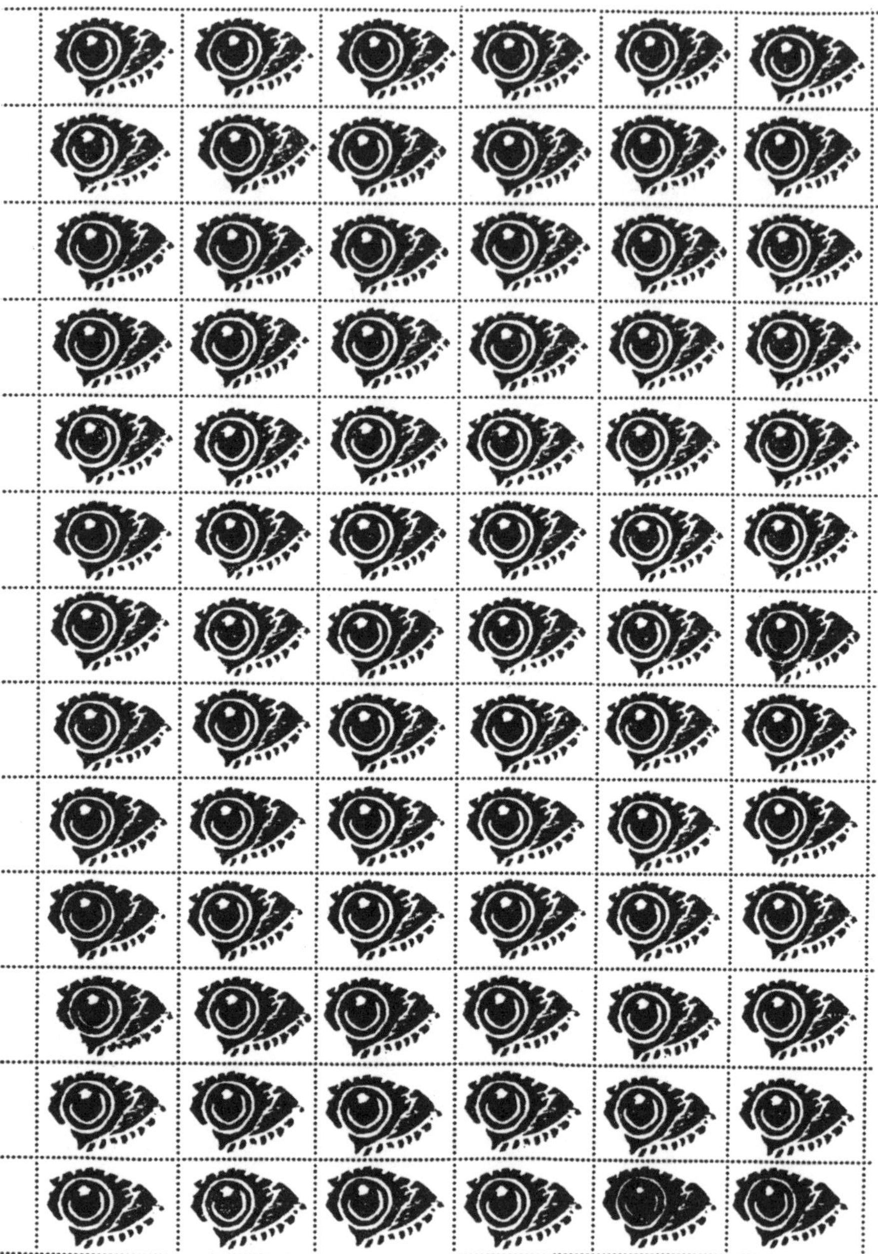

120

Series

Kawara's serial postcards would appear to have provided Waanders a model for the series of postcards he mailed on a daily basis to Peter Foolen from January 17th to February 1st, 1997. [*See pages 128–129*] The picture side of each postcard consists of sixteen kingfisher postage stamps designed by Waanders. These match exactly the number of days (and number of postcards) that Waanders mailed Foolen. In terms of numerical significance, Waanders' choice of the number sixteen remains unclear. One can speculate endlessly on what that number symbolises in the larger scheme of his solipsistic cosmos. However, it is just as possible that the dimensions of the postcard and his stamps arbitrarily determined the conceptual constraints of Waanders' mailings. Thus, if, for example, the postcard could have accommodated twenty stamps, Waanders may have posted twenty postcards over a twenty-day period. If so, it is another instance of Waanders responding pragmatically to the creative opportunities of coincidence.

Despite the uniformity of the single image of *Alcedo atthis* that Waanders uses on his postage stamp, its colour varies across the sixteen cards. (Again, one can only conjecture whether there is an overarching "pattern" or "code" to these combinations of colours as they occur across the sixteen postcards.) The information that Waanders provides on the reverse side of these postcards is minimal and, like Kawara's postcards, entirely rubberstamped. "BIRDLIFE" is stamped in blue with a serial number (1 to 16 successively), followed by "hans wanders / 1997". Again like Kawara, Waanders never signs his cards or provides any additional information, handwritten or otherwise. On each card Peter Foolen's name and address is also rubberstamped, but in black.

The postcards themselves are taken primarily from a series, entitled 'Birdlife', issued by the South African faction of the global conservation organisation BirdLife International. The purpose, as printed on the back of each of card (in English and Afrikaans), is to showcase "Some of the many and varied birds to be found in the contrasting climes of this vast subcontinent".* Waanders' stamps obscure entirely each postcard's original image. However, and perhaps most likely in allusion to Waanders' formative kingfisher sightings, three of

* The entire series of the *Birdlife* postcards can be viewed on Peter Foolen's blog, *Peter Foolen: Editions, Publishing, and Bookdesign.*

the *Birdlife* cards break from this serial uniformity. *Birdlife 2*, *Birdlife 5*, and *Birdlife 13* retain enough information to reveal that these are postcards of kingfishers separate from the other South African BirdLife cards in the series. *Birdlife 13*, a Dutch postcard that includes a lengthy description of *IJsvogel*, is especially notable as Waanders includes another of his own stamp designs (a white silhouetted kingfisher against a blue background), collaterally cancelled (thus sanctioned and legitimised) due to its position next to the official postage stamp [*See page 129*]. This fleeting appearance of the king-fisher in *Birdlife 13* might be conceived as an equivalent of, or allusion to, the 1982 experience: an illuminative rupture or hiatus in an other-wise monotonous routine.

The solipsistic nature of the *Birdlife* cards is repeated throughout Waanders' work in various forms and practices. For example, *Eyes*, which Waanders began in 1990, consists solely of one rubberstamped image of the kingfisher's eye stamped repeatedly to form a block of perforated artiststamps. Waanders would daily stamp the same image to "equal the number of days that have passed since he saw the kingfisher, on October 4, 1982" [*See page 120*].[1] The personal expe-rience motivating *Eyes*, coupled with the tacit pun between the bird's eye and the pronoun "I", implies a self-centered solipsism that marks time and ritualistically recapitulates—or, indeed, *observes*—a private, subjective moment in time. With the significance of this ritual practice resting largely on Waanders' own private frame of refer-ence, only mortality, it seems, will put *closure* (another pun, perhaps, on eyes and lids) on such observance. The rationale of *Eyes* may be solipsistic (if not hermetic), but the very nature of this serial prac-tice communicates something else, something more universal about meaning-making. Like the Greek notion of *dromenon* (the "thing done"), the "meaning" of *Eyes* is in the means and the practice of its making, and not simply in the end that it anticipates or the original subjective experience that it monotonously recapitulates.

Solipsism also informs Waanders' book *IJsvogelwiel (Kingfisherpond)* (1989). Using the same method as in *Bloody Tracks*, Waanders uses his arm, post-surgery, as a brush to paint with. Partly covering his arm in blue ink, Waanders makes four prints on semi-transparent layers of Japanese (washi) paper that "form together a triangle".[2] Speculating on this triangular form and "the symbolic significance of the number three", Kristine Stiles considers "the Holy Trinity, tran-substantiation, and the Eucharistic" among other possible "esoteric and theological references".[3] The trinitarian significance of this book might also allude to Waanders' third sighting of *Alcedo atthis* at the "kingfisherpond" in 1982. Thus, *IJsvogelwiel* might therefore be read as an invocatory rite that attempts to summon, or better still, re-call the kingfisher.

An enduring mystery of Waanders' work is why the third sighting of *Alcedo atthis* should, not withstanding the element of coincidence, have been such a transformative experience. However, with the 1982 sighting initiating what is essentially Waanders' "new life" in art, it is difficult to ignore certain suggestions of Dante and the symbolic emphasis the Italian poet puts on the number three in his 'Book of Memory', the *Vita nuova* (*The New Life*).[4] In Dante's time, as Thomas Rendall notes, "three was the number of God" and, for Dante, symbolic of the miraculous Trinity.[5] Dante first sets eyes upon his beloved Beatrice at the age of nine, a number associated with miracles.* "Nine times already since my birth the heaven of light had circled back to almost the same point when the now glorious lady of my mind first appeared to my eyes", Dante writes in the *Vita nuova*.[6] It is a further nine years until he sees Beatrice again: notably, at three o'clock in the afternoon, which is also the ninth hour of the day. Furthermore, Dante recounts how Beatrice's "wholly noble soul departed in the first hour of the ninth day of the month; and according to the custom of Syria, she departed in the ninth month of the year, since the first month there is Tixryn the First, which for us is October"[7]—the same month that Waanders saw his third kingfisher, Yves Klein made his leap into the Void, and the Soviet Union launched Sputnik 1 into space.

Regardless of its accuracy or credibility, Dante's elaborate number symbolism—not unlike the solipsistic systems of conceptual art—provides the means for structuring, ordering, and arranging memory and experience. One might compare this numerological certitude with the methods and practices underpinning Waanders' own "romance". Indeed, the sense of fate that Dante conveys through his number symbolism is echoed in the way that Waanders "claimed to be able to foretell the future". Collecting "sufficient quasi-scientific knowledge allowed him to be able to predict the return of his original kingfisher", Jean Poussin suggests, "*a priori* rather than by experience".[8]

---

* The idea of *Alcedo atthis* as Waanders' Beatrice might not seem quite so hyperbolic when the species name of the bird is taken into account. According to David Chandler *Atthis* refers to "a particularly attractive lady" that the poet Sappho loved and, subsequently, lost. As Dante did Beatrice, Sappho immortalised her beloved in her verse, with her absence provoking melancholic contemplation. "Atthis has not come back to me: truly I long to die", Sappho writes in one poem: "Do not forget me, for you know how I love you." David Chandler, *Kingfisher* (London: New Holland, 2010), p.26; Sappho, 'Love Poems and Fragments', trans. Edward Storer, pp.153–155, *The Egoist* 10.2 (October, 1915), p.153.

Comparing Waanders' methods to Liebniz's belief that "all substances (by this he meant roughly all 'living beings') contain their future from the moment they come to life", Poussin claims that "Hans Waanders' and the kingfisher's paths were bound to cross; for it had been written in the stars since the dawn of time". Such a notion finds some qualification in Waanders' book *Picture Index* (1994) in which Waanders modifies an old Asian lottery prediction guide so that "the kingfisher's infiltration of the forecasting system", gives fate a blue twist.[9] Method, or "right practice", meets coincidence, reiterating a tacit notion that runs throughout Waanders' work—namely, that the fateful blue encounter on October 4th, 1982 was perhaps as much fate as it was chance.

The veracity of such a claim, however, is not as important as the logical reason underpinning such "a wild idea", as Jean Poussin explains:

> This is because Hans Waanders believes in order; a worldly order that may be invisible at first sight but one that even a kingfisher ultimately has to obey. Hans Waanders' courage comes from his belief and he is never sidetracked by chance.

Adopting Leibniz's thesis, Poussin suggests that, in a cosmos, "in an ordered universe, everything can be predicted":

> Leibniz recognises the visible confusion in the world around us. But he suggests that the disorder we see (e.g. unkempt weeds and grasses growing on the banks of the river Maas) is not due to an error of nature but to lack of intelligence on our part. We simply do not possess the necessary tools to understand. Hans Waanders set out patiently and bravely to construct those tools, steadily, without rushing, in the sure knowledge that the kingfisher must confirm to its own specific laws.[10]

A corollary of this faith in order might be the sanguine pulse of Waanders' work which, as *Bloody Tracks* and his series of perch interventions illustrate, express a tenacious confidence in the return of *Alcedo atthis*.

Another signal work of Waanders' in this respect is *Orde: Coraciiformes – Familie: Alcedinidae*, which Waanders begun working on in 1983. Prompted by Waanders' sighting of *Alcedo atthis* the previous year, *Orde: Coraciiformes* is an incipient "tool" in Waanders' endeavor to find cosmos in the form of the kingfisher. Waanders consulted numerous bird guides for basic information about the kingfisher—its field marks, mating behavior, feeding habits—which he transcribed by hand onto large sheets of paper. The scope of the research increasingly broadened as Waanders collated more specialised information on his subject. Waanders did so in the belief of eventually gaining sufficient knowledge to intimately understand the bird's behavior and thus, as Teeuwen explains, enable him "to know the time and place of its appearance".[11]

The constraints that Waanders imposes on this project, however, distinguish it from the ornithology that he consulted. "Turning his back on riverside observation, he delved into nature guides, dictionaries and encyclopaedias", Poussin writes, "not through any desire to become an expert on kingfishers but simply as a means to catch sight of his original kingfisher once more". Thus, like the imposed procedures and constraints of conceptual art, Waanders only returned "to the spot where he last saw the tiny bird" (near the river Maas) "several times a week". According to Tjeu Teeuwen, Waanders "decided to continue the investigation until the moment he would see a kingfisher again". This, however, took another seven years. In 1990—the same year that he commenced on *Eyes*—Waanders eventually saw, not one, but two kingfishers—only this time "in the centre of 's-Hertogenbosch" on the river Aa.[12]

Although it was evidently not the return of his original kingfisher, this sighting was sufficient enough for Waanders, while "working on page 188", to conclude *Orde: Coraciiformes*.[13] The result of his labour was a boxed collation of 188 large (50 x 30cm) unbound handwritten sheets of research that Waanders then worked over with washes of blue ink. The tone of the work is fluidity. The long flowing lines of Waanders' initial text, washed in various shades of blue, evoke the ripples of the kingfisher's ideal feeding condition (slow-moving water), as well as the reflections and refractions of light on its surface. Notions of depth and surface are also implicit in the way that the blue ink, as Tjeu Teeuwen suggests, serves to "distract the reader's attention from the literal text", so that Waanders' text is both looked at and looked through, as one might the water of a stream or pond.[14] This unique work is therefore aptly reflective—or, rather, self-reflexive—of the motives that prompted such an undertaking. If Waanders wanted to re-invoke *Alcedo atthis* and experience again a fleeting moment in time, the river metaphor of *Orde: Coraciiformes* tacitly recalls the familiar Heraclitean adage that one can never step twice into the same river.

Collecting—in this instance, collecting information, knowledge, and data—does not reclaim what has been lost; neither does it result in the autonomous world or private totality that Baudrillard attributes to the collection. Instead, Waanders' collection of facts, as John Elder and Roger Cardinal suggest of collections more generally, "shuns closure and the security of received evaluations and instead opens its eyes to existence—the world around us, both cultural and natural, in all its unpredictability and contingent complexity".[15] Waanders' search for order seems therefore to have inversely accentuated such unpredictability and contingency rather than control it. Not unlike Richard Burton's great exhaustive cento of 1621, *The Anatomy of Melancholy*, the accumulative nature of Waanders' research resists closure and instead spurs further exposition and reasoning. In this respect, *Orde: Coraciiformes* is perhaps closest in spirit to the pre-Linnaean historian whose task, Foucault writes, "was to establish the great compilation of documents and signs—of everything, throughout the world, that might form a mark as it were": "His existence was defined not so much by what he saw as by what he retold, by a secondary speech which pronounced afresh so many words that had been muffled."[16]

The information that Waanders compiled and "retold" over the duration of *Orde: Coraciiformes* would galvanise rather than satiate his pursuit of *Alcedo atthis*. One has only to consult the bibliography included in *Kingfishers and Related Works* to see this. Consisting over a hundred books and articles (in numerous languages) relating to the kingfisher family, Waanders it seems, left no bibliographic stone unturned in his search for his bird. Thus, if *Orde: Coraciiformes* started out as an attempt to reify the object of Waanders' inquiry, it became instead an incipient synecdoche for the "flow of works", to use Cathy Courtney's apposite phrase, that proceeded it.[17]

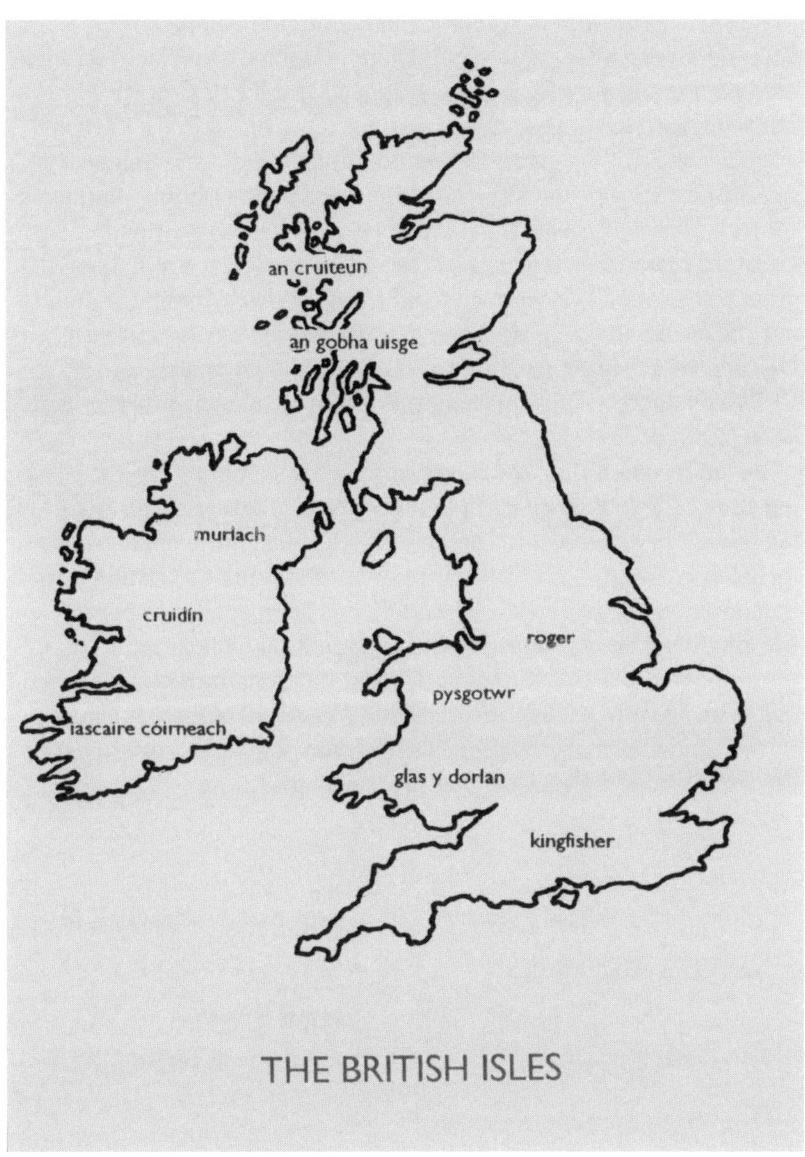

THE BRITISH ISLES

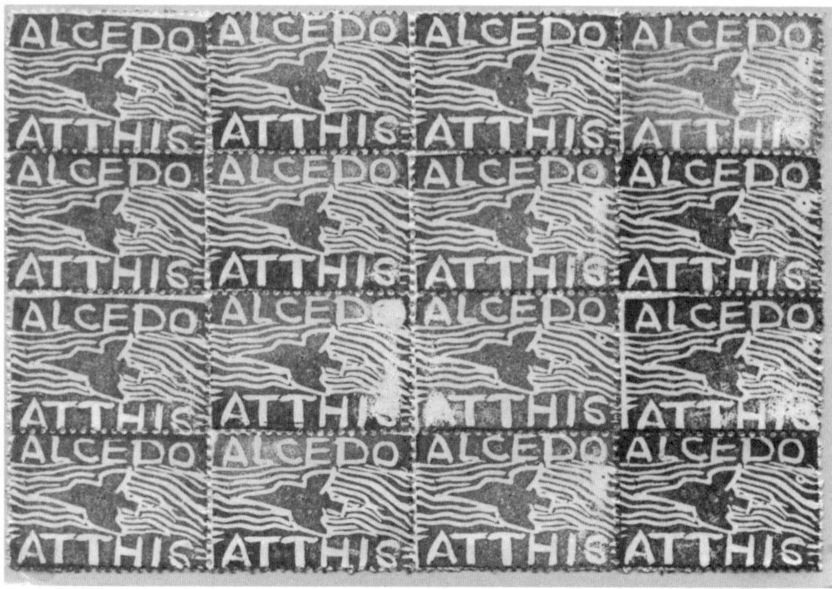

ALCEDO ALCEDO ALCEDO ALCEDO
ATTHIS ATTHIS ATTHIS ATTHIS
ALCEDO ALCEDO ALCEDO ALCEDO
ATTHIS ATTHIS ATTHIS ATTHIS
ALCEDO ALCEDO ALCEDO ALCEDO
ATTHIS ATTHIS ATTHIS ATTHIS
ALCEDO ALCEDO ALCEDO ALCEDO
ATTHIS ATTHIS ATTHIS ATTHIS

POST CARD
POSKAART
COPYRIGHT
NEDERLAND
80c
ART PUBLISHERS (PTY) LTD. DURBAN • JOHANNESBURG • CAPE TOWN
BIRDLIFE
1
hans waanders
97
PETER FOOLEN
NIJENRODE 107
5653 JD
EINDHOVEN
BIRDLIFE:
Some of the many and varied birds to be found in the contrasting
climes of this vast sub-continent.
VOËLLEWE:
Enkele van die baie en verskeidenheid voelsoorte wat aangetref word
in die wisselende klimaat van hierdie uitgestrekte vasteland.

IJSVOGEL.

Deze vogel heeft het meest felgekleurde verenkleed van alle bij ons broedende vogels.
De veldkenmerken zijn: bovenzijde fel staalblauw, oranje - bruine onderkant, witte keel en vlek aan weerszijden van de hals.
Het voedsel van de IJsvogel bestaat voornamelijk uit voorntjes en stekelbaarsjes, waterkevers en libellelarven.
De IJsvogels hebben het in strenge winters zeer zwaar. Vele komen om van de honger, doordat hun hoofdvoedsel, vis, onbereikbaar is door het ijs.
's Winters ziet men ze wel bij wakken in het ijs, vandaar de naam IJsvogel waarschijnlijk.
De opvallende kleuren van de IJsvogel hebben een funktie bij de zelfverdediging.
De IJsvogels graven hun nest meestal uit in zanderige of leemachtige rivieroevers. De legtijd is van april tot augustus. Er zijn meestal 6 à 7 eiëren, die 19 tot 21 dagen door beide vogels worden bebroed. De jongen, door zowel mannetje als vrouwtje gevoerd, vliegen na 23 - 27 dagen. De IJsvogel heeft meestal 2 broedsels per jaar.

BIRDLIFE
13

hans waanders
97

Uitgeverij DE STULP-Leidschendam

Serie 550

PETER FOOLEN
NIJENRODE 107
5653 JD
EINDHOVEN

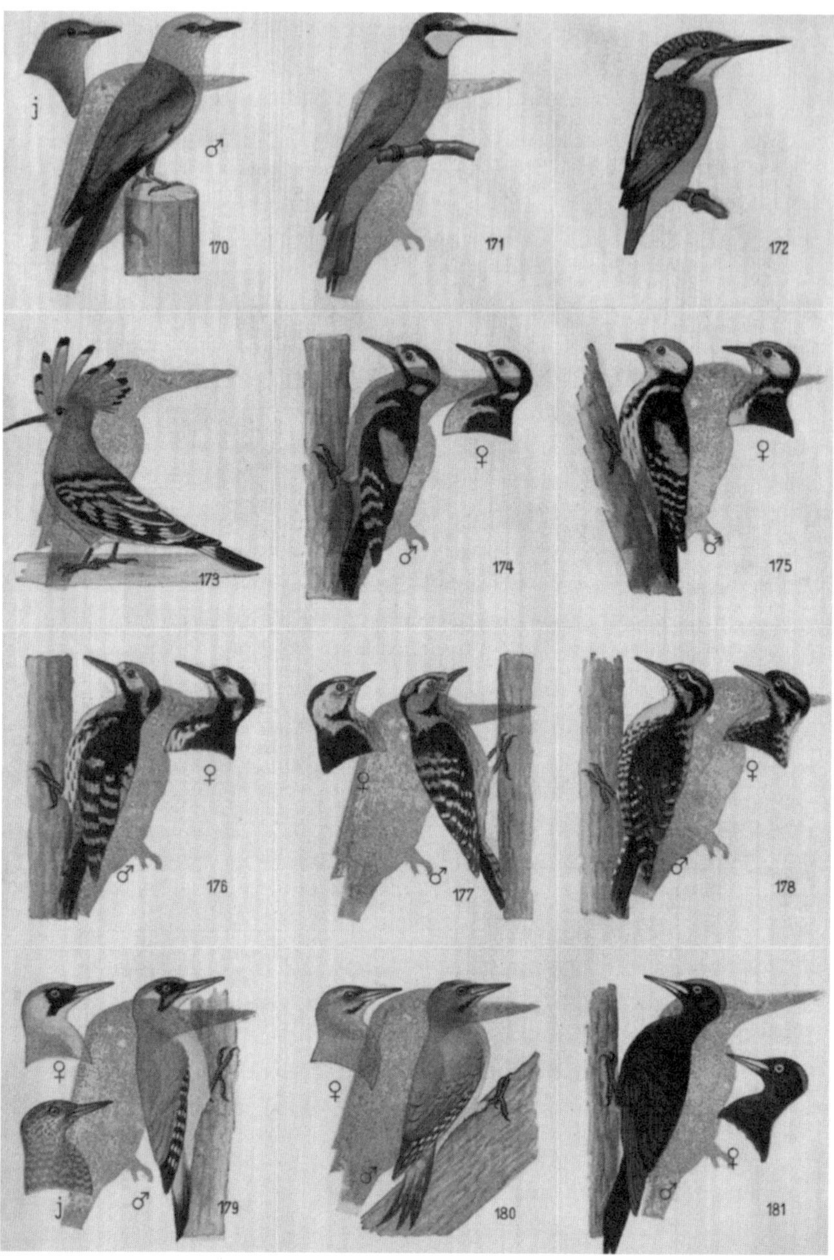

j
♂
170
171
172
173
♀
174
♀
175
♀
176
♂
♀
177
♂
♀
178
♀
j
♂
179
♀
180
181
♀
♂

Rite

The insistent, systematic progression of *Orde: Coraciiformes* is pres-
cient of the ways in which temporality and order inform Waanders'
work. The procedural modes of these works also reflect his awareness of what Susan Stewart calls the "temporality of everyday life".
Temporality, she claims, "is held to be ongoing and nonreversible and,
at the same time, characterised by repetition and predictability".[1]
As well as inflecting the melancholic idiom of Waanders' work, this
emphasis on time and repetition also gives his work a subtle, yet
distinctive, sense of what the historian of religions Jonathan Z. Smith
calls "ritual and its capacity for routinisation" which, according to
Smith, occurs when "significance and regularity" is projected on an
event or object.[2]

At its most rudimentary level, Lucy R. Lippard proposes, ritual is
about "perpetuating belief and history" via the complex "relationship
of belief to the forms that convey it". Images and activities, Lippard
continues, are "ritual in the true sense only when filled by a commu-
nal impulse that connects the past (the last time we performed this
act) and the present (the ritual we are performing now) and the
future (will we ever perform it again?)". Echoing the idea of *dromenon*, this temporal awareness, Lippard suggests, also constitutes
a praxis of "knowing through doing and communicating through
participating".[3]

Jonathan Z. Smith also emphasises the practical dimension of ritual
when he suggests that ritual "represents the creation of a controlled
environment" which puts a focusing lens on ordinary, commonplace
activities: *"Ritual is a means of performing the way things ought to be
in conscious tension to the way things are in such a way that this ritualised perfection is recollected in the ordinary, uncontrolled, course of
things."*[4] Not unlike the "right practice" that Karen Davidson finds in
Waanders' work, ritual, as conceived by Smith, "provides an occasion
for reflection and rationalisation on the fact that what ought to have
been done was not done".

> Ritual relies for its power on the fact that it is concerned with
> quite ordinary activities, that what it describes and displays is,
> in principle, possible for every occurrence of these acts. But it
> relies, as well, for its power on the fact that, in actuality, such
> possibilities cannot be realised.[5]

Both *Orde: Coraciiformes* and *Eyes* might be understood from such a perspective which gives to their solipsistic procedures "a significance which [their] rules express but are powerless to effectuate".[6]

Another example of this ritualised perfection is Waanders' rubber-stamped field guide interventions. In these détourned texts, Jenny Brownrigg suggests, the rubberstamped "symbol of the kingfisher colonises pages in a methodical take-over" which "mimics the real life preoccupation of the artist engaged in his own search for the next glimpse of this bird".[7] [*See page 130*] Waanders' ritualistic stamping might therefore, to recall Smith's thesis, be perceived as the ritualised perfection or performance of *"the way things ought to be in conscious tension to the way things are"*.

Describing the repetition of the kingfisher's rubberstamped image as "the required incantation in the artist's quests to become closer", Brownrigg echoes what Tjeu Teeuwen notes about *Orde: Coraciiformes*, namely that this endeavor to "conjure the kingfisher", tactitly evokes his interest in the prehistoric cave paintings at Altimira or Lascaux.* The crude elegance of Waanders' rubberstamp images of the kingfisher might therefore be perceived as his equiva-lent of the charcoal drawings and polychrome paintings of animals found at these Paleolithic sites, just as Waanders's arm prints in *IJsvogelwiel* and *Bloody Tracks* might suggest the hand prints and stencils found at these same locations. Furthermore, with his rubber-stamps frequently being devoid of any ambient context, Waanders carved kingfisher images also recall how the Paleolithic cave painter, as the writer Geoffry Grigson speculates, "gives all his effort to the solitary image" and "leaves the environment of the animal to be inferred".[8] [*See page 2*]

The zoomorphic images of the cave painter have provoked consid-erable speculation and debate regarding their purpose. One popular interpretation considers the representations of animals in parietal art as a form of "hunting magic", which, according to the psychologist Joseph Lyons, "developed as a practical means of securing magical control over the hunted animal and thus insuring success in the hunt".[9] As an art "meant to deliberately invoke", the cave paintings and drawings at Lascaux and Altamira might, therefore, appeal to or summon what is absent.[10]

The poet Gustaf Sobin makes a similar case in his 1999 essay collection *Luminous Debris*, a book that gathers the American

* Waanders visited Spain's prehistoric caves in in 1987 and, in 2000, visited Font-de-Gaume in Dordogne, south-west France. Waanders' interest in prehistoric cave art is also evident in his book *La Grotte de Lascaux* (1993), which repurposes an old schoolbook of the more famous prehistoric cave in Dordogne from the perspective of the kingfisher.

writer's reflective, lyrical readings of the pre- and proto-historical
vestige and artifacts of Provence and Languedoc. To be confronted
by the "graphic gestures", and "hesitant outlines" of these "first
invocations", Sobin suggests of the region's cave paintings, is to be
"in the presence of an articulated absence, or, more exactly, of an
interval that seems to span the space between the manifest and the
imagined, to oscillate between the *here* and the *there*, the *now* and
the ever-imminent *then*. Between, that is, desire and gratification,
supplication and response." These parietal artists, Sobin reasons,
"didn't paint what they saw but what they needed", with each
zoomorphic subject being "conjured—graphically summoned—
as a metaphysical entity" and "a *wish*".[11]

In contrast to these theories of invocation, Jonathan Z. Smith
considers such "'mimetic' or 'sympathetic hunting magic,' especially
as it occurs in relation to preparation for the hunt", as further exam-
ples of how ritual represents "the idealised and controlled paradigms
of otherwise contingent everyday practices".[12] "It is not", Smith
clams, "that 'magical' rituals compel the world through representation and manipulation", but rather that "they express a realistic
assessment of the fact that the world cannot be compelled":

> The ritual is incongruent with the way things are or are likely
> to be, for contingency, variability, and accidentality have been
> factored out. The ritual displays a dimension of the hunt that
> can be thought about and remembered in the course of things.[13]

Recalling the solipsist artist's "(nearly magical) systems" that seek to
"keep the outside at bay", it is perhaps Smith's conception of ritual
as incongruent praxis that speaks most pertinently to Waanders'
work.[14] In particular, it is Waanders' "ritualised mark-making" that
suggests the ritual of iterative, habitual practice.[15] The suggestion
that Waanders' ritual stamping might answer or react to a world
that cannot be compelled is accentuated by the bureaucratic connotations of the rubberstamps he employs. This otherwise innocuous
form, as Ulises Carrión suggests, wields the power "to validate or
invalidate something" and thus "control and direct our lives".[16] The
act of stamping might therefore be seen as a prime expression of the
implicit monomania in Waanders' work and the "malevolent spirit",
as Jean Poussin refers to the kingfisher, which compels, controls and
directs, it. At the same time, however, to recall Bachelard's notion
of the poetic object, the impersonal authority of Waanders' rubberstamps also puts the world more emphatically under the sign of the
kingfisher. The world is sanctioned and sanctified by means of this

discreet symbol of power and its attempt at yielding a full, total control of things.

What Jonathan Z. Smith deems the refocusing lens of ritual finds an equivalent in the "binocular vision" of the modern bird field guide. The sanitised visual representations of birds in these guides, as Spencer Schaffner suggests, reflect "a taxonomic, focused way of seeing and thinking about individual parts of 'nature'" which seeks to "render the things around us as recognizable, classifiable, and predictable".[17] Like the cave painter's animal depictions, the generic illustrations used in field guides depict "decontextualised specimens […] drawn in paradigmatic fashion and with a minimum or absent reference to naturalistic surroundings".[18] Recalling Smith's notion of ritual preparation for a hunt, the field guide seeks to overcome any "problems with perspective, acuity, and luck" likely to occur in the field—the "contingencies which cannot be found in even the most detailed inspection of their pages"—by way of an idealised systematic method of observation.[19]

Like ritual, however, there is in field guides a notable contrast between the way things ought to be and the way they really are. As Jeremy Mynott's example of the eagle in *Birdscapes* suggests, there is a notable lacuna between the idealised representation of the bird in the field guide and what is actually encountered out in the field:

> The fine distinctions that look so clear on the page of a field guide can easily be obscured and overwhelmed by the sheer eagleness of these dramatic birds in the field, even if you are concentrating on them hard as a species.[20]

Likewise, an "occurrence that is highly unlikely in reality", Jenny Brownrigg remarks, "becomes commonplace on the page" of Waanders' field guides.[21] Thus, what J. A. Baker calls the "systematic watching" of the birder, methodically organised by the field guide, becomes, in Waanders' interventions, systematic stamping.[22] Not unlike the solipsist's "obsessive recourses to systemicity" which, Johanna Burton claims, tend to be conceived "as methods employed to lessen the brunt of stimulus, to literally slow down and thus re-make not so much the *real* as one's relationship to it", Waanders, by repurposing the field guide's "iterable organisation" of phenomena, attempts to make *his* world (the world according to *Alcedo atthis*) a manageable cosmos.[23]

Юрий Алексеевич
ГАГАРИН
Первый в мире
космонавт

THE KINGFISHER—

ísfugl

kunin
kungsfiska

isfågel

Cpuroín kingfisher isfugl

pysgotwr eisvogel

moualh-arhant ijsvogel *ledňáček* žimor

martin-pêcheur jégmade

martiñeta pu

martin pescador piombina vodon

pica-peixe alción

martin pescatore

ἀλκυών

رفراف

لَئ

رفراف

kingfisher martin-pêcheur

kingfisher

kingfisher

martín pescador

fisherman

fisman

martín pescador

ma

cĩ-na-ɜùya

kingfisha

ndege mɜu

martin-pescador

alcião

unongo

isiv

ysvoë

martín pescador

kalastaja

обыкновенный зимородок

ek

оче

ircik

çapkını

lagothi

skin ruva

dein-nyin

chim bói cá

raja udang

pĕkakak chichit
burung udang

tèngkèk

tsui niao

翠鳥

魚狗

カワセミ

물총새　翡翠

KAWASEMI

sana kama mdiria

SEM-MIN

kingfisher

berrimilla

teepookana

boondoon　tete

kingfisher

kotare

lo

oa

VPRO | **DINSDAG RADIO 1**

09 JUNI 1992

PRIMULA OM IN COSMOS

22.53 De 1% regeling
4 minuten en 58,4 sec. beeldende kunst voor het oor.

1
AM (kHz): 747 Flevoland, (402 m).

Elk heel uur (NOS) Nieuws

KRO

7.07 **Echo-magazine**
Nieuwsoverzicht.
7.30 (NOS) **Nieuws**
7.34 **Echo-magazine**
Actualiteiten.
8.35 **Kruispunt**
9.05 **Dingen die gebeuren**
10.05 **M/V-magazine**
11.05 **Schone kunsten**
12.05 **Echo-magazine**
Nieuws, actualiteiten, achtergronden en muziek. Om 12.30 (NOS) Nieuws; 12.55 (NOS) **Mededelingen voor land- en tuinbouw**

VOO

14.05 **Nieuwsradio**
Om 17.30 (NOS) **Nieuws**
19.04 **Sportradio**
Met interviews, rechtstreekse verslagen en reportages.
20.04 **Confrontatie**

VPRO

21.04-22.58 **DE PLANTAGE**
Vervolg van Radio 2.
21.04 **God zij met ons**
Programma dat vragen stelt. Mmv Piet Vroon en Stan van Houcke.
22.53 **De 1% regeling**
4 minuten en 58,4 sec. beeldende kunst voor het oor. Vandaag: *Hans Waanders*, met 'Tweegesprek tussen een ijsvogel en Gagarin'.
Samenstelling: Wim Brands.
23.07 (NOS) **Met het oog op morgen**

VARA

0.02 **For the record**
2.02 **Geen tijd**
4.02 **Rock & Roel**
5.02-7.00 **Ochtendhumeur**

2
FM stereo (MHz): 87,7 Wieringermeer; 87,9 Goes; 88,0 Smilde; 88,2 Roermond; 91,4 Markelo; 92,1 Hulsberg; 92,6 Lopik.

Elk heel uur (NOS) Nieuws

AVRO

7.04 **Sugar in the morning**
Vervolg van Radio 1, met om 7.04 Radiojournaal; 7.30 Nieuwsoverzicht; 8.04 Radiojournaal; 8.30 Financieel nieuws.

EO

9.04 **De muzikale fruitmand**
10.04 **Ik zou wel eens willen weten**
10.30 **Vrouw zijn**
12.04 **Lunchtime**
13.04 **Tijdsein**
13.30 **Als mensen veranderen**
13.54 **Metterdaad**

14.04-22.58 **DE PLANTAGE**
Culturele radiobijlage. Produktie: Leonie Smit, Astrid Nauta, Jan Vermaas, Nienke Fels en Mia Beerends. Stemmen: Cor Galis en Anton de Goede. Eindredactie: Wim Noordhoek. Vanaf 14.04 elk heel uur Programmaoverzicht.
14.10 **'t Nut v/h algemeen**
Programma dat de culturele gemoederen peilt.
Samenstelling: Ad Fransen.
14.43 **De Jazz van Pete Felleman**
Coleman Hawkins: Don't Take Your Love From Me.
(Met Milt Jackson, Lockjaw Davis en Tommy Flanagan, herh.).
15.04 **Het spoor terug**
De geschiedenis opnieuw verteld door ooggetuigen.
Serie portretten.
Afl 4: *Cathrien Eimers en Derk Ploeger:* De Wapens Neder, De Vrije Socialist, De Coöperatie, De Bond van Geheelonthouders, De Dageraad, De Vonk, De Vlam: idealistische bewegingen uit een ver verleden, waaraan het echtpaar Ploeger-Eimers uit Groningen zich met hart en ziel gewijd heeft.
Samenstelling: Kiki Amsberg.
16.04 **Ischa**
Interview.
16.53 **Vrije geluiden**
17.04 **Het nabije westen**
Kunstprogramma. In juni, Borátmaand, een mooie montage van de Borátnacht van 7 januari 1984. In de hoofrollen: Kermit de Kikker, Wim Schippers en Harko Wind.
Samenstelling: Rik Zaal.
18.04 **Boeken**
Nieuws en informatie van het boekenfront. Samenstelling: Wim Brands.
19.04 **Passages, passanten**
Interview van Tanneke de Groot met de bekende Indonesische popmusicus Rhoma Irama
20.04 **Timboektoe**
Tekst en muziek van ver over den einder.
Samenstelling: Dave van Dijk.
Redactie: Karin Bjärvall.
De Plantage gaat door op Radio 1.

TROS

21.04 **Music all in**
Terug in de muziek.
22.00-7.00 **Zie Radio 1**

3
AM (kHz): 675 (444 m) Lopik. FM stereo (MHz): 89,8 Wieringermeer; 90,9 Roermond; 91,8 Smilde; 95,0 Goes; 96,2 Markelo; 96,8 Lopik; 103,9 Hulsberg.

Elk heel uur (NOS) Nieuws

VARA

6.02 **Doorloper**
7.04 **Carola op de radio**

VPRO

9.04 **Denk aan Henk**
12.04 **Steen & been show**
14.04 **Twee meter de lucht in**
16.04 **Happy hour**
18.04 (NOS) **De avondspits**
19.04 **Dubbeltjes**
20.04 **Vuurwerk**
21.04 **Popkrant**
22.04 **Poppodium**
0.00 **Sluiting**

5
AM (kHz): 891 (337 m) Hulsberg; 1008 (298 m) Flevoland

6.30-6.50 (NOS) **Scheepvaart- en marktberichten;**
uitgebreid weerbericht
7.00 **Overname Radio 2**
8.30 (IKON) **Vroeg**
8.55 (IKON) **Snippers**
9.00 (NOS) **Nieuws**
9.02 (NOS) **Sportief**
9.25 (NOS) **Waterstanden**
9.30 (RVU) **De wereld in Nederland**
Over het ontwikkelingsproject Gast aan tafel.

NCRV

10.00 **De wereld zingt Gods lof**
10.50 **Tekst en uitleg**
11.00 **Studio 55**
12.00 (NOS) **Nieuws**
12.05 **Rondom het Woord**
12.30 **Middagpauzedienst**
13.00 (NOS) **Nieuws**
13.10 **De verdieping**
Met o.a. Hoogstpersoonlijk en Tussen droom en daad (Jouw teder mond een en al kus, van Marina Tsvetajeva.)
14.10 **Dagvaardig**
14.30 (TELEAC) **Cursus**
Van kloostertuin tot Floriade (introductie).
15.00 (NOS) **Radio Vrijplaats**
16.00 (NOS) **Recht**
17.35 (Overheidsvoorlichting)
Postbus 51 Radiomagazine
17.55 (NOS) **Mededelingen en schippersberichten**
18.00 (NOS) **Nieuws**
18.10 (NCRV) **Relevant**
Drs. Niek Schuman.
18.20 (Politieke Partijen) GL
18.30 (KRO) **Vertel me wat**
18.40 (KRO) **Taal en teken**
Negendelige serie over de betekenis van H. Andriessen voor de kerkmuziek (6).
19.00 (NOS) **Nieuws en actualiteitenrubriek**
Om 19.00 in het Turks; 19.30 in het Marokkaans en Berbers; 20.15 in het Chinees.
20.30 (TELEAC) **Cursussen**
20.30 Britse en Amerikaanse literatuur (9). 21.00 Kelten (5).
21.30 **Sluiting**

Territory

The ritualistic rubberstamping of Waanders' appropriated field guides are also assertions of territory. The playwright and science writer Robert Ardrey in *The Territorial Imperative*, published in 1966, defines territory as an "area of space, whether of water, of earth or air", that is possessed and defended "as an exclusive preserve".[1] In the context of human agency, the geographer Anssi Passi suggests that the "idea of 'territory' usually refers to classifying and controlling things and ideas in material and metaphorical spaces, and how it is located in the fuzzy area that brings patterns of nature and culture together to form specific landscapes".[2] This is perhaps most explicit in terms of spatial control and geographical assertions of power. As a classifying and controlling instinct, territory is, however, also more broadly implicit in the solipsist's aspiration *"to manage the unmanageable"* which, according to Johanna Burton, involves a level of appropriation (of making a thing private property).[3] "Make it flat, *make it mine*, hold it at arm's length, rotate it, catalogue it, ingest it (but only in pieces)", Burton proposes: "In other words: pretend, suspend, assume."[4] In this way, the solipsist, "so invested in the world", marks out a space—a bounded system, a microcosm—as means for understanding and contending with it.[5]

In a similar spirit, Waanders' rubberstamps methodically colonise and appropriate (make their own) what belongs to others. The organising power of the rubberstamp in Waanders' interventions, its bureaucratic associations with validation and cancelation, impresses more emphatically the combative nature of the bird as well as well as the key note of taxonomy: elimination.* To successfully identify one species requires eliminating and discounting all the other possible species that it may resemble. Difference, not commonality, is key.

"System fights system", in Waanders' interventions, Jenny Brownrigg writes, but unlike the Peterson system of the field guide, Waanders "seeks to expand rather than reduce".[6] In his desire to extend the bird's bibliographical preserve, Brownrigg suggests, Waanders' practice of rubberstamping "shares territorial traits with the kingfisher, which establishes its territory with its call":

---

* "How territorial is the Kingfisher?" David Chandler asks: "In a word—very. Don't be fooled by its gorgeous colours—the Kingfisher is a feisty creature, and many defend breeding and winter feeding territories." *Kingfisher*, p.64.

He forges his own terrain within a space belonging to another;
his process violates the sanctity of the autonomous printed book.
The symbol of the kingfisher colonises pages in a methodical
take-over. Frequently its image is overtly war-like; a dive-bombing
kingfisher stamped onto a series of birds in flight.[7]

Each reclaimed field guide therefore becomes contested territory and
"the ideal place, habitat, nature and conditions for his chosen bird to
establish itself in".[8]

Waanders invokes the kingfisher's "aggressive call" more explicitly
in *Atlas* (1994), a book which maps the local voice of the kingfisher as
it has been phonetically transcribed in all the global regions where
it can be found.[9] [*See pages 59–62*] Like his airmail stamps, in *Atlas*
Waanders reasserts the cosmopolitan nature of the kingfisher by
appropriating the bird's instinctive habit of establishing and main-
taining its territory with the aggressive call (a repeated high pitched
whistle) that it makes while in flight. As well as being "very aggressive to others of its species throughout most of its life", David Boag
notes, *Alcedo atthis* is also quick to challenge other species that will
encroach on its territory: "The kingfisher can also be very possessive
about its favourite perches and I have seen a robin chased away and,
on another occasion, a grey wagtail was put to flight."[10] The kingfisher's defensive call and its aggressive behaviour is recast by Waanders
as a way to assert its global presence. By evoking these territorial
habits in *Atlas*, diversity is accentuated at the same time that it is
aggressed as a threat to the kingfisher's territorial sovereignty and
solitary status.

Atlas therefore implicitly questions what the geographer Doreen
Massey, in her book *For Space* (2005), deems the "modern, territorial,
conceptualisation of space" wherein "geographical difference [is]
constituted primarily through isolation and separation".[11] "First the
differences between places exist, and then those different places
come into contact", Massey writes: "The differences are the products
of internal characteristics."[12]

The territory-making of Waanders' bird shows more affinity for
Massey's anti-essentialist conception of space. In this context, space
is percieved as "an emergent product of relations, including those
relations which establish boundaries, and where 'place' in consequence is necessarily meeting place, where the 'difference' of a
place" is established through "the constant emergence of uniqueness
out of (and within) the specific constellations of interrelations within
which that place was set".[13] Not unlike the sychronous scope of a

collection, Massey's conception of space accomodates the juncture (rather than inflexible oppositions) of different elements and qualities within boundaries that are continually subject to change and metamorphosis.

The multilingual nature of Waanders' work—for example, in the repurposed texts of *Field Guide* or the centos of reference material in *Kingfishers and Related Works*—attests to such spatial plurality and interrelations, as does the silkscreen print *Map of the World* (1996). [*See pages 136–137*] Instead of demarcating international regions and territories by their political names and dominions, *Map of the World* uses the veracular nomenclature of local kingfisher species to demarcate territory. In one respect, Waanders' map displays an "urge towards classification, order, control and purification" that, according to the cultural geographer Denis Cosgrove, most modern forms of cartographic representation share.[14] Thus, in the spirit of his work more broadly, Waanders delimits and measures the world according to *Alcedo atthis* by limning the broad territory that the bird inhabits. Yet, at the same time, Waanders dissolves and unsettles the "stability" and the "aesthetics of closure and finality", that Cosgrove associates with "conventional mapping (whose *sine qua non* is the bounding frame)".[15]

While the regional nomenclature still retains a political dimension (for example, the imperial and colonial history implicit in the conspicuous European names occupying non-Western territories) Waanders' map charts a more fluid sense of place. The only borders on this otherwise boundless map are the constellations of names that meet, morph, and mutate through local appelation and mutual themes such as fishing, sovereignty, ice, and the fabled halcyon. With their suggestion of interrelation through movement and dialogue—of birds, people, and cultures—these names measure "the spatialities of connectivity, networked linkages, marginality and liminality, and the transgression of linear boundaries and hermetic categories". In short, Waanders' map articulates the concept of "spatial 'flow.'"[16]

Recalling Massey's notion of "open interactional space" in which "there are always connections yet to be made, juxtapositions yet to flower [and] relations which may or may not be accomplished", the multilingual world of *Alcedo atthis* in *Map of the World* is a provisional one.[17] Waanders' poetic object is not the site of homogenised unity but a fluid trace of diversity, deferral, and variance. Far from sovereign independence, the bird's cosmopolitan world is defined by interdependence and interrelation—even when those relations, like the birds', might be intrinsically antagonistic. "At the edges", as John R. Stilgoe maintains in his recent book *What Is Landscape?*, is where "things clash and merge".[18]

Defined by proximity rather than division and mutuality rather than exclusion, the territory that *Map of the World* maps is reflective of how, in Waanders' work, the world is not divided into difference (as the taxonomy of the field guide supposes), but constituted by it. In the spirit of the dialectical tension (the brilliant absence) of his work, Waanders' geographical imaginary straddles what Doreen Massey calls "two apparently self-evident truths, a geography of borderlessness and mobility, and a geography of border discipline".[19] Although Brownrigg suggests that the repeated rubberstamping in Waanders' field guide interventions "becomes a ritual, reinstating the potential for a limitless and boundless space", it is possible to see Waanders adopting a more nuanced approach to these questions of space.[20] By means of *Alcedo atthis*, Waanders not only challenges the divisive rigidity of enclosed borders and boundaries—as they occur geographically, taxonomically, and (in the form of the collection) mentally—he also tempers the fantasy of free global mobility and limitless, unbounded space.

The cosmopolitan mobility of Waanders' bird might therefore be described as a freedom or flow that is also grounded. Such a paradox of flight and alighting finds salient expression in a key determinant of the kingfisher's territorial behavior: the perch. These strategic hunting stations in the form of twigs, branches, posts, exposed roots, and sedges are the stakes of a bird's hunting ground. And, as Waander's card *Border – Perch* (1999) suggests by evoking cartographic border lines, perches are also the markers of territory and a key resource its effort to survive and endure. [*See page 65*] Thus, where *Atlas* and *Map of the World* evoke the kingfisher's territorial behaviour, Waanders' perch installations, as documented in *Fishing Perches* and *Perches*, incite it.

These perches, which Waanders installed along various waterways located "at the edge of the European kingfisher's natural habitat, such as the Borders of Scotland", pertinently recall the Dutch conceptual artist Jan Dibbets' exploration of frontiers and borders in *Robin Redbreast's Territory / Sculpture*.[21] Published as a slim systematic artist's book by Seth Siegelaub in 1970, *Robin Redbreast's Territory / Sculpture* documents Dibbets' attempt in 1969 to extend the territory of a European robin (*Erithacus rubecula*) in Amsterdam's Vondelpark.

An experiment described by David Lack in his book, *The Life of the Robin*, first published in 1943, forms the basis of the project:

The territory is a song area, and many robin territories have
natural boundaries where song-posts stop, as, for instance, at the
edge of a wood bordering a field. Indeed the size of one territory
was increased by the erection of some scaffolding at the edge of
a wood, for the bird then sang regularly from the scaffolding.[22]

Dibbets, who had read Lack's book as well as Ardrey's *The Territorial
Imperative*, manipulated the bird's aggressive territorial habits
(which, according to Lack are a "psychological necessity") by situating five posts on the edges of its territory.[23] "After I had carefully
staked out the territory", Dibbets writes of the first stage of his
sculpture, "I placed poles 1 and 2 close to the edge of the clump of
trees at the spot where the bird often perched, but just far enough
outside of its territory so that, its curiosity piqued, it would fly to the
pole."[24] By gradually displacing all five posts, Dibbets incrementally
extended the bird's song area. The robin's manipulated movements
consequently shaped Dibbets' sculpture, which, he claims, "can never
be seen in its entirety".[25]

Dibbets' book is both the record and the means of representing
what was otherwise an ephemeral sculpture. "Only its documentation can reconstruct it in the viewer's imagination", Dibbets notes.[26]
"Although the book is printed documentation", Clive Phillpot writes,
"it approaches the status of art in absence of the artwork".[27] Another
notable absence in this absent artwork, and a further indication of
its ephemerality, is the robin in the photographs, which, by Dibbets'
own admission, was a dead one that he had put on a stick.[28]

Dibbets' use of perches to construct "a sculpture", his careful
research and his consultation of specialist literature on the bird, and
the difficulty he experienced in "capturing" his subject on paper,
all speak pertinently to Waanders' perch installations. Above all,
however, it is Dibbets' claim that *Robin Redbreast's Territory / Sculpture*
was not so much about the robin's "biological facts" as it was his
own "desire to explore the boundaries of the visual arts" which reso-
nates most pertinently with Waanders' work.[29] Dibbets' sculpture
restates how boundaries and borders—like categories and defini-
tions—are contingent and mutable rather than irresolute and fixed.
Like the robin that instinctively extends the bounds of its territory,
Dibbets pushes against the prescribed parameters of what contains
and constitutes "art". The behavior of *Erithacus rubecula* thus
becomes analogous of larger processes and dynamics that demarcate, distinguish, and discriminate between here and there, art and
non-art, nature and artifice.

As a bird perched "on the edge of existence", Waanders' kingfisher, like Dibbets' robin, alights at the boundaries of its world, simultaneously displacing and delimiting its territory. One might compare this territory to the "many circles" in Wallace Stevens' poem 'Thirteen Ways of Looking at a Blackbird':

> When the blackbird flew out of sight,
> It marked the edge
> Of one of many circles.[30]

Like the "circumscribed area" of a collection—"the locking of individual items within a magic circle"—Waanders' pursuit of *Alcedo atthis* might imply a system of thought that draws a circle around itself and closes down any meaningful relationship with world beyond it.[31] However, in the spirit of Stevens' and Dibbets' respective birds, Waanders' kingfisher remains perennially at the limits of its world, on the edge of existence. This world is not a definite one, neither is it a closed one, but, as "one of many circles", its edges are the prospective frontiers "established by the limits of the processes which create it".[32]

"For the future to be open", Doreen Massey writes in *For Space*, "space must be open too":

> Space can never be that completed simultaneity in which all interconnections have been established, and in which everywhere is already linked with everywhere else. A space, then, which is neither a container for always-already constituted identities, nor a completed closure of holism.[33]

Closure might, as Jean Poussin implies, be a terminus sought by Waanders, but his work is a search that is never fulfilled or completed. To the credit of its blue cast, all of Waanders' processes, procedures, and practices that are otherwise predisposed toward closure and self-containment—from collecting and taxonomy, to solipsism and ritual—enlarge the world rather than contain it. With its beak compassing futurity, Waanders' kingfisher opens up space rather than closes it, and flies beyond conclusion.

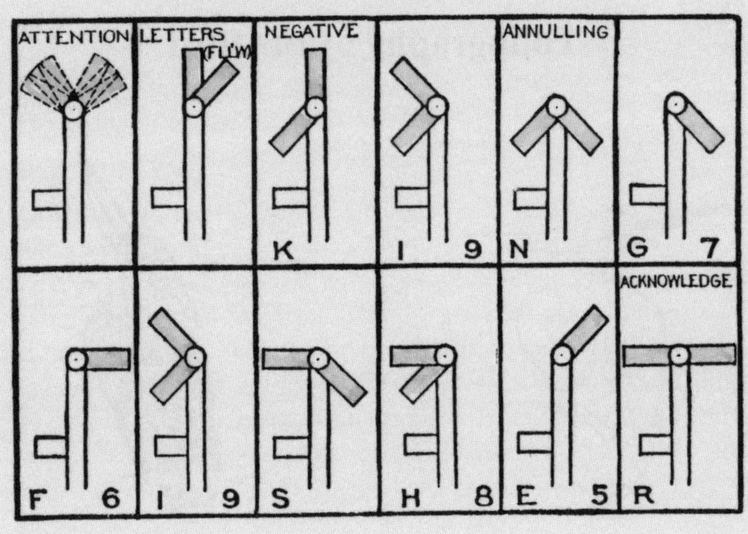

THE TWO-ARM SEMAPHORE CODE.
ATTENTION
LETTERS
(FL.W.)
NEGATIVE
ANNULLING
ACKNOWLEDGE
K
I 9
N
G 7
F 6
I 9
S
H 8
E 5
R

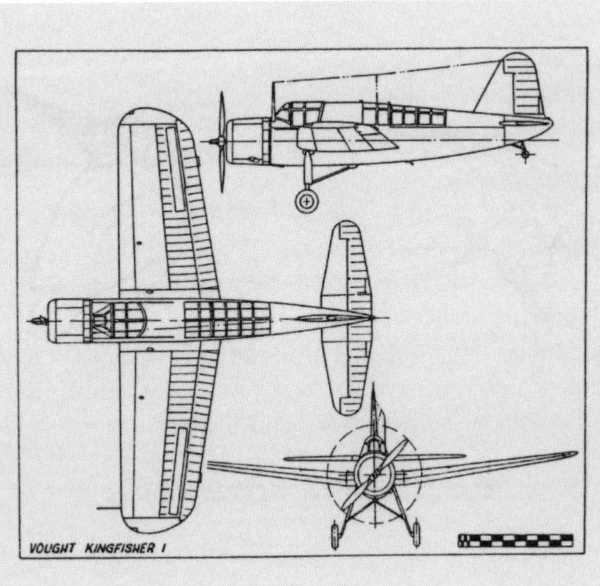

VOUGHT KINGFISHER I

Topography of the Bird

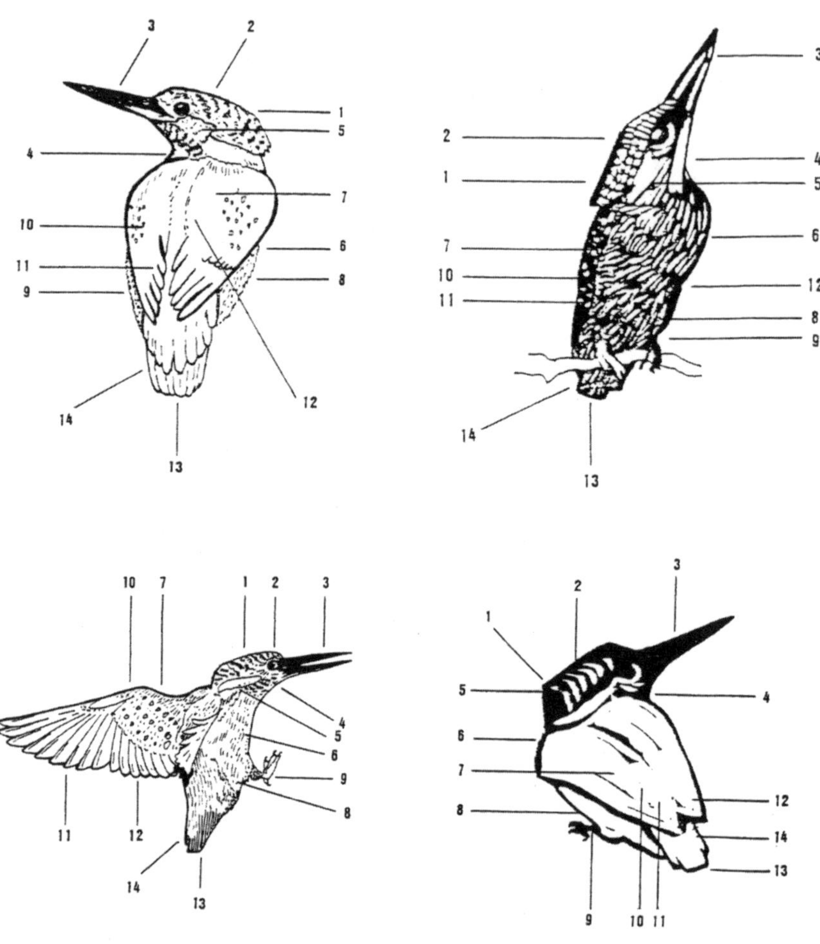

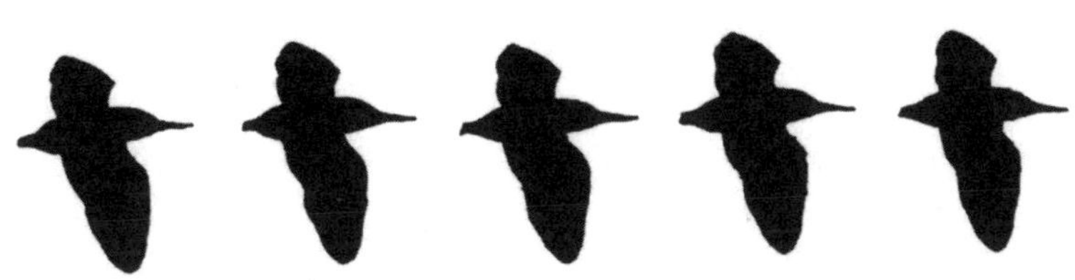

зиморо́док (*птица*); ~vor-
f. образова́ние лединико́в

.... иместч ев
ijsvogel:
ijswater: banioe n (to

ijs'vogel, m., -s, ψαροπούλι, τό ⌶ ψα-
    ροφάγος, ὁ
ij'ver, m., ζῆλος, ὁ ⌶ προθυμία, ἡ ⌶
    King'dom, n.   مملكة ‖ عَهْد
    King'fish'er, n. طير أزرق يصطاد بالبحيرات

ijsvogel (*zoöl*) [de] [*sjaldak*]   שַׁלְדָג ּ

ijsvlakte, *v.* campo de hielo *m.*
ijsvogel, *m.* martín pescador *m.*, alción *m.*, guar-
    darrío *m.*

KAWASE, カハセ, 川瀬, *n.* The rapids of
    a river, a swift current.
KAWASEMI, セハセミ, 翡翠, *n.* A king-
    fisher. Syn. ni-szi, soni.
KAWASHI,-*sz*,-*sh'ta*, カハス, 交, *t.v.* To

dowe, · lodowisko ´ *n*; ~-
vogel *m* -s zimorodek *m*;
~water *n* woda z lodem;
~zak *m* -ken woreczek

ijs'veld h. (-en) buz sahası
ijs'vogel d. (-s) *zo.* yalıçapkını, iskelekuşu,
    emircik
ijs'vrij s. buzlanmaz

kingfisher, n. glas y dorlan, pysgotwr.

hans waanders
noordwal 31 NL
5211 rn den bosch

Fuglinn flaug. (The bird *flew.*)

Envoi

"Birds begin and end beyond us", the nature writer Tim Dee observes in *The Running Sky*, "out of our reach and outside our thought; and we see them doing things apparently without feeling or thinking, but—and because of this—they make us think and feel".[1] "Perhaps that is why a select group of people return to birds as if they were unfinished business", David Callahan in *A History of Birdwatching in 100 Objects*, similarly writes, "time after time, never getting to the heart of their fascination but always loving in its pursuit".[2] The broader implications of both Dee's and Callahan's sentiments are best summarised by Jeremy Mynott's belief that "our experience of birds [can] take us outwards into other domains".[3]

Taking him from the domains of observation and classification to the errant blue-sky flights of the imagination, *Alcedo atthis* enabled Waanders, as Kristine Stiles writes, to "see feeling and think seeing". "Imagination allows us to leave the ordinary course of things", Gaston Bachelard writes, in *Air and Dreams*: "Perceiving and imagining are as antithetical as absence and presence. To imagine is to absent oneself, to launch out toward a new life." One might recall Thomas A. Clark's suggestion that, in Waanders' work, the kingfisher's "flight is a cut in facts", and not simply an iteration of them. Yet, neither is it a transcendence of them. Waanders' work does not so much leave the course of ordinary things as imaginatively probe and dissect them, finding metaphor in fact and exposing the aleatoric depths—the contingency and coincidence—in the ambits of the most ordered phenomena. Indeed, as a dialectician of blue, Waanders' pursuit of a small bird, "lost while half-seen" (as A. Y. Campbell writes) near a small pond one early October day in 1982, remains, for all its single-minded solipsism, more heuristic than obsession, more experiment than solitary romantic quest.[4] "By solving small problems we teach ourselves to solve large ones", Bachelard claims.[5] Waanders may have never solved the problem of seeing the same kingfisher at the *ijsvogelwiel* in 1982, but in his attempt to, he not only explored broader questions about how we perceive, understand, and navigate the world—how we might make of it a *cosmos*—but also how we might *be* (and orient ourselves) in it.

Notes

Origin

1 Hans Waanders, *Kingfishers and Related Works* (Edinburgh / New York / Eindhoven: Morning Star, Pont La Vue Press, October Foundation, 1999), p.127.

2 Karen Davidson, 'In Memoriam Hans Waanders, 1951–2001', pp.39–40, *Umbrella* Vol. 24, no. 2 (2001), p.39.

3 Cathy Courtney, 'Artists' Books Unbound', pp.42–43, *Art Monthly* 206 (May 1997), p.42.

4 Kristine Stiles, 'Quiet Heart Storm', pp.1–5, *Hans Waanders* exhibition catalogue (Raleigh, North Carolina: City Gallery of Contemporary Art, 1995), p.2, p.1.

5 Alec Finlay, 'Perches', in Hans Waanders, *Perches* (Edinburgh / New York / Eindhoven / Grizedale / Limoges: Morning Star, Pont La Vue, October Foundation, Grizedale Arts, & Sixtus Editions, 2001), n.p.

6 Thomas A. Clark, 'A Flower and a Bird', *Sealevel* 1/4 (February 2002), n.p.

7 Craig Saper, *Networked Art* (Minneapolis & London: University of Minnesota Press, 2001), p.xii

8 Ken Friedman, 'The Early Days of Mail Art: An Historical Overview', pp.3–16, *Eternal Network: A Mail Art Anthology*, ed. Chuck Welch (Calgary, Albert: University of Calgary Press, 1995), p.3.

9 Ibid., p.3.

10 Stiles, 'Quiet Heart Storm', p.2.

11 Clive Phillpot, *Booktrek: Selected Essays on Artists' Books (1972–2010)* (Zurich & Dijon: JRP | Ringier & Les Presses du Réel, 2013), p.186.

12 Johanna Drucker, *The Century of Artists' Books* (New York City: Granary Books, 2004), p.3–4.

13 Ulises Carrión, *Second Thoughts* (Amsterdam: Void Distributors, 1980), p.25.

14 Stiles, 'Quiet Heart Storm', p.2

15 Robert C. Morgan, 'Systematic Books by Artists', in *Artists' Books: A Critical Anthology and Sourcebook*, ed. Joan Lyons (New York: Visual Studies Workshop Press, 1985), pp.207–222, p.207.

16 Michael Hampton, *Unshelfmarked: Reconceiving the Artists' Book* (Axminster: Uniformbooks, 2015), p.91.

17 Stiles, 'Quiet Heart Storm', p.5.

18 Ibid., p.2.

19 Peter Foolen, 'Editorial', *Sealevel* 1/4 (February 2002), n.p.

20 Drucker, *The Century of Artists' Books*, p.25.

21 Tjeu Teeuwen, 'Hans Waanders: The Kingfisher – *Alcedo atthis*', *Sealevel* 1/4 (February 2002), n.p.

22 Waanders, cited in Mathieu, Didier, 'On Hans Waanders', in *Herman de Vries, Lefevre Jean Claude, Oxo-Pascal Le Coq, Hans Waanders, Eric Watier* (Saint-Yriex-la-Perche / Mariemont: Centre des livres d'artistes / Musée royal, 2007), p.4.

23 Foolen, 'Editorial', n.p.

24 Jenny Brownrigg, 'The Field Guides of Hans Waanders', pp.142–154, *The Libraries of Thought & Imagination: An Anthology of Books and Bookshelves*, ed. Alec Finlay (Edinburgh: Pocketbooks / Morning Star Publications, 2001), p.144.

25 John Berger, Sven Blomberg, Chris Fox, Michael Dibb, and Richard Hollis, *Ways of Seeing* (London: BBC & Penguin, 1972), p.10.

26 Brownrigg, 'The Field Guides', p.144.

27 Richard Stamelman, *Lost Beyond Telling: Representations of Death and Absence in Modern French Poetry* (Ithaca, New York: Cornell University Press, 1990), p.10, p.11.

28 Maurice Rickards, *Collecting Printed Ephemera* (New York: Abbeville Press, 1988), p.18.

29 Thomas A. Clark, 'In Search of the Kingfisher', photograph by Peter Foolen (Eindhoven: October Foundation, 2001), postcard.

30 Mark Cocker and Richard Mabey, *Birds Britannica* (London: Chatto & Windus, 2005), p.300.

31 Eastman, *The Kingfisher* (London: Collins, 1969), pp.22–23.

32 Ibid., p.22.

33 Alfred Tennyson. *The Complete Works* (New York: Frederick A. Stokes Company, 1891), p.454.

34 Davidson, 'In Memoriam', p.39.

Life

1 Patrick Barkham, 'Cold Blood: Adventures with Reptiles and Amphibians', *The Guardian* (May 9, 2014), online.

2 Susan Cerulean, *Tracking Desire: A Journey After Swallow-tailed Kites* (Athens, Georgia: University of Georgia Press, 2005), p.1.

3 Ibid., p.1.

4 Cocker and Mabey, *Birds Britannica*, p.300.

5 David Callahan, *A History of Birdwatching in 100 Objects*, ed. Dominic Mitchell (London, New York: Bloomsbury, 2014), p.155.

6   J. A. Baker, *The Peregrine* (New York: New York Review Books 2005), p.13.

7   Baker, *The Peregrine*, pp.11–12

8   Hetty Saunders, *My Life of Sky: A Life of J. A. Baker* (Dorchester, Dorset: Little Toller Books, 2017), p.146.

9   Davidson, 'In Memoriam', p.40.

10 Norie Neumark, 'Introduction: Relays, Delays, and Distance Art/Activism', pp.2–25, *At A Distance: Precursors to Art and Activism on the Internet*, eds. Anne Marie Chandler and Norie Neumark (Cambridge, Massachusetts: MIT Press, 2005), p.3.

11 Saunders, *My Life of Sky*, p.15.

12 Robert Macfarlane, 'Violent Spring: The Nature Book that Predicted the Future', *The Guardian* (April 15, 2017), online.

13 John Law and Michael Lynch, 'Lists, Field Guides, and the Descriptive Organization of Seeing: Birdwatching as an Exemplary Observational Activity', pp.271–303, *Human Studies* 11, 2/3 (April–July, 1988), p.274.

14 Robert Macfarlane, 'Introduction', in J. A. Baker, *The Peregrine* (New York: New York Review Books, 2005), pp.vii–xv, p.ix–x.

15 W. H. Hudson, *Birds In Town & Village* (New York: E. P. Dutton & Company, 1920), p.30.

16 Stiles, 'Quiet Heart Storm', p.1.

17 Foolen, 'Editorial', n.p.

18 Clark, 'A Flower and a Bird', n.p.

19 Julia Kristeva, *Black Sun: Depression and Melancholia*, trans. Leon S. Roudiez (New York: Columbia University Press, 1989), p.6.

20 Davidson, 'In Memoriam', p.40.

21 Teeuwen, 'Hans Waanders', n.p.

Quest

1   Macfarlane, 'Introduction', pp.vii–viii.

2   Helen Macdonald, *Falcon* (London: Reaktion Books, 2006), p.8.

3   Jan Verwoert, *Bas Jan Ader: In Search of the Miraculous* (London: Afterall Books, 2006), pp.2–3, p.6.

4   Ibid., p.6.

5   Ibid., p.14.

6   Hans Waanders, cited in Annette Embrechts, 'Leven op de rand van het bestaan' ('Living on the Verge of Existence'), *De Volkskrant* (30 Jun 2000), online.

7   Henry David Thoreau, *A Year in Thoreau's Journal: 1851*, ed. by H. Daniel Peck (Harmondsworth: Penguin, 1993), p.147.

8   Stanley Cavell, *The Senses of Walden: An Expanded Edition* (Chicago & London: The University of Chicago Press 1992), p.98

9   Ibid., p.98.

10 Law and Lynch, 'Lists, Field Guides, and the Descriptive Organization of Seeing', p.273.

11 Davidson, 'In Memoriam', p.39.

12 Alexander von Humboldt, *Cosmos: A Sketch of a Physical Description of the Universe*, trans. E. C. Otté (London: Henry G. Bohn, 1864), p.52.

13 Hans Waanders, cited in Annette Embrechts, 'Leven op de rand van het bestaan', online.

14 Edward Hussey, *The Presocratics* (London: Duckworth, 1972), p.18; Robin Waterfield, *The First Philosophers: The Presocratics and Sophists* (Oxford & New York: Oxford World's Classics, 2000), p.37; Davidson, 'In Memoriam', p.39.

15 Samuel Sambursky, *The Physical World of the Greeks* (London: Routledge & Kegan Paul, 1956), p.4.

16 Lucy R. Lippard, *Six Years: The Dematerialization of the Art Object from 1966 to 1972* (Berkeley & Los Angeles: University of California Press, 1997), p.xv.

17 William Wordsworth, 'Preface', pp.v–xxii, *Lyrical Ballads, with other Poems*, vol.1 of 2 (Philadelphia: James Humphreys, 1802), p.xvii.

18 Alec Finlay, 'And So Books Entered Our Lives…', pp.13–19, *The Libraries of Thought & Imagination: An Anthology of Books and Bookshelves*, ed. Alec Finlay (Edinburgh: Pocketbooks / Morning Star Publications, 2001), p.14.

19 Jeremy Mynott, *Birdscapes: Birds in Our Imagination and Experience* (Princeton & Oxford: Princeton University Press, 2009), pp.22–23.

20 James Clifford, *The Predicament of Culture: Twentieth-Century Ethnography, Literature, and Art* (Cambridge, Massachusetts: Harvard University Press, 1988), p.219.

21 Gaston Bachelard, *The Poetics of Space*, trans. Maria Jolas (Boston: Beacon Press, 1994), p.84.

22 Michel Foucault, *The Order of Things: An Archaeology of the Human Sciences* (London & New York: Routledge, 2004), p.146.

23 Bachelard, *The Poetics of Space*, p.134.

24 Stiles, 'Quiet Heart Storm', p.1.

25 Davidson, 'In Memoriam', p.39.

Object

1   David Boag, *The Kingfisher* (Poole, Dorset: Blandford Press, 1982), p.16.

2   W. H. Hudson, *Birds and Man* (London: Duckworth & Co., 1920), p.12.

3   Ibid., p.12.

4   S. Vere Benson, *The Observer's Book of British Birds* (London & New York: Frederick Warne & Co., 1937), p.110.

5   Hans Waanders, *Field Guide to the Books of*

Hans Waanders, 4th ed. (Den Bosch: The World Publishing Company, 1997), item no.9, n.p.

6   Gaston Bachelard, *Air and Dreams: An Essay on the Imagination of Movement*, trans. Edith R. Farrell and C. Frederick Farrell (Dallas: The Dallas Institute Publications, 2002), p.165.

7   Stiles, 'Quiet Heart Storm', p.5

8   Bachelard, *Air and Dreams*, p.166.

9   Novalis (Friedrich von Hardenberg), *Heinrich of Ofterdingen: A Romance* (Cambridge, Massachusetts: John Owen, 1842), p.23.

10 Maggie Nelson, *Bluets* (London: Jonathan Cape, 2017), p.45.

11 Jeanne Riou, *Imagination in German Romanticism: Re-thinking the Self and Its Environment* (Oxford, Bern, Berlin: Peter Lang, 2004), p.93.

12 Gail M. Newman, *Locating the Romantic Subject: Novalis with Winnicott* (Detroit: Wayne State University Press, 1997), p.65.

13 Clark, 'A Flower and a Bird', n.p.

14 Ibid., n.p.

15 Gaston Bachelard, *The Poetics of Reverie: Childhood, Language, and the Cosmos*, trans. Daniel Russell (Boston: Beacon Press, 1971), p.154.

16 Jean Poussin, 'Hans Waanders ou La Conquête du monde sur les ailes du Martin-pêcheur' / 'Hans Waanders or Conquering the World on Kingfishers' Wings', trans. Jonathan Bass (Saint-Yrieix-la-Perche: Centre des livres d'artistes, 2001), p.6.

17 Finlay, 'Perches', n.p.

Privation

1   Hans Waanders, cited in Davidson, 'In Memoriam', p.39.

2   Jacques Derrida, *Speech and Phenomena and Other Essays on Husserl's Theory of Signs*, trans. David B. Allison (Evanston: Northwestern University Press, 1973), p.156.

3   Stéphane Mallarmé, *Selected Poetry and Prose*, ed. Mary Ann Caws (New York: New Directions, 1982), p.76.

4   Stiles, 'Quiet Heart Storm', p.2.

5   Brownrigg, 'The Field Guides', p.144.

6   Clark, 'A Flower and a Bird', n.p.

7   Bachelard, *Poetics of Reverie*, p.14, p.15.

8   Teeuwen, 'Hans Waanders', n.p.

9   Spencer Schaffner, *Binocular Vision: The Politics of Representation in Birdwatching Field Guides* (Amherst & Boston: University of Massachusetts, 2011), p.3.

10 Roger Tory Peterson, *A Field Guide to Western Birds: Field Marks of all Species Found in North America West of the 100th Meridian, with a Section on the Birds of the Hawaiian Islands* (Houghton Mifflin, 1961), p.27.

11 Roger Tory Peterson, *A Field Guide to the Birds Eastern and Central North America* (Boston: Houghton Mifflin Company, 1980), p.7.

12 Schaffner, *Binocular Vision*, p.55.

13 Ibid., p.57.

14 Law and Lynch, 'Lists, Field Guides, and the Descriptive Organization of Seeing', p.277.

15 Ibid., pp.277–78.

16 Thomas R. Dunlap, *In the Field, Among the Feathered: A History of Birders and Their Guides* (Oxford & New York: Oxford University Press, 2011), p.98.

17 Poussin, 'Hans Waanders', p.5.

18 Mynott, *Birdscapes*, pp.67–69.

19 Ralph Waldo Emerson, *Nature and Selected Essays*, ed. Larzer Ziff (Harmondsworth: Penguin, 2003), p.268.

20 Poussin, 'Hans Waanders', p.6.

21 Foucault, *The Order of Things*, p.19.

22 Poussin, 'Hans Waanders', p.4, p.6.

23 Brownrigg, 'The Field Guides', p.144

24 William H. Gass, *On Being Blue: A Philosophical Inquiry* (New York: New York Review Books, 2014), p.21.

Melancholy

1   Gass, *On Being Blue*, p.74.

2   Aristotle, cited in ibid., p.74.

3   Stamelman, *Lost Beyond Telling*, p.3, p.4.

4   Ibid., p.22.

5   Ibid., p.x.

6   Nigel Fabb, 'Complex Implied Form, Leisure Pursuits, and Cultural Studies', pp.105–120, *Changing Philologies: Contributions to the Redefinition of Foreign Language Studies in the Age of Globalization*, ed. Hans Lauge Hansen (Copenhagen: Museum of Tusculanem Press, 2002), p.118.

Halcyon

1   Eastman, *The Kingfisher*, p.25.

2   Boag, *The Kingfisher*, p.106, p.105.

3   C.f. Hans Waanders, 'Marlowe' card (1997), *Kingfishers and Related Works*, p.38.

4   Waanders, *Field Guide*, item no.13, n.p.

5   Phil Robinson, *The Poets' Birds* (London: Chatto & Windus, 1883), p.252.

6   Ibid., p.125.

7   J. H. Wiffen, *Aonian Hours; And Other Poems* (London: Longman, 1820), p.104.

8   Robinson, *The Poets' Birds*, p.4.

9   Ibid., p.63.
10 Ibid., pp.252–53.

Reverie

1   T. S. Eliot, *Collected Poems 1909–1962* (London: Faber & Faber, 1974), p.194.
2   Stiles, 'Quiet Heart Storm', p.5.
3   Poussin, 'Hans Waanders', p.4.
4   Bachelard, *The Poetics of Reverie*, p.14.
5   Eva T. Brann, *The World of Imagination: Sum and Substance* (Lanham, Boulder, New York: Rowman & Littlefield, 2017), p.182.
6   Bachelard, *The Poetics of Reverie*, p.153.
7   Bachelard, *The Poetics of Space*, p.xvi.
8   Ibid., p.xxxviii.
9   Bachelard, *Poetics of Reverie*, p.13,
10 Ibid., p.154, p.14.
11 Ibid., p.8.
12 Ibid., p.12.
13 Ibid., p.158, p.155, p.14.
14 Ibid., p.13, p.12, p.155
15 Gaston Bachelard, *The Psychoanalysis of Fire*, trans. Alan C. M. Ross (London: Routledge & Kegan Paul, 1964), p.14.

Collection

1   Ronald Johnson, 'Hurrah for Euphony: Dedicated to Young Poets'. *The Cultural Society*, 14 January 2002. Online.
2   Bachelard, *The Poetics of Reverie*, p.158.
3   Jean Baudrillard, *The System of Objects*, trans. James Benedict (London, New York: Verso, 2002), p.87.
4   Walter Benjamin, *Illuminations*, trans. Harry Zohn (London: Fontana Press, 1992), p.62.
5   Baudrillard, *The System of Objects*, p.88.
6   Ibid., p.85, p.96.
7   Susan M. Pierce, *Museums, Objects and Collections: A Cultural Study* (London & New York: Leicester University Press, 1998), p.66.
8   Ibid., p.66.
9   Susan Stewart, *On Longing: Narratives of the Miniature, the Gigantic, the Souvenir, the Collection* (Durham & London: Duke University Press, 2003), p.151.
10 Hans Waanders, *Standard Catalogue* ('s-Hertogenbosch: Hans Waanders, 1992), n.p.
11 Stewart, *On Longing*, p.153.
12 Henk Woudsma, 'The Book Itself (I): The Process of Arranging', trans. Taco Hidde Bakker, in *Sequence 1: Dutch Artists's Books in International Perspective* (Groningen: Academie Minerva, 2015), p.20.
13 Davidson, 'In Memoriam', p.40.
14 Alfredo José Estrada, *Havana:*

Autobiography of a City (New York: St Martin's Press, 2007), p.78.
15 Stewart, *On Longing*, p.23.
16 Ibid., p.92.

Blue

1   Charles James Phillips, *Stamp Collecting: The King of Hobbies and the Hobby of Kings* (New York: H. L. Lindquist, 1936).
2   Neumark, 'Introduction: Relays, Delays, and Distance Art/Activism', p.7.
3   Gustav Schenk, *The Romance of the Postage Stamp: An Illustrated History of Stamps and Stamp Collecting* (New York: Doubleday, 1962), pp.140–141.
4   Carrión, *Second Thoughts*, p.54.
5   Davidson, 'In Memoriam', p.39.
6   Rebecca Solnit, *A Field Guide to Getting Lost* (London: Penguin, 2005), p.41.
7   Ibid., p.29.
8   Ibid., p.39.
9   Ibid., p.29.
10 Finlay, 'Perches', n.p.
11 Yves Klein, *1928–1962: Selected Writings*, trans. Barbara Wright (London: Tate Gallery Publications, 1974), p.35.
12 Solnit, *A Field Guide*, p.159.
13 Ibid., p.56.
14 Ibid., p.169.
15 Hannah Weitemeier, *Yves Klein* (Köln & London: Taschen, 2001), p.48.
16 John Held Jr., *Small Scale Subversion: Mail Art and Artiststamps* (Breda: TAM Publications, 2015), p.75.
17 Walter Benjamin, *One-Way Street and Other Writings*, trans. Edmund Jephcott and Kingsley Shorter (London: NLB, 1979), p.92
18 Neumark, 'Introduction', pp.4–5.
19 Teeuwen, 'Hans Waanders', n.p.
20 Jamie Doran and Piers Bizony, *Starman: The Truth Behind the Legend of Yuri Gagarin* (London: Bloomsbury, 2011), p.159.

Space

1   Stiles, 'Quiet Heart Storm', p.3.
2   Solnit, *A Field Guide*, pp.30–31.
3   Ibid., pp.30–31.
4   Lauri Twitchell, email to the author, April 28, 2018.
5   Lauri Twitchell, email to the author, May 15, 2018.
6   *International Code of Signals for Visual, Sound, and Radio Communications*, United States Edition, 1969 (Annapolis, Maryland: Lighthouse Press, 2005), pp.3
7   John Burroughs, *Birds and Poets, with Other Papers* (New York: Hurd & Houghton, 1877), p.10.

8 Hans Waanders, *There Are Still Kingfishers*, card, n.d.
9 Stiles, 'Quiet Heart Storm', p.2.
10 Poussin, 'Hans Waanders', p.6.

Catalogue

1 Michael Bidner, cited in Rosemary Gahlinger-Beaune, 'A World of Artistamps: Remembering Michael Bidner', pp.55–58, *Eternal Network*, p.56.
2 Chuck Welch, editor's preface to Gahlinger-Beaune, 'A World of Artistamps: Remembering Michael Bidner', p.55.
3 Waanders, *Field Guide*, item nos.16, 17, n.p.
4 Clifford, *The Predicament of Culture*, p.219.
5 Benjamin, *Illuminations*, p.60.
6 Ibid., 62.
7 Davidson, 'In Memoriam', p.39.
8 Elliott Coues, *Handbook of Field and General Ornithology; A Manual of the Structure and Classification of Birds with Instructions for Collecting and Preserving Specimens* (London: Macmillan & Co., 1890), p.91.
9 Paul Lawrence Farber, *Finding Order in Nature: The Naturalist Tradition from Linnaeus to E. O. Wilson* (Baltimore & London: The Johns Hopkins University Press, 2000), p.21.
10 Foucault, *The Order of Things*, p.148.
11 Ibid., p.148.
12 Ibid., p.146.
13 Callahan, *A History of Birdwatching*, p.33.
14 John Elsner and Roger Cardinal, 'Introduction', in *The Cultures of Collecting*, eds. John Elsner and Roger Cardinal (London: Reaktion Books, 1997), pp.1–6.
15 Dunlap, *In the Field*, p.48.
16 John M. Swales, 'Field Guides in Strange Tongues: A Workshop for Henry Widdowson', pp.215–228, *Principle & Practice in Applied Linguistics: Studies in Honour of H. G. Widdowson*, eds. Guy Cook and Barbara Seidlhofer (Oxford: Oxford University Press, 1995), p.219; Thomas J. Lyon, 'A Taxonomy of Nature Writing', pp.276–281, *The Ecocriticism Reader: Landmarks in Literary Ecology*, eds. Cheryll Glotfelty and Harold Fromm (Athens & London: University of Georgia Press, 1996), p.276, p.277.
17 Spencer Schaffner, 'Field Guide to Birds: Images and Image/Text Positioned as Reference', pp.95–122, *Ecosee: Image, Rhetoric, Nature*, eds. Sidney I. Dobrin and Sean Morey (Albany: SUNY Press, 2009), p.97.
18 Courtney, 'Artists' Books Unbound', p.42.
19 C.f. Roger Tory Peterson, *How to Know the Birds* (Boston: Houghton Mifflin Co., 1949), p.7.
20 John Bevis, 'The Observer', in Colin Sackett, *Observer's Marginalia* (Axminster, Devon: Colin Sackett, 2011), pp.9–10.
21 Ludwig Wittgenstein, *Tractatus Logico-Philosophicus*, trans. D. F. Pears and B. F. McGuiness (Abingdon, Oxon: Routledge, 2001), p.5.
22 Mel Bochner, 'Serial Art, Systems, Solipsism', in *Minimal Art: A Critical Anthology*, ed. Gregory Battcock (Berkeley, Los Angeles, London: University of California Press, 1995), p.94, p.99.
23 Ibid., p.100.
24 Johanna Burton, 'Mystics Rather than Rationalists', pp.64–80, *Open Systems: Rethinking Art c.1970*, ed. Donna De Slavo (London: Tate Publishing, 2005), p.74.
25 Ibid., p.74.
26 Baudrillard, *The System of Objects*, p.96, p.86.
27 Bevis, 'The Observer', p.9.
28 Lippard, *Six Years*, pp.49–50.
29 Ibid., p.50.
30 Jonathan Watkins 'Where 'I Don't Know' Is the Right Answer', pp.42–109, *On Kawara*, ed. Jonathan Watkins (New York: Phaidon, 2002), p.92.

Series

1 Teeuwen, 'Hans Waanders', n.p.
2 Waanders, *Field Guide*, item 12.
3 Stiles, 'Quiet Heart Storm', p.3.
4 Dante Alghieri, *Vita Nuova*, trans. Mark Musa (Oxford & New York: Oxford University Press, 1999), p.3.
5 Thomas Rendall, 'The Numerology of Dante's Divine Vision', pp.151–154, *The Explicator* 68.3 (2010), p.151.
6 Dante, *Vita Nuova*, p.4.
7 Ibid., p.61.
8 Poussin, 'Hans Waanders', p.5, p.4.
9 Davidson, 'In Memoriam', p.39.
10 Poussin, 'Hans Waanders', p.5.
11 Teeuwen, 'Hans Waanders', n.p.
12 Ibid., n.p.
13 Ibid., n.p.
14 Ibid., n.p.
15 Elsner and Cardinal, 'Introduction', pp.5–6.
16 Foucault, *The Order of Things*, p.142.
17 Courtney, 'Artists' Books Unbound', p.42

Rite

1 Stewart, *On Longing*, p.14.
2 Jonathan Z. Smith, 'The Bare Facts of Ritual', pp.112–127, *History of Religions*, 20.1/2 (August–November, 1980), p.113.
3 Lucy R. Lippard, *Overlay: Contemporary Art and the Art of Prehistory* (New York: Pantheon Books, 1983), p.160.

4   Smith, 'The Bare Facts', pp.124–125., p.125.
5   Ibid., p.125.
6   Ibid., p.127.
7   Brownrigg, 'The Field Guides', p.143.
8   Geoffrey Grigson, *Painted Caves* (London: Phoenix House Ltd, 1957), p.69.
9   Joseph Lyons, 'Paleolithic Aesthetics: The Psychology of Cave Art', pp.107–114, *The Journal of Aesthetics and Art Criticism*, 26.1 (Autumn, 1967), p.109.
10 Ibid., p.109.
11 Gustaf Sobin, *Luminous Debris: Reflecting on Vestige in Provence and Languedoc* (Berkeley: University of California Press, 1999), pp.19–20.
12 Smith, 'The Bare Facts', p.126.
13 Ibid., p.127.
14 Burton, 'Mystics Rather than Rationalists', p.73.
15 Davidson, 'In Memoriam', p.39.
16 Carrión, *Second Thoughts*, p.33.
17 Spencer Schaffner, *Binocular Vision*, p.3, p.1.
18 Law and Lynch, 'Lists, Field Guides, and the Descriptive Organization of Seeing', p.278.
19 Ibid., p.291.
20 Mynott, *Birdscapes*, p.288.
21 Brownrigg, 'The Fields Guides', p.142.
22 Baker, cited in Saunders, *My House of Sky*, p.90.
23 Burton, 'Mystics Rather than Rationalists', pp.72–73; Law and Lynch, 'Lists, Field Guides, and the Descriptive Organization of Seeing', p.273.

Territory

1   Robert Ardrey, *The Territorial Imperative: A Personal Inquiry into the Animal Origins of Property and Nations* (London: Collins, 1967), p.3.
2   Anssi Paasi 'Territory', pp.274–276, *Patterned Ground: Entanglements of Nature and Culture*, eds. Stephan Harrison, Steve Pile, and Nigel Thrift (London: Reaktion Books, 2004), p.278.
3   Burton, 'Mystics Rather than Rationalists', p.74.
4   Ibid., pp.74–75, emphasis added.
5   Ibid., p.74.
6   Brownrigg, 'The Field Guides', p.144.
7   Ibid., p.143.
8   Ibid., p.143.
9   Boag, *The Kingfisher*, p.24.
10 Ibid., p.21, p.22.
11 Doreen Massey, *For Space* (Los Angeles & London: Sage, 2005), p.68.
12 Ibid., p.68.
13 Ibid., p.68.
14 Denis Cosgrove, 'Introduction', pp.1–23, *Mappings*, ed. Denis Cosgrove (London: Reaktion Books, 1999), p.4.
15 Ibid., p.2.
16 Ibid., pp.4–5.
17 Massey, *For Space*, p.11.
18 John R. Stilgoe, *What is Landscape?* (Cambridge, MA: MIT Press, 2015), p.219.
19 Massey, *For Space*, p.86.
20 Brownrigg, 'The Fields Guides', p.143.
21 Finlay, 'Perches', n.p.
22 David Lack, *The Life of the Robin* (London: H. F. & G Witherby, 1946), p.133.
23 Ibid., p.136.
24 Jan Dibbets, *Robin Redbreast's Territory / Sculpture 1969* (Brest, France: Zédélé Editions, 2014), n.p.
25 Ibid., n.p.
26 Ibid., n.p.
27 Phillpot, *Booktrek*, p.198.
28 Jan Dibbets, in Christophe Cherix, *In & Out of Amsterdam: Travels in Conceptual Art, 1960-1976* (New York: The Museum of Modern Art, 2009), p.72.
29 Dibbets, *Robin Readbreast's Territory / Sculpture*, n.p.
30 Wallace Stevens, *Collected Poetry and Prose*, eds. Frank Kermode and Joan Richardson (New York: The Library of America, 1997), p.76.
31 Benjamin, *Illuminations*, p.62.
32 Anne Whiston Spirn, *The Language of Landscape* (New York & London: Yale University Press, 1998), p.119.
33 Massey, *For Space*, pp.11–12.

Envoi

1   Tim Dee, *The Running Sky: A Birdwatching Life* (London: Vintage, 2016), p.4.
2   Callahan, *A History of Birdwatching*, p.209.
3   Mynott, *Birdscapes*, p.6.
4   Waanders, *There Are Still Kingfishers*.
5   Bachelard, *The Poetics of Space*, pp.134–135.

Biography

1951—Hans Waanders is born on 4th January, Enschede, Netherlands.

1955—Started collecting matchbox marks and cigar bands.

1963—Saw first kingfisher during a trip in Overijsel, Netherlands.

1972—Settled in Groningen, studied at Academie Minerva. First journey to Czechoslovakia.

1974—Second journey to Czechoslovakia (Prague, Bohemia).

1975—Trip to London. Spent much time making watercolours at the Wadden Sea in the north of the Netherlands. Third journey to Czechoslovakia (High Tatras, Mala Fatra, Bratislava).

1976—Journey to Scandinavia (Copenhagen, Vänern)

1977—Graduated from Academie Minerva. Moved to 's-Hertogenbosch. Made a small painting of a kingfisher. Painted many detailed watercolours, with vegetation, birds and water. Saw a kingfisher along the river Amblève, Belgium. First one-man exhibitions in Asten and Gemert, Netherlands.

1978—Teacher at several institutes: graphics, oil, paint, watercolour. Exhibition in Drimmelen, Netherlands. A journey by bike to Arles, Corse, Sardinia, Vinci, Rome, Florence, Barcelona and Perpignan. Made drawings and wrote a diary.

1979—Teaching art history in 's-Hertogenbosch. Exhibition in Geldrop, Netherlands.

1980—Journey by bike to Amiens, Isle of Wight, Stonehenge and London. Start of the trips along the river Maas near 's-Hertogenbosch. First 'water-series'.

1981—Journey to Iceland. 'Icelandic Waters', a large number of works, combination of collage and watercolour.

1982—Exhibition in Oss, Netherlands. Showed the 'Icelandic Waters' for the first time. Diaries with waterdrawings, the names of ships and birds. Observation of a kingfisher on 4th October, flying across a small pond near the river Maas. Start of the writing of *Orde: Coraciiformes-Familie: Alcedinidae*.

1983—Journeys to Köln and Antwerp. Worked near St. Malo, France. Co-founded artists' initiative ARTIS.

1984—First show of *Orde: Coraciiformes-Familie: Alcedinidae*, until page 136. Second journey to Iceland. Photographic project *In Search of the Kingfisher* on Iceland. Start of making books.

1985—Journey by bike to Connemara and the Aran Islands, Ireland. In search of the kingfisher at the west coast of Ireland, many drawings and photographs.

1986—Journey by bike in Portugal. In search of the kingfisher near Cabo de são Vicente. Made large books. *Kingfishers & Queens* series.

1987—Journey by bike to prehistoric caves in northern Spain. Experiments with arm-prints: Made large images of flags and the wings of the kingfisher. *Bloody Tracks* in different versions.

1988—Exhibition *Le Temps Perdu*, 's-Hertogenbosch. Exhibition at Boekie Woekie, Amsterdam.

1989—Experiments in woodcut. Foundation of an artists' books department in Kunst & Vliegwerk arts bookshop in 's-Hertogenbosch. Publication of a portfolio *Three Irish Rivers. A Travel Survival Kit.*

1990—Saw two kingfishers along the river Aa, in the centre of 's-Hertogenbosch on 24th February. Stopped with the writing of *Orde: Coraciiformes-Familie: Alcedinidae*. Found a shop 'Le Martin Pecheur' along the river Seine in Paris. Guest Lecturer at Academy of Art, 's-Hertogenbosch. Guest Lecturer at Academy of Art, Kampen, together with Gerrit Jan de Rook. Saw the kingfisher in the *Garden of Delights* of Bosch, in the Prado, Madrid.

1991—Start of carving kingfisher stamps. Printed them by hand on large sheets and in books. Books: *Mobile* and *Martin Pescador* (with Estampa, Madrid).

1992—Radio production on 9th June: 'A discussion between a kingfisher and Yuri Gagarin', broadcasted on Radio 1, Netherlands. Books: *Gagarin* and *Icarus*.

1993—Stampwork *Compass*, directly printed on a wall of the Van Abbemuseum in Eindhoven. First complete show of *Orde:*

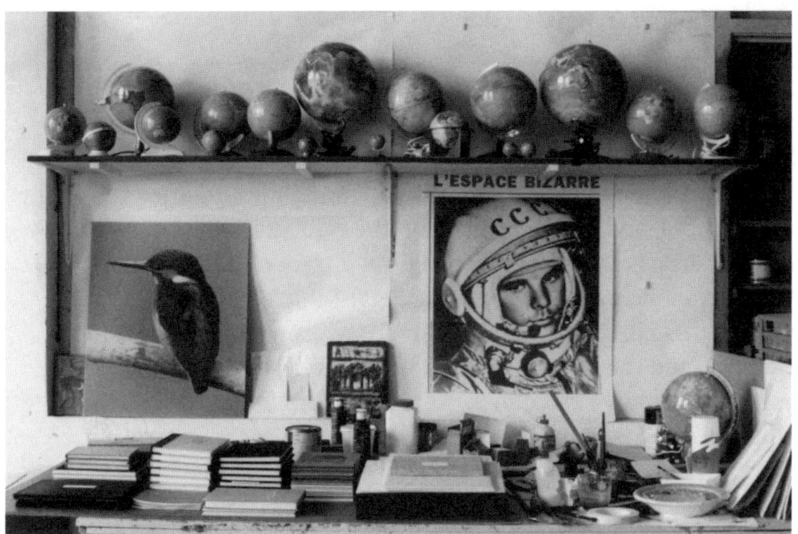

Coraciiformes-Familie: Alcedinidae in ARTIS. Books: *Recognition* (with Philip Elchers, Groningen) and *La Grotte de Lascaux*.

1994—Visited a kingfisher exhibition in the museum of Natural History in Denekamp, Netherlands. Books: *Atlas*, *Inimicus-Praeda*, *Picture Index*, *The Lincoln Stamp Album*.

1995—Carving of many kingfisher stamps, later collected in books and on large prints. 'Kawasemi', with Alec Finlay, Edinburgh. A large wall painting with kingfishers in Raleigh, USA. Saw a belted kingfisher near Pittsboro, USA. Start of the 'Topography' series.

1996—*Drie ijsvogels* (*Three kingfishers*), with the Academy of Fine Arts, Maastricht, Netherlands. Many kingfishers at the National Museum of Natural History, Leiden Netherlands. Research in the library of the museum. The call of the kingfisher on bridges in Eindhoven Netherlands. In search of the kingfisher at a trout farm in Nailsworth, England. New *Dictionary* and *Dictionnaire de pôche*.

1997—Many kingfishers at the National Museum of Natural History in New York. In search of a belted kingfisher near Bloomington, USA. Got a feather and a pellet of a kingfisher. The bills of all kingfishers, printed on paper. Books: *Correo Aereo* (with Morning Star, Edinburgh), *Dagger*, *Laika*, *Kosmonaut*.

1998—Arranged a conversation between a Belted Kingfisher and a European Kingfisher. Inspection of breeding holes in De Biesbosch, Netherlands. Gîtes de pêche in La Creuse, France. A kingfisher at the Rau de l'Etang de Clavérolles, France. Drawings of obstacles in water. Chinese exercise books, and *Boctok* (with Morning Star, Edinburgh).

1999—Gîtes de pêche in Calvados, France. Return to the Overijsselsch kanaal, in search of the kingfisher (1963). Rivers and bridges at the English-Scottish border. Fishing perches in Grizedale, England. A kingfisher walk in Kentmere, England. *Edinburgh kingfishers* and *Fishing Perches* (with Pont la Vue, New York).

2000—Fishing perches in Belgium and Germany. A walk in the Neanderthal, Germany. Visit to prehistoric cave Font de Gaume, Dordogne, France. Fishing perches at Vézère and Auvézère, France. Many bird guides.

2001—In search of kingfishers along Yarrow Water and Ettrick Water, Scotland. Field Guides in Dundee, watercolours in Edinburgh. Publication of *Perches*. Hans Waanders dies on 24th June.

Adapted from the biographies included in *Kingfishers and Related Works, Standard Catalogue, Hans Waanders* exhibition catalogue (Raleigh, North Carolina: City Gallery of Contemporary Art, 1995), and the website *hanswaanders.nl*.

Acknowledgements

The work of Hans Waanders, like his kingfisher, has been as elusive as it has compelling to pursue. I cannot, therefore, thank the following people enough for generously answering my enquiries, providing me material, and for putting me on the right track in the course of my searches: Petra van Koppen and the Estate of Hans Waanders, Wieke Waanders, Johan Deumens, Peter Foolen, Thomas A. Clark, Lauri Twitchell, Kristine Stiles, Karen Davidson, Simon Cutts, Helen Douglas, and the library staff at Chelsea College of Arts (UAL). Especial thanks go to Colin Sackett of Uniformbooks, whose keen editorial eye has, in so many ways, made this book; and to Laurie Clark, who first put me onto the trail of Hans Waanders.